GENESES OF DISASTER

GENESES OF DISASTER

Ramifications and Ameliorations

K.S. Gulia

KALPAZ PUBLICATIONS
Delhi-110052

Geneses of Disaster

Rs. 680

ISBN: 81-7835-283-4

Published in 2004 in India by
Kalpaz Publications,
C-30, Satyawati Nagar, Delhi-110052
E-mail : Kalpaz@hotmail.com

Laser Typesetting at : Shree Vaishnavi Creations, Delhi
Printed at : Mehra Offset Press

Contents

List of Tables, Figures and Slide

Figures

Tables

Slide

Preface

As I chance upon the journalists breaking astounding news, and as I read through the news paper headlines announcing breath taking advances in scientific achievements, with each new development I regress into the past. I regress into a pre-human world of silent but lively forests, crowded oceans, the mighty dinosaurs and the everlasting balance in the nature. I am drawn into post regression, and there I see a mirror image of the future sans the human elements.

The earth's ecosystems strive for balance, prior to the dawn of modern civilized society the balancing forces of the nature could conveniently cope with minorfractures here and minor shifts there, within the earth's ecosystems and the biomes. With the progress of time massive urbanization and industrialization commenced to take its toll on the balancing forces. The nature lost control over the massive shifts and the balance within the life giving forces of the natural ecosystems commenced regression for the worse. Thus, commenced the beginning of 'Thc End'. The disasters began. Today they are the order of the day.

This book is about the Geneses of Disasters as seen through history of Civilisations commencing from the growths of civilizations, travelling through the breakdowns and fracturing of certain great civilizations that ultimately disintegrated and then vanished. Successions of civilizationsoccurred upon the ruins of the older ones. The challenge of the environments was the stimulus for growth. Loss of command over the same environment was the cause of disintegration and vanishing.

Today we are on the threshold of another breakdown. Our civilization has advanced beyond the carrying capacity of Space Ship Earth. The earth's crust has been punctured and ecavated. The extractable resources have been sucked dry all minerals excavated, all forests logged down, the ozone umbrella in the stratosphere irreparably damaged, and the earth's biosphere heated beyond sustenance temperatures of living species. The earth is on the threshold of dying.

Our civilization is on the brink of a disaster. Broadly, there are two facets to forces that may bring about this impending disaster. I try to classify these under two categories:

- The first category refers to disasters which have a long gestation period and which can be foreseen. This category includes elements such as ppopulation explosion, pollution on ground, water and air, loss of species, climate change, etc. All of these are known to the governing elites and the intelligentsia. Yet, the greed of the human species forces the civilization to get into an ostrich act. Awareness exists. Global meetings take place. Pledges are made. Protocols are signed. Pace of degradation and march towards disintegration, however, continues unabated. This disaster, when it occurs will be irreversible. the current civilization may simply be wiped off. The balancing powers of the nature will ultimately be left ot themselves under ho,oeostatic controls. May be,one day another civilization grows and nourishes over the ruins that the current civilization will create.
- The second category of disasters is as we commonly understand it. These are events triggered by natural or man made causes that lead to sudden disruption of normalcy within society causin widespread damage to life and property to such an extent that normal social and economic mechanisms available are not adequate to restore normalcy.

The second category as one would see is a derivative of the first. While the disasters of first category encompass the entire globe, the events of second category are merely agents and catalysts leading to the ultimate first.

This book is an attempt to discuss the geneses of both the categories of disasters, I have tried to collate, correlate and simplify the data collected from the works of great historians, geographers, life and the physical scientists and so also the massive data available in the realms of global organisations such as the WHO, UNDP, FAO and UNDAC etc.

As we tread along, through the pages of this book we understand the value of being a human, and the futility of actions of the humans that bring forth the cycles of growth, breakdowns, dicimation and resurgence of civiliations on the Planet Earth. Did the God Almighty design and ordain that it to be so!!!

K.S. Gulia

Acknowledgements

The genesis of this book takes roots from a Seminar on the same subject in the aftermath of the 2001 Republic Day earthquake in the Kutch district of Gujarat. I am greatly indebted to Colonel Dev Arvind Chaturvedi and his team of research enthusiasts form First Third Gorkha Rifles who contributed heavily with mind and matter during the collection, collation and synthesis phase of this work. I am grateful to the staff of Gujarat State Disaster Management Association for their help in locating documents for initiating this study.

I depended and drew heavily on the WHO and UNDAC publications for latest collection of data on road traffic hazards, and the hazards of climate change, which I gratefully acknowlege.

Among the many other individuals who provided help of various kinds, I must especially mention the following; Satish Tyagi, Sanjeev Shukla, Pawan Chaddha, Sanjay Bajpai, Mrs Aparna Gain, R Ravi Kumar, BS Killer and Sajesh V.

My wife Santosh, daughters and sons-in-law followed the course of this work with interest and a growing exasperation. Their support at all times has been critical.

Finally I acknowledge my thanks to Kalpaz Publications for their rich contribution in publishing this work.

K.S. Gulia

1

Introduction

General

This book is about power, violence and destruction through the civilisations and now into the wake of the third millennium. It deals with natural and human initiated disasters, and the role they play in our lives. It is about new paths to living, managing, and dying, opened by the world in an upheaval.[1]

I admire Arnold J Toynbee,[2] whose analysis of the rise and fall of civilisations has been acknowledged as an achievement without parallel in modern scholarship. His famous creation 'A Study of History', an event of intellectual importance inquires into creations, disasters and breakdowns of civilizations. He sums up the breakdowns into three factors :-

(a) **Loss of Command over Environment**:
- ***The Physical Environment***. Through natural catastrophes.
- ***The Human Environment***. Through social disintegration.

(b) **The Impact on the Sense of Unity of Religion**. Understanding or misunderstanding the meaning of Jehad, Hindutva etc, and limits of tolerance.

(c) **The Power Shift**. Rise of the industrial nation states brought the systematic monopolization of violence and the sublimation of violence into law. Populations continued to grow more dependent on money. Elites became wealthier, especially so, after the monopolized violence of two World Wars. Today there is a fundamental change in the mix of violence, wealth and knowledge employed by elites to maintain control.[3]

The non-elites meanwhile, whether they are religious zealots or certain aspiring third world nations with "Legalized Kings or Despots" emphasise on creating situations of catastrophic and disastrous nature.

A social change itself may contain the metabolics of disasters. As early as 322 BC, the Greek Philosopher Aristotle, after studying the constitutions of 158 states of past and present had concluded the endless cycles of changes, which passed through a chain of disasters:-[4]

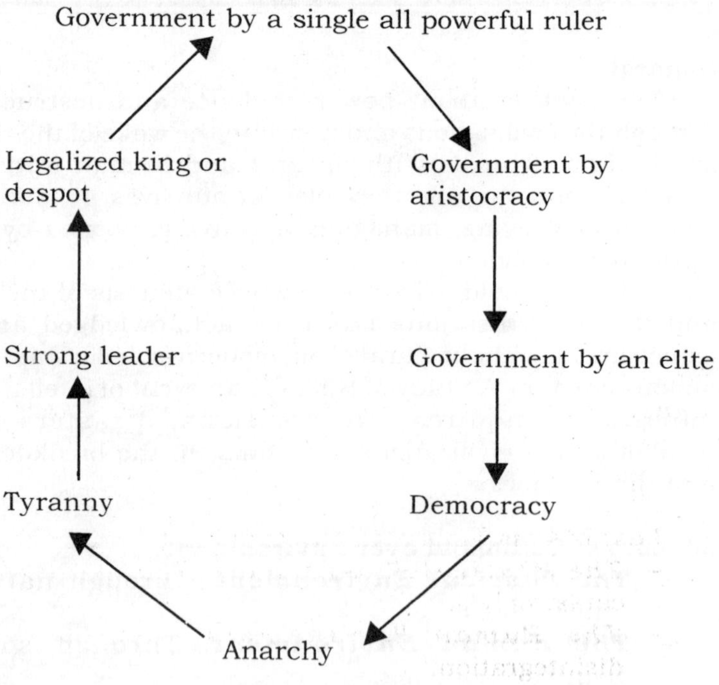

The basic intellectual attitudes that accompanied each

phase (disastrous or otherwise) were :-[5]

All pervading faith. Truth handed down from a supernatural source.

↓

Organized, systematic faith backed up by reasons.

↓

Emphasis on human relationships and conduct in religion. Science important.

↓

Science all-important. Doubting and questioning. Right and wrong no longer overriding, but related to circumstances.

↓

Selfishness, distrust, lack of faith

↑

Trust in factions. Short-term gains by any means.

↑

Trust in deliverers and saviors.

↑

Truth from prophecy, Oracles, and other Supernatural channels.

↑

(back to: All pervading faith. Truth handed down from a supernatural source.)

Development, Decay and Collapse

The 'J' Curve of the Yeast in Glucose Jar. The population ecology of the yeast in a jar filled with glucose water is typical. It is typical of development, multiplication and finally a mutated end of the population. Initially, as the availability of glucose is large, the yeast bacteria consumes and multiplies at a fast pace, until the supply of glucose is exhausted. With exhaustion of nutrient resources, there is an alarming decrease of population, aiding in total annihilation. The humans have developed similar systems of development, followed by decay and disaster.

The Second and Third Wave Revolution. The industrial revolution and evolutionary theories of the 19th Century, of which Darwin's was the most important, had a powerful influence on sociology. Most important of all, the developments led to an intellectual climate in which expectations were altered. Thomas Babington Macualay in 1850 had this to say :-[6]

- Science has lengthened life.
- Mitigated pain.
- Extinguished diseases.
- Increased fertility of soil.
- Given new securities to the mariner.
- Spanned bridges over great rivers, barriers and estuaries.

Decay. The optimism of Macaulay did not last long. By 1950, voices of doubt and concern were beginning to rise. As far back as 1798, Thomas Robert Malthus had predicted that as a result of human actions, universal prosperity, and abundance of resources were mirages that recede as fast as we approach them. He predicted "famine, distress, havoc and dismay."[7]

Collapse Theory and Limiting Factors. The total rate of exploitation of the earth's ecosystem has some upper limit, which reflects the intrinsic limit of the ecosystem's turnover rate. If this rate is exceeded, the system is eventually driven to collapse. This is firmly established by everything that we know about ecosystems.

Hence it follows that there is an upper limit to the rate of exploitation of the biological capital on which any productive system depends. Since the rate of use of this biological capital cannot be exceeded without destroying it, it also follows that the actual rate of use of the total capital (i.e., biological capital plus conventional capital, or the means of production) is also limited. Thus, there must be some limit to the growth of total capital, and the productive systems must eventually reach a "no-growth" condition, at least with respect to the accumulation of capital goods designed to exploit the ecosystem, and the product which they yield. Exploitation beyond limiting factors opens itself to a disastrous catastrophe.[8]

Evolution of Human Related Disaster and its Management

"It is eminently natural for humanity to create a "second nature" from its evolution in "first nature." By second nature, I mean the development of uniquely human culture, with a wide variety of institutionalized human communities, effective human techniques, richly symbolic languages, and carefully managed sources of nutrients. Dualism, in all its forms, has opposed these two natures to each other, as antagonists. Monism, in turn, often dissolves one into the other – be it liberalism, fascism, or more recently, the biocentrism that so closely approximates misanthropic antihumanism. These monist ideologies differ primarily in whether they want to dissolve first nature into second or second nature into first."[9]

What these dualisms and monisms have in common is an acceptance of domination. Classically, the counterpart of the "domination of nature by man" has been the "domination of man by nature."[10] Creation of 'second nature' through evolution from 'first nature' seems eminently natural. Similarly, inter-dominance of various islands of power created in the 'second nature' of the human evolution is equally evolutionary. This evolution includes mixes of liberalism and extremism. The most extreme of extremism is a human created disaster. Just as creation of a disaster is a part of 'second nature', so is the management of such a disaster. Both are evolutionary.

The Pollution Disaster[11]

Donora, 1948. Between 27 and 31 October 1948 the small town of Donora, in Pennsylvania, USA, lived through an air pollution disaster. With a population of 14,000, and heavily industrialized, Donora was situated in a basin. Meteorological conditions, during the period, prevented normal dispersion of the industrial emissions and stagnation occurred. As a result more than 6,000 of its residents were adversely affected, 10 per cent of them seriously. There were 200 more deaths than was normal for the period.

London Air Borne Muck, 1952. On Friday, 5 December 1952 weather conditions in greater London held the cities air close to the ground and a high pressure system prevented the formation of winds. The various air pollutants generated, which were normally dispersed, started accumulating at ground level. For five days the greater London area was blanketed with airborne muck. There were 4,000 more deaths than normal, hospital admissions were 48 per cent higher. Eighty-four per cent of those who died had pre-existing heart or lung diseases. Hospital admissions for respiratory illness increased three-fold and deaths due to chronic respiratory disease increased ten-fold.

Minamata, Japan, 1960. In 1950s, the incidence of nervous system and brain damage increased significantly at Minamata, Japan. A marked increase in retarded and blind babies was also observed. Eventually, these cases were identified as severe mercury poisoning and named Minamata disease. It was found that a chemical factory was discharging its wastes containing mercury into the local waters. The mercury concentrated in the fish that the residents caught and consumed. Between 1953 and 1960, 111 persons were seriously affected, of which 45 died. Nineteen babies with congenital defects were born to mothers who had consumed the fish.

Love Canal, USA, 1978. In 1978, the New York State Department of Health, based on evidence of high incidence of reproductive problems among women and high levels of chemical contamination, ordered the evacuation of pregnant women and children from 239 homes in the community of Love Canal in upstate New York. Eventually, most of the 900 families living in Love Canal were relocated at a total relocation and cleanup cost of over 200 million dollars.

During the 1920s, a partially completed channel between the upper and lower Niagara rivers came into use as a municipal and chemical waste dump. In 1953, the channel was filled and subsequently homes and schools were built on and around the site. In time the chemicals began to resurface and residents often complained of strange odours. Traces of toxic chemical residues in the air and water were identified in 1976. High levels of carcinogenic polychlorinated biphenyls (PCBs) were detected in the storm waster system. With mounting evidence, the Department of Health finally had to evacuate the area.

Bhopal, India, 1984. On a cold December night, in 1984, the Union Carbide pesticide plant in Bhopal, India, accidentally released a cloud of deadly methyl isocyanite over the sleeping neighbourhood. It left 200,000 people fleeing for their lives and about 2,500 dead. One hundred thousand people are still suffering from side-effects ten years later, which include blurred vision, disabling lung diseases, intestinal bleeding, and neurological and psychological disorders.

Chernobyl, 1986. In April 1986 an explosion and fire at the Chernobyl Nuclear Power Station in the Soviet Union caused a partial melt down of plant reactor core. More than seven tons of radioactive material escaped into the environment contaminating land, food, and water throughout Europe. Twenty-eight people died of acute radiation poisoning within 75 days, while another 300 were treated for serious radiation exposure. More than a hundred thousand people were evacuated from their homes, and more than 2,000 square kilometers of land became uninhabitable.

The six episodes outlined in the preceding paragraphs are all pollution related and have became famous, or rather infamous. Perhaps these could be described as 'accidents', but they could all have been prevented, or at least mitigated to a large extent by proper planning, engineering, operations, and surveillance. Apparently these 'accidents' are on the rise worldwide. And for each episode mentioned there are many, many more which have not been reported. We are familiar with the accidental oil spills in our waters that wreck havoc with the ecosystem. Of course there is the planned or deliberate release of pollutants into the environment by homes, communities, industries, and nations.

Environmental Emergencies

What is an Environmental Emergency? "It is a sudden onset of an event out of the normal course of events that has the potential to significantly affect the environment, and the human health." And here, we are being anthropocentric, even at the levels of as high as the UN Body. Perhaps the additions of life within that part of the biosphere would have been more meaningful and bio-centric. Anthropocentricity has been the root cause of the present day crisis, and we in our own vision, at levels no less than the UN General Assembly continue to march on blind folded, in spite of all the hind sight. We are 'QUICK FIXERS'. Hence, we shall continue to face the environmental emergencies as soon as the 'quick fix' has seen its threshold.

There is a need to understand the possibility of various kinds of environmental emergencies. These could be :

- Classic environmental emergency situation, e.g., spill, leak or other releases.
- Other types of disasters with significant environmental impacts, e.g., forest fires, natural disasters such as earthquakes, floods, cyclones etc.
- Combination of above.

Human Related Terror Disasters

Disaster managers must get to know and learn to match the disaster creators, that they intend to target. The human society at large may not be interested in the disaster creating terrorist; never the less, the human society is the prime target of such terror prowlers. Much of the literature in this part of the presentation may be acknowledged to Alvin and Heidi Toffler, co-authors of *War and Anti War*. Many faces of terror violence as seen by Toffler are narrated in succeeding paras.[12]

Rogue Nations. Some First and Second Wave (Wave as described by Toffler in his book *The Third Wave*) nations have been seeking to acquire Third Wave weaponry from the West. This includes the inventories of the WMD also. Professior A Q Khan of Pakistan is much known for his notoriety of this kind.

Parallel Violence. High-tech nations on the way to developing brain-force economics could find themselves either sucked into Third World conflicts, or thrown into war as a result of internal 'smash–ups'. USA finds itself deeply rooted into Afghanistan and now Iraq after 9/11 catastrophe.

Niche Wars. A nation defeated a conventional War may find that its disintegrated elements are engaged in a large number of groups wars. Niche wars of Afghanistan continue even today. In a future, should Pakistan or any such nation faces a comprehensive defeat, the number of Niche War groups may be even higher. With acquisition of WMDs, as in the case of Pakistan, be at stake, the Niche Wars may be extremely disastrous.

The Mercenaries and the Drug War Lords. Highly trained soldiers may be drifted or weaned away from their prime employers. There exist elite units of this kind in USA, UK, Pakistan, and even India. Such mercenaries may market their skills anywhere. Today it is J&K. Tomorrow it could be Gujarat. The 'Drug War Lords' bring the money. Actions could be as disastrous as :

– Ethnic cleansing, e.g., Kashmiri Pandits from the Valley.
– Hostages.
– Smuggling of WMDs.
– Narco–trafficking.

'Spin Doctors' and 'Key Board Terrorists'. The press/ media have their share of terrorist infiltrators. Such 'spin doctors' specialise in deception and disinformation. Then, you have the smart 'Key Board Operating Terrorists', who may cause crisis of disastrous nature through computers, by means of :-

– Implant false messages.
– Alter records.
– Engage in espionage.
– Search and transmit data to adversaries.
– Arm, disarm and re-target weapons.
– Push buttons on WMDs.

Polarization and Divine Sanction. When cruel quacks get to absolute power, they consider it 'Divine Sanction' upon themselves of cleansing the humanity. President Idi Amin of Uganda was one, Hitler another. We have few more today. Their direct obedience of 'Orders from God' requires a direct intervention from the society as a whole, from within, and also from beyond the geographical frontiers of that country.

What do We Do ?
Two Possibilities

– ***Generalist***. Do not be an innocent bystander. Keep an eye, and raise alarm as necessary, environmental considerations when involved in a mission addressing broader issues, such as natural or man made disaster situation.

- ***Expert***. Do bring to bear some form of specialized expertise within the context of a given emergency.

Assessment Steps. You need to ascertain :-

- Nature of incident.
- Location of actual or potential hazard/threat.
- Hazard identification.
- Assessment of hazard implications.
- Identify response requirements.
- Short and long term environmental considerations, e.g., EIA and EA.

Where are the Threats ?

(a) ***Classic Environmental Emergencies***. Usually the result of human error. Can occur anywhere hazardous products are used :-

- Hospitals. (Pathogenic wastes and faulty decomposition).
- Construction sites. (MAP is coming up in a big way).
- Chemical and manufacturing plants (Amn factories and Ordnance Depots).
- Ware houses.
- Rail and road accidents.
- Aircraft ramming high rise buildings or industrial estates.
- Mining facilities (Chasnala incident of Bihar).
- Water treatment facilities.

(b) ***Natural Disasters***

- Flooding/Cyclones.
- Earthquakes.
- Droughts.
- Breaking New Paths and Awakening

Breaking New Paths and Awakening

We need to be awake. We are already forewarned. Remember, as a conclusion, there are four types of hazardous events that put societies at risk :-

- Those based in nature : Earthquakes, droughts, floods, avalanches, etc.
- Those based in violence : War, armed conflict, physical assault, etc.
- Those based in deterioration : Declining health, education and other social services ; environmental degradation etc.
- Those based in the failings of industrialised society: Technological failures, oil spillage, factory explosions, fires, gas leakage, transport collisions.

Chronology of a Disaster

- Failure to comply with regulations or violation of laid down precautions.
- Incubation Period.
- Precipitation Event.
- Onset of the Disaster.
- Rescue and Salvage.
- Full Cultural Re-adjustment.

Human Capacity for Creation of Disaster

The awareness of man's dependable upon nature has a long ancestory; but a sense of man as the maker and unmaker of nature has only more recently dawned upon us, and with it an awesome sense of our own capacity for mischief and mayhem.

- Arnold and Guha

References

1. Toffler, Alvin; *Powershift*, Bantam Paperback Edition, Bauxam Double Day Publishing Group, Inc, New York, USA, (1991). (pp. xix).
2. Toynbee, Arnold, (–) J; *A Study of History*, Dell Publishing Co. Inc, 750 Third Avenue, New York, USA, (1946) (pp. 286 - 413).
3. Toffler, Alvin; *ibid*, (pp. 58-65).
4. Ross – Macdonald, Malcolm; *Life in The Future*, Interiberica, S.A., Madrid, Spain, 1976 (p. 16).
5. Ross – Macdonald, Malcolm, *ibid.*, (p. 16).
6. Ross – Macdonald, Malcolm, *ibid.*, (p. 17).
7. Ross - Macdonald, Malcolm, *ibid.*, (p. 17).
8. Nico Nellissen, Straaten and Klinkers (eds); *Classics in*

Environmental Studies, Kusum Publishing, New Delhi, 2001 (p. 193).

9. Bookchin, Murray; *The Philosophy of Social Ecology*, Rawat Publications, Jaipur, (1996). (p. 119).
10. Bookchin, Murray, *ibid.* (p. 119).
11. Chakraverty, Chiranjit; *Environment for Everyone*, Augustan Publishers and Distributors,Delhi,1996 (pp. 44-46).
12. Toffler, Alvin and Heidi; *War and Anti –War*, Little Brown and Company, Canada and USA, 1993.

2

Evolution of Man The Beginning of the End

"When all the story is finished, what's the news?
In luck or out the toil has left the mark :
That old perplexity an empty purse,
Or the day's vanity, the night's remorse".

W.B. Yeats

Life and Chance – Passing on of Genes

In the cavernous interiors of the Roulette Plazas, the world over, there are ranks of gambling machines lined up like the army soldiers on parade, each one to a common design, though subtly different. They invite you to play or at least to make a close inspection. The machines are designed to be close to human height. You place yourself before them on skimpy stools, or stand to attention inspecting the arcane rules that govern how you may be paid back richly as you gamble. The winner takes all. The winner is chanced against many odds.

Chance events play a critical role in ecology. The opening of a gap in a forest canopy after a storm will have a major impact on the ecology of the fauna and flora of the forest floor, but it is unpredictable in either time or location. Similarly, the dynamics of sand dune and rocky shore species is dominated by the random destruction and creation of new, bare colonizing surfaces. The decline of the passenger pigeon which was so numerous in North America in the eighteenth century, that flocks passing overhead blocked out the sun for minutes at a time, was largely caused by over-hunting. However, extinction was finally caused by the chance combination of disease and a harsh winter. The role of chance is also integral to the evolutionary past of organisms. The importance of chance events in ecology does not mean ecological patterns are wholly unpredictable but it necessarily places boundaries on the potential level of predictive detail.

The gambling dens are similar temples of chance. Between the machines are roulette wheels, spinning symbols of chance itself. Punters cluster intently around the wheels, seeking by willpower alone to guide the little ball into the numbered haven of their choice. There are various ways in which to place your bets. The long shot is to bet on a single winning number, with the faint possibility of major returns. Or, alternatively and more conservatively you could bet on red or black. Whatever you do, the table has the edge. The odds can be evaded temporarily – enough to fund an occasional small fortune. But the odds will reassert themselves in the end with the inexorability of a mathematical certainty.

Prospective punters are drawn like flies over sweet meat into these gambling strips in the scenic spots situated in hugging vicinity of sprawling suburbs. As the humans retire to rest during the heat of the day in the deserts or frozen silence of the mountains by night, the elements of the nature take over. These creatures lacking in presumption but rich in qualities required for survival against the odds would inherit the strips. For the meek survive even if they do not inherit the Earth.

Life – as we all know–is a gamble. Chance promotes or damns according to the whim of history. The analogy of permutations in a game of chance has long been applied to genetic mutations, spontaneous changes in the genetic code. Like vast ranks of gamblers who come away with nothing, most mutations also lead to nothing. They do not result in an increase in fitness. Some are lethal – as might be the production of a wingless butterfly. Others might put the mutant at a disadvantage–a new colour pattern might not be favoured by a potential mate, for example. But those rare mutations that hit upon an advantageous combination produce the big pay off–the jackpot. They are rewarded not in the grass currency of rupees or dollars but in the irresistible coins of many successful offspring. Unlike the lucky gambler, the luck of the successful gene is passed on to make luck for future generation.

Survival and Mutation of Genes through Geological Ages

Through the 3,700 million years of life's history we may have tread upon countless possible paths. Richard Fortey the renowned natural historian recounts *'luck'* as one recurring motif for survival and succession of species. Those animals and plants that survived the death of the dinosaurs did not prosper because of a small change in genes at the critical time. They already 'had' what was needed to survive–by another sort of luck. Small warm–blooded mammals and birds, together with insects and magnolias, survived the crisis at the end of the cretaceous that extinguished dinosaurs and ammonites because they were already equipped to survive, and not because they invented some wheeze at the last minute.

The whole course of life hinged on the fact that some of the animals that appeared in the Cambrian were unlucky enough not to survive, and thus failed to propagate their designs into their descendants. The geological splitting and rearrangement of the continents as the great plates that make up the Earth's surface cruise in their leisurely fashion over the surface of the mutable globe. It is luck–must be luck–which determines which animals, when and where are attached to a particular continent. As Antarctica was carried towards the South Pole, its cargo of terrestrial animals was doomed to die. Rare fossils tell us that there were mammals there before the ice caps grew. Doubtless there were mutations galore, some of which favoured cold–tolerant species over less tolerant ones, as the climate deteriorated. But that was useless in the face of implacable ice and everlasting winters, a cold that freezes blood. This was pure bad luck for species on board to the frozen continent of Antarctica.

Humans Colonize Geographical Wonders

Geography can be just as creative. When the island of Hawaii was born from the eruption of oceanic basalt lavas it was isolated within the young Pacific Ocean, far from the nearest continent. It was a rare beauty upon which nature might write. A tropical climate almost guaranteed that it would be fruitful. Volcanic soil is rich and capable of nourishing any plant that can reach it. Some did. Seeds floated, brought by storms, other seeds blew in, light as thistledown, borne in upon delicate parachutes carried by the breeze. Distance was selective–very few species of animal landed safely. For birds it may have been less difficult to reach the freshly green island, but even so, the founding species were less in number. There may have been as few as seven insect species to reach out. But good luck here provoked a fever of creative evolution–the opposite of Antarctic blight. From the few species that arrived in this evolutionary Eden, dozens of species arose. Since change could only work upon what material was to land, wonders happened. Harmless pollow-eaters evolved into predators; small insects became large; many specialists arose to eat the newly native flora. None of these unique species was found outside Hawaii, Good luck was fenced off from the rest of the world.

But it has become bad luck, now that the contact has been established with the world, thanks to human colonisation. For, in a tragic mirror–image of that original creativity, introduced animals such as the rat, are forcing out the erstwhile lucky ones from their private Eden: it is a reversal of fortunes.

Australia also carried its cargo of diverse species southwards, and it evolved richly. Man's arrival as part of the Diaspora of *Homo Sapiens* also coincided with the decline of some large marsupial herbivores, but more damage has been done by the greedy ways of modern human.

Growth of the Human

The shape and tempo of the story of life on Earth as a whole resembles that of the history of mankind, a single species. It makes you think of an orchestra display which starts slowly, uneventfully, a long series of slight variations upon a recurrent theme, gradually gathering pace, shifting from one instrument to another, while an underlying pulse goes on and on. From time to time there are shifts in key, then more instruments join in, and the pace and excitement build, until, at the end, it is a scurrying, swirling mass of interwoven instrumental activity.

The slow growth of brain size in humans took several millions of years. To be sure, the innovation of tool making was a threshold, but how similar those tools remained for more than a million years, slowly turning changes on familiar themes. But technology built itself up and interactions between a growing population increased, until there was a sudden flowering of stone tool types, building techniques, and domestication of animals and plants. In a geological instant society mushroomed in all its uncountable complexity.

Similarly, for thousands of million of years the bacterial and algal world slowly, almost imperceptibly changed – a long, leisurely theme repeated, and slowly modified–while within the last 500 million years the richness of life has increased a thousand folds again. The growth of the humans in geological terms hereinafter was stupendous. This marked the beginning of the civilisations.

Inhumanity of the Humans

Where civilisation starts, prehistory is blurred into history. This is the moment when the records begin, when humble hutments or grandiose monuments tell the mankind's inhumanity, or his aspirations to Godliness. Appropriately enough, the earliest writings are biographical inscriptions trumpeting the achievements of kings. The truth of life also depends upon selection of its incidents, no less than does an account of a civilisation. As such unnatural selection proceeds, there is also the possibility of lies and unwitting deception; although Nature is full of camouflage, we are the first animal ever to deceive ourselves.

In spite of the humans, life will probably cope.
But disasters have their probability factors too.

3

Breakdown and Disintegration of Human Civilisations

Hunter – Gatherers as Ecologists

Early man was a successful practicing ecologist. He survived in a rich and competitive biotic community, and his relationship to this community was continually intimate. He was by no means the strongest, the swiftest and the hardiest among his congeners but he possessed several distinct advantages. He had a close effective social organisation, an unusual manipulative ability, and of course, an emerging intelligence. Thus, he developed tools and fire in early Palaeolithic time (500,000 to 1,000,000 years ago), and he accumulated knowledge at a faster rate than other primates.

Much of this knowledge was ecological. It was knowledge of his environment and the most effective use of it. It was detailed knowledge of food and water resources, some of which can still be seen in the "primitive" peoples of today. The Kalahari bushmen, for example, can find water in a barren desert where other men would surely die of thirst. The Australian aborigine can locate grubs and lizards in the Australian deserts far better than a modern biologist. Elton (1933)[1] pointed out that, "The Arawak of the South American equatorial forest knows where to find every kind of animal and catch it, and also the names of the trees and the uses to which they can be put." Bates (1960)[2] found on the Micronesian atoll of Ifaluk that the native people had a detailed ecological knowledge of the plants on the islands and the use to which each could be put in terms of food, medicine, construction and ornament. They also possessed detailed knowledge of the reefs and sea around them. In all societies of hunter-gatherers there was strong selective pressure against the nonecologist. This rigorous natural selection prevailed throughout the two million years of Palaeolithic man, and before that the 10 to 15 million years of Pliocene and Miocene hominids and protohominids, the forerunners of man.

There is increasing evidence that early man was well adapted to his environment. The popular conception that he barely clung to life through a precarious and difficult struggle is definitely misleading (Lee and DeVore 1968)[3]. Recent studies of both ancient and modern hunter-gatherers have shown that they frequently have had an abundant life, with very ample resources and sustenance. Some present-day primitive peoples are declining, of course, but usually as a result of modern forces–a deteriorating environment or competition from agricultural peoples. Other studies on former hunter-gatherers have shown that malnutrition was rare, starvation infrequent, and chronic diseases, as we know them today, of relatively low incidence–all evidence of sound ecological balance in their way of life (Dunn, 1968; Neel, 1970)[4]. There was, however, high infant mortality, primarily through infectious disease, and high "social mortality" (infanticide, geronticide, warfare, etc.), and these served as primary mechanisms of population regulation.

The ecological ability of early man does not necessarily mean that he was a good conservationist. Guthrie (1971)[5] has pointed out that the concept of early man living in blissful harmony with his environment is a serious distortion of facts. Early man knew enough practical ecology to survive and even prosper, but he exploited his environment at every opportunity. He was a persistent forager and relentless hunter whose primary goal was survival. He was often nomadic "in part because prolonged habitation in any one area depleted game and firewood and accumulated wastes to the extent that the region was no longer habitable" (Guthrie, 1971)[6]. Some scholars have felt that the overzealous hunting of early man contributed to the widespread extinction of animals in the Pleistocene Epoch (Martin and Wright, 1967)[7]. Although this is a controversial hypothesis, there is some evidence that early man was not always conservative in hunting or environmental protection. For example, plain Indians of North America were known to have killed many more bison than they could utilise by driving them over cliffs. Apart from some of these extravagances, early man did feel a close kinship with nature, and considered himself a small part of a vast scheme.

As pointed out by Lee and DeVore (1968)[8]: "Cultural man has been on earth for some 2,000,000 years: for over 99 per cent of this period he has lived as a hunter-gatherer. Only in the last 10,000 years has man begun to domesticate plants and animals, to use metals, and to harness energy other than the human body".

The civilisations of agricultural and industrial man have a long way to go before they can match the longevity of primitive man.

Desertification Through Animal Domestication

With the rise of civilization and its elaborate divisions of labour, more niches for the nonecologist became available. The weaver, potter and tool-maker did not require the same broad ecological knowledge as the hunter and gatherer. The most significant ecological achievement of civilized man was, of course, the domestication of plants and animals for greater productivity and control over the means of subsistence. Thus, the development of pastoral and agricultural life, in the Neolithic period of 10,000 B.C., to 6,000 B.C. altered the entire pattern of human existence. Permanent villages became established, inter group cooperation and trade routes developed and a demand arose for a new type of ecological knowledge, that was associated with the husbandry of plants and animals. Economics displaced ecology as the vital key to survival success.

The beginning of recorded history, about 3,000 B.C., showed civilizations in Egypt and Mesopotamia with cities and a high degree of vocational specialisation. The Bronze Age, shortly after 3,000 B.C., and the Iron Age, starting about 1,000 B.C., accelerated agriculture, exploration and conquest but did little for man's general ecological knowledge. Environmental exploitation expanded without a comparable increase in environmental harmony. Major land changes occurred. Forests were cut, fields cleared, pastures grazed and ploughed, and the landscape was carved to fit the new economic demands of man. A general increase in aridity occurred throughout much of the world then occupied by civilised man. Some of the great land barrens of our modern world probably developed during this time (Marsh, 1864; Sauer, 1938; Sears, 1935; Thomas, 1955-1956)[9].

There have been, in general, two theories to explain the development of these great land barrens, especially those in the Middle East and North Africa. The theories differ in their views on the role of man. One has viewed man as the victim of climatic change while the other has viewed man as the perpetrator of climatic change. Thus, as per one view, man had to adapt to desert conditions imposed upon him by great continental forces of climate and geography while in the other view, man himself was the major desert-making force.

The "man-as-victim" view has probably prevailed in most academic circles until recent years, not so much because of positive evidence to support it, but mainly because it seemed more logical and definitely kinder to the man's ego. There is now increasing evidence from archaeology and ecology that man's role as a desert-making force has been underestimated. Rather than being a passive victim of climatic change, man's influence in inducing this change has been significant and perhaps critical. This view does not assert that man's activities have been the sole forces in desert formation but it does assert that they were influential in accelerating and intensifying desert formation.

Desertification Through Agriculture

Agricultural man set into motion several major forces which had significant geographic and meteorologic consequences: deforestation, overgrazing, intensive burning, and land scarring. Geographic consequences came about through increased erosion, soil loss and declining water tables; meteorologic consequences resulted from reductions in atmospheric humidity and cloud cover, increased heat reflectivity and a lowering of rainfall. Ecological studies have shown that forests help to maintain the level of rainfall necessary for their own existence, and that deforestation results not only in an immediate lowering of ground water levels, but also in long-term lowering of rainfall. Forests recycle moisture back into their immediate atmosphere by transpiration where it again falls as rain. Transpiration return from an acre of forest may reach 2,500 gallons per day (McCormick, 1959)[10] and thus create a natural system of water reuse. If the forest is removed, this natural reuse cycle is broken, and water is lost through rapid run-off. Grasslands perform the same function to a lesser degree, and operate with a smaller amount of available moisture. It is interesting to examine Middle Eastern history in light of this principle.

Disintegration of Civilisation of the Middle East, North Africa and the Mediterranean

The span of history from 5,000 B.C. to 200 A.D., which we know primarily as the period of great civilization–Sumerians, Babylonia, Assyria, Phoenicia, Egypt, Greece and Rome–was also a period of unprecedented environmental disturbance. We tend to concentrate our attention on the superb achievements of these civilisations in literature, art, government and science, while we virtually forget their incompetence in land management. Perhaps this is not surprising since we seem to ignore our own shortcomings in the same area. Nevertheless, the fact remains that these golden civilisations prospered at the expense of their environments. They left a landscape which has never recovered, and a legacy to future civilisations which ushered forth a period of dark ages for more than a thousand years.

As specific examples of the destructive nature of these civilisations, we can cite critical landscape changes in many areas of the Middle East, North Africa and Mediterranean lands. As late as 7,000 B.C., the headwaters of the Tigris and Euphrates Rivers were covered with forests and grasslands (Saggs, 1962)[11].. In fact, most of the area now occupied by Iran and Iraq was productive and well-watered (Sauer, 1938)[12]. Domestic cattle appeared in the seventh millennium B.C., probably around 6,300 B.C. (Perkins, 1969)[13]. Thus herds of domestic cattle, sheep and goats found very favourable pasture in these virgin grasslands. Their great success provided a major stimulus for the developing civilizations of Mesopotamia and Sumerians, but it also provided the first significant onslaught on these grasslands and their adjacent forests. The herdsmen prospered, utilising the stored capital of thousands of years, and the upsurge of prosperity was followed by more people and larger herds. Forests were cut to provide additional pasture and more land was exposed to the increasing livestock populations. Residential communities developed around 4,000 B.C., and further deforestation occurred to provide timbers for developing cities. Elaborate agricultural practices ensured with irrigation canals extending the reach of the rivers. At first the erosion and silt load of the canals was manageable, and the alluvial soil along the rivers was remarkably fertile. With passing generations, however, siltation increased and it became necessary to occupy great numbers of slaves and labourers with the job of maintaining irrigation channels free of silt (Dasmann, 1968)[14]. After 3,000 B.C., the increased silt of the Tigris and Euphrates filled in the Persian Gulf 180 miles from its origin. All of these changes–loss of vegetation and soil, lowered water tables, declining agricultural productivity, diminishing rainfall and the added economic burden of siltation in the irrigation canals–were significant factors in the fall of the great Babylonian empire (Saggs, 1962)[15]. Successive waves of invaders–kassites, Elamites, Assyrians and eventually Persians–conquered this tragic land and increased its devastation.

At the same time of the Sumerian and early Babylonian empires in the Middle East, there was a thriving civilization in the Indus valley of present-day Pakistan. A prosperous and advanced culture existed at the site of Mohenjo-Daro in the Province of Sind (Wallbank, 1958)[16]. There is evidence of an urban civilization with well-planned streets, dwellings, municipal halls, palaces and a well-engineered drainage system. An advanced governmental structure apparently existed. There was skilful use of bronze, copper, silver and lead, and there was also beautifully glazed pottery, delicate jewellery and carefully woven cotton textiles. This prosperous civilisation came to an abrupt end about 2,500 B.C. No one knows the reason for its total collapse, but there was again a loss in the means of subsistence. The Sind today is mostly desert, except in those portions bordering the Indus River and its related irrigation canals.

Man, over a period of 3,000 years, in the sixth to the third millennia B.C. had become a major force in environmental change. Although his powerful civilisations and glorious cities had flourished, they were intimately dependent upon the land which gave them birth. When the pastoral and agricultural riches of the land were destroyed, the civilisations could no longer be supported, decline began, and they became more vulnerable to invading armies.

In Africa, similar patterns have been found. Even the Sahara within written history has not been as extensive as it is now. In Egypt and the Sudan, Davidson (1959)[17] found abundant evidence of former productivity within historical times:

Even as late as the third millennium large numbers of cattle are known to have found grazing in lower Nubia (formerly Ethiopia, now part of Sudan) where, as Arkell says, "desert conditions are so severe today that the owner of an ox-driven water-wheel has difficulty in keeping one or two beasts alive throughout the year". And anyone who has travelled in these dusty latitudes will have noticed how the wilderness of sand and rock that lies to the west of the Nile, far out upon the empty plains, is scored with ancient wadi beds which must once have carried a steady seasonal flow of water, but are now as dry as the desert air.

Throughout Saharan Africa, there are "lost cities" of former grandeur in areas now too arid to support life

(Davidson, 1959)[18]. It would be extravagant and incorrect to claim that man's activities produced the Sahara desert, for it was largely the result of great climatic shifts over the course of geological history. But the evidence is clear that man extended Saharan conditions and forced once productive and well-watered areas to become barren wastelands.

The Sahara is still actively extending its arid conditions-in some areas at the rate of one mile per year (Rienow and Rienow, 1967)[19]. In recent centuries, over 250 million acres (3,90,000 square miles) in Africa have been converted from agricultural and pastoral production to nonarable desert, primarily through the agent of man and his livestock. Similarly, the great Thar Desert of western India has increased its size by 60,000 square miles within the last 100 years (Ehrlich and Ehrlich, 1970)[20].

According to Sauer (1938), the second great period of human destruction upon the landscape occurred during the latter days of Rome. Phoenicia, Greece and Rome all prospered on the riches of the Mediterranean lands. One of the best accounts of this Roman exploitation is provided by Marsh (1864)[21], who pointed out:

The Roman Empire, of the period of its greatest expansion, comprised the regions of the earth most distinguished by a combination of physical advantages. The provinces bordering on the principal and secondary basins of the Mediterranean enjoyed a healthfulness and equability of climate, a fertility of soil, a variety of vegetable and mineral products, and natural facilities for the transportation and distribution of exchangeable commodities, which have not been possessed in an equal degree by any territory of like extent in the Old World or the New. The abundance of the land and of the waters adequately supplied every material want . . . . the luxurious harvests of cereals that waved on every field from the shores of the Rhine to the banks of the Nile, the vines that festooned the hillsides of Syria, of Italy, and of Greece....

Even much of North Africa was rich and productive, clothed in cedar forests which provided further wealth for Rome. But Marsh hastened to add a more recent description of these lands, as he observed them in the mid-nineteenth century during his tenure as United States Ambassador to Italy.

If we compare the present physical conditions of the countries of which I am speaking, with the descriptions that ancient historians and geographers have given of their fertility and general capability of ministering to human uses, we shall find that more than one-half of their whole extent–including the provinces most celebrated for the profusion and variety of their spontaneous and their cultivated products, and for the wealth and social advancement of their inhabitants–is either deserted by civilised man and surrendered to hopeless desolation, or at least greatly reduced in both productiveness and population. Vast forests have disappeared from mountain spurs and ridges; the vegetable earth accumulated beneath the trees by the decay of leaves and fallen trunks, the soil of the alpine pastures which skirted and indented the woods, and the mould of the upland fields, are washed away; meadows, once fertilised by irrigation, are waste and unproductive....

Besides the direct testimony of history to the ancient fertility of the regions to which I refer–Northern Africa, the greater Arabian peninsula, Syria, Mesopotamia, Armenia, and many other provinces of Asia Minor, Greece, Sicily, and parts of even Italy and Spain – the multitude and extent of yet remaining architectural ruins, and of decayed works of internal improvement, show that at former epochs a dense population inhabited those now lonely districts.

It appears, then, that the fairest and fruitfulest provinces of the Roman Empire, precisely that portion of terrestrial surface, in short, which, about the commencement of the Christian era, was endowed with the greatest superiority of soil, climate and position, which had been carried to the highest pitch of physical improvement, and which thus combined the natural and artificial conditions best fitting it for the habitation and enjoyment of a dense and highly refined and cultivated population, is now completely exhausted of its fertility, or so diminished in productiveness, as, with the exception of a few favoured oases which have escaped the general ruin, to be no longer capable of affording sustenance to civilised man.

The decay of these once flourishing countries is partly due, no doubt, to that class of geological causes, whose action we can neither resist nor guide, and partly also to the direct violence of hostile human force; but it is, in far greater proportion, the result of man's ignorant disregard of the laws of nature ......

World-Wide Environmental Destruction

The same phenomenon has been discussed at length by Paul Sears (1935)[22], Fairfield Osborn (1948)[23], and Carl Sauer (1967)[24]. They have shown that the environmental destructiveness of man has not been limited to the Middle East, Africa and the Mediterranean, but has, in fact, occurred throughout China, India, sub-Saharan Africa and the New World. In India, for example, the original vegetation of Rajasthan and the southern borders of the Gangetic basin–areas which are now arid and semi desert–was deciduous forest and far richer in natural soil moisture than at the present time (Champion, 1937)[25].

In northern India, the magnificent city of Fatehpur Sikri, just 23 miles west of Agra, was built in the sixteenth century, only to be abandoned within two decades due to a lack of water. It was overcome by the arid landscape its people helped to create. Looking at Fatehpur Sikri today in the midst of an oven-like desert, it is hard to envisage the productive and well watered environment which gave it birth 400 years ago.

In north America, the present desolate shifting sand areas bordering the Colorado river were rich grassland pastures as late as the seventeenth century (Sauer, 1967)[26]. Mexico was extensively forested over vast areas now occupied by dry and rocky plains (Osborn, 1948)[27]. Of all these destructive changes wrought by man, Sears (1935)[28] writes:

Wherever we turn, to Asia, Europe, or Africa, we shall find the same story repeated with an almost mechanical regularity. The net productiveness of the land has been decreased. Fertility has been consumed and soil destroyed at a rate far in excess of the capacity of either man or nature to replace.

Fairfield Osborn, in 'Our Plundered Planet' supports these views and points out that destructive land use practices have not been confined to ancient people and former centuries, but have in fact been very recent phenomena as well. This can be seen in Australia, where forest destruction, overgrazing and unlimited burning have greatly accelerated wind erosion and have thus, extended the Australian deserts within the last 100 years. The present-day expansions of the Sahara and Thar deserts are largely due to excessive grazing and land misuse. The American dustbowl of the 1920's and 1930's is an other well-documented story of land misuse, changing a once fertile grassland into a dusty pit of ecological tragedy. Throughout much of present-day Latin America and in many tropical or subtropical regions of the world, the dangerous game of "slash and burn" agriculture is actively practiced. This denudes forested tracts rapidly, permits a few years of productive agriculture, and leaves a wake of destruction. The forest that may have taken 1,000 years to develop can be destroyed in two or three years. In the tropics, where natural soils are thin and very susceptible to rapid leaching and erosion, the entire organic ecosystem may be irreparably damaged in less than a decade. We have either ignored the lessons of ecologic history or are too blinded by the economic pressures of life to appreciate their importance to us.

Considerable progress in a positive direction has been made in recent years by the well-publicised "Green Revolution." Many countries throughout Asia, Africa and Latin America have made dramatic advances in agricultural production through the development of irrigation, new varieties of seeds and increased fertiliser production (Horsfall, 1970)[29]. India, for example, became self-sufficient in food grain production in food grain production in 1971 for the first time in more than 20 years. The Philippines became self-sufficient in rice production in 1970 (Athwal, 1971)[30]. It remains to be seen, however, if this progress of the Green Revolution can be maintained or if it will simply provide additional spurts to population growth. The chemical fertilisers used for higher yields, have however resulted in a stunted growth in the long run. The agro- industry now awaits new turns in bio-technology and genetic-engineering.

Conclusion

There is little doubt that many environments throughout the world have been rendered barren and inhospitable by excessive pressures from the axes, ploughs and hoofed animals of man. The pioneer civilizations altered their own biotic and physical environments and displayed man's ability to trigger ecological changes leading to his own downfall.

In the decade of the new millennium there is very little evidence that man recognises this aspect of his own history or realises its applicability to his present predicaments. In country after country around the world I have seen the conservation movement losing ground, either through neglect or ridicule. In Malaysia and Indonesia, deforestation is occurring at increasing rates, and the people believe that their forests are unlimited. In India, overgrazing and hydroelectric power development schemes are invading the few National Parks and Forest Reserves which still exist. In the Himalayan Mountains, the landscape is being carved within an inch of its life to support a burgeoning and none-too-healthy human population. In Africa and Latin America, slash and burn agriculture is encroaching upon natural areas which have existed in ecological balance for thousands of years.

Much of this environmental destruction is done in the name of economic development. The pressures of increasing populations place a greater burden than ever on the finite blanket of life that covers this earth. That blanket is getting torn and shredded in thousands of places. Like a wound or a burn on the skin, its ability to heal depends upon the extent of the lesion and the health of the surrounding tissue. A point can be reached where the healing capacity is lost.

References

1. Elton, C.S. *The Ecology of Animals.* London: Methuen, 1933.
2. Bates, M. The Forest and the Sea. *A look of the Economy of Nature and the Ecology of Man.* New York: Menton Books, 1960.
3. Lee, R.B. and I. De Vore (ed.). *Man the Hunter.* Chicago: Aldine, 1968.

4. Dunn, F.L. Health and Disease in hunter gatherers. Chap. 23 In *Man the Hunter,* Lee and DeVore (eds.), Chicago: Aldine, 1968, pp. 221-228.
   Neel, J.V. Lessons from a "Primitive" People. Science, 170: 815-822 (1970).
5. Guthrie, D.A. Primitive Man's Relationship to Nature. *Bioscience,* 21:721-723 (1971).
6. Guthrie, D.A. Primitive man's relationship to nature. *Bioscience,* 21:721-723 (1971).
7. Martin, P.S. and H.E. Wright. Pleistocene Extinctions. Proc. 7th Cong. Int. Assoc. for Quarternary Res., Vol. 6. New Haven: Yale University Press, 1967.
8. Lee, R.B. and I. DeVore (ed.). *Man the Hunter.* Chicago: Aldine, 1968.
9. Marsh, G.P. *Man and Nature.* D. Lowenthal (ed.), Cambridge: Harvard University Press. 2nd Printing, 1967. Org. Publ. 1864.
10. McCormick, J. *Forest Ecology.* New York : Harper & Bros., 1959.
11. Saggs, H.W.F. *The Greatness that was Babylone.* New York : Hawthorn Books, 1962.
12. Sauer C.O. Theme of Plant and Animal Destruction in Economic History. *Jour. Of Farm Econom.* 20 : 765-775 (1938).
13. Perkins D. Jr. Fauna of Catal Huyuk : Evidence for Early Cattle Domestication in Anatolia. *Science,* 164:177-179(1969).
14. Dasmann, R. *Environmental Conservation.* New York : Wiley, 1968.
15. Saggs, H. W. F. *The Greatness that was Babylone.* New York : Hawthorn Books, 1962.
16. Wallbank, W.T. *A Short History of India and Pakistan.* New York : Scott Foresman, 1958.
17. Davidson, Basil. *The Lost Cities of Africa.* Boston : Little, Brown, 1959.
18. Davidson, Basil. *The Lost Cities of Africa.* Boston : Little, Brown, 1959.
19. Rienow, R. and L.T. Rienow. *Moment in the Sun.* New York: Ballantine Books,1967.
20. Ehrlich, P.R. and A.H. Ehrlich. *Population, Resources*

Environment : Issues in Human Ecology. San Francisco : W.H. Freeman & Co., 1970.
21. Marsh, G.P. *Man and Nature.* D. Lowenthal (ed.), Cambridge, Harward University Press. 2nd Printing,1967. Org. Publ. 1864.
22. Sears, P.B. *Deserts on the March.* Norman : University of Oklahoma Press,1935.
23. Osborn, F. *Our Plundered Planet.* Boston : Little Brown, 1948.
24. Sauer,C.O. Land and Life. *A selection from the writings of Carl Ortwin Sauer.* John Leighly (ed.). Berkeley: University of California Press, 1967.
25. Champion H.G. A Preliminary Survey of the Forest Types of India and Burma. *Indian Forest Records (Silviculture series), Vol. 1, No.1, 1936.*
26. Sauer,C.O. Land and Life. *A selection from the writings of Carl Ortwin Sauer.* John Leighly (ed.). Berkeley: University of California Press, 1967.
27. Osborn, F. *Our Plundered Planet.* Boston : Little Brown, 1948.
28. Sears, P.B. *Deserts on the March.* Norman: University of Oklahoma Press, 1935.
29. Horsfall, J.G. The Green Revolution: Agriculture in the Face of the Population Explosion. In *The Environmental Crisis,* H.W. Helfrich, Jr., New Haven: Yale University Press, 1970, pp. 85-98.
30. Atwal, D.S. Semi-dwarf Rice and Wheat in Global Food Needs. *Quart. Rev. of Biology,* 46:1-34(1971).

4

Attitudenal Breakdowns

Early Man

We can imagine that the world was a baffling place to early man. His attitudes towards his environment were probably shaded by reverence, awe and fear-fear of storms, disease wild animals, earthquakes, volcanos, celestial phenomena and countless other events which were not understood. This primitive sense of fear and loneliness has been poetically described by the eminent Bengali writer Tagore :

When in the depth of the night
in the phantasmal light of the sick-bed
appears your wakeful presence,
it seems to me
that the countless suns and stars
have guaranteed my little life:
then I know that you will leave me
and the fear spreads from sky to sky,
the fear of the terrible indifference
of the All.@

Note : @ "Fear" from the anthology, Boundless Sky by Rabindranath Tagore. Calcutta: Visva-Bharati, 1964.

Amid the accountrements of modern civilisation it is impossible to project ourselves fully into the mind of early man, but perhaps we can visualise the awesome nature of the African veldt or the Malaysian forest throughout the cycles of storm and drought, heat and cold, night and day, disease and health. It is no wonder that mysticism and religion arose in virtually all people to help explain the unexplainable. Man felt himself to be a close integral part of his world and subject to its whims. He recognised his dependence upon nature and held it in awe. A unity of life existed and man considered himself one small part of a vast and complex scheme of nature. Again Tagore conveys this feeling in the song offerings of Gitanjali, one of which reads:

The same steam of life that runs through my
veins night and day runs through the world and
dances in rhythmic measures.
It is the same life that shoots in joy
through the dust of the earth in numberless blades
of grass and breaks into tumultuous waves of leaves
and flowers.

It is the same life that shoots in joy
through the dust of the earth in numberless blades
of grass and breaks into tumultuous waves of leaves
and flowers.

It is the same life that is rocked in the ocean-
Cradle of birth and death, in ebb and in flow.
I feel my limbs are made glorious by the
touch of this world of life. And my pride is from
*the life-throb of ages dancing in my blood this moment.**

These are modern writings, of course, since Tagore was born in Calcutta in 1841 and died in 1941, having received the Nobel prize for literature in 1913 and British Knighthood in 1915. Many of his writings, however, capture the ancient philosophies of India, and they may, in fact, mirror the sensitivities of early man towards his environment.

Note : * From The Song Offerings of Gitanjali by Rabindranath Tagore. New York and London : Mac-Millan and Co., 1964.

The Judaic-Christian Tradition

Gradually, throughout the rise of agricultural civilisations in the last 10,000 years, man has increased his confidence and ability to control his means of subsistence. Religion became more a means of establishing a favoured relationship with the unknown, and less a means of survival per se. Landscape became property and the concept of proprietary ownership developed. The Judaic-Christian Philosophy in particular portrayed land as the God-given property of man (White, 1967)1. Nature existed for man, to be used by him and exploited for his own good. Man no longer considered himself merely one part of the biotic community, interacting with it in a humble and mutually beneficial way. He was now its owner and master, capable of treating it like any other property. According to White (1967)[1], Christianity arose as "the most anthropocentric religion the world has seen". The egocentricity of man could be seen long before the time of Christ. For example, the famous passage from Genesis 1:28 exemplifies the favoured status which religion bestowed on man:

And God blessed them, and God said to them, "Be fruitful and multiply, and fill the earth and subdue it; and have dominion over the fish of the sea and over the birds of the air and over every living thing that moves upon the earth".

The writer of Deuteronomy (8:7-9) continued this theme:

For the lord your God is bringing you into a good land, a land of brooks, of water, of fountains and spring, flowing forth in valleys and hills, a land of wheat and barely, of vines and fig trees and pomegranates, a land of olive trees and honey, a land in which you will eat bread without scarcity, in which you will lack nothing, a land whose stones are iron, and out of whose hills you can dig copper.

This was the Promised Land and man was now the master, for he represented God on earth (Genesis 1:26)

And God said, " let us make man in our image after our likeness: and let them have dominion over the fish of the sea, and over the fowl of the air, and over the cattle, and over the all earth, and over every creeping things that creepeth upon the earth."

These aspects of the Judaic-Christian tradition are considered by White (1967)[1] to be the philosophic basis for the complete exploitation of land for the benefit of man. Nature, in fact, existed for no other reason than to serve man. Hence, White calls this, *The Historical Roots of our Ecologic Crisis*, and he feels that our modern problems of land destruction and pollution originated in the Judaic-Christian philosophies.

This specific thesis might be contested on several grounds: (1) much ecologic damage had occurred long before the first formulation of the book of Genesis in the Old Testament (the Yahwist text of Genesis was written between 850 B.C and 750 B.C. according to Anzou, 1963)[2] and (2) misuse, exploitation and destruction of the landscape have occurred with equal severity in non-Christian parts of the world.

We have seen in the previous chapter how the destructive influence of man upon his environment was by no means confined to the areas of Judaism and Christianity. It occurred throughout broad reaches of Asia and Africa, certainly in China, India, and the Sudan, in areas subject to highly varied religious influences, and even in the Middle-East long before the time of Judaic-Christian influence.

Hence, it is doubtful if the ecological ills of the world can be blamed on any single religious or philosophic foundation. Nonetheless, the persistence and growth of the exploitation of land as property, existing solely for the use of man, was certainly fostered by the Judaic-Christian concepts of land ownership.

The geographer Carl Sauer believed that there were three great periods of habitat destruction in the history of man: First, a period at least three to four thousand years ago, when the great herds of pastoral man and the early successes of agriculture caused extensive land scarring, erosion, and irreversible aridity in Africa, the Middle East and Asia. Second, the latter days of Rome and the disorderly period that immediately followed, when many of the Mediterranean lands were despoiled. Third, the transatlantic expansion of European commerce and people into the New World, when rapid and disastrous land exploitation occurred throughout the Americas. Sauer documented these views in an important book first published in 1938 and reprinted in a recent anthology (Leighly, 1967).[4]

Does this mean that each major advance of man carries with it the possibility of some destructive force,? Keeping in mind the domestication of hoofed animals, the expansion of the Roman empire, the invasion of the New World, the development of gunpowder, the rise of modern medicine, the internal combustion engine, and now the advent of the atomic age–all major technologic achievements which also contained destructive capabilities, one is tempted to believe the above statement may have sober elements of truth.

The Industrial Revolution and the Baconian Creed

The industrial revolution of the eighteenth and nineteenth centuries, and certainly the technologic revolution of the twentieth century, continued to foster the ideas of proprietary ownership and economic exploitation of the land. Man has generally viewed land as existing for his own benefit and profit potential. The widespread practice of shifting cultivation and the agricultural techniques of slash, burn, cultivate, and then move on, have characterized much New World agriculture until recent times, and tragically these practices still prevail in tropical regions.

The technological revolution has gone several steps further in moulding the attitudes of man. The Baconian creed, that scientific and technologic knowledge means control and power over nature, arose from the writings of Francis Bacon in the early seventeenth century, but it has found its fullest expression in the last one hundred years. The developments of electrical energy and the internal combustion engine gave man unprecedented power for transportation, production, and environmental modification. These new tools, as products of scientific technology, furthered the belief that science held sovereignty over nature.

The Rise and Fall of Twentieth Century Optimism

During the twentieth century the Baconian creed has given man the optimism that he can achieve all things. He can control and eliminate diseases, produce unlimited food, develop comfortable housing and clothing for all, and enter a golden age of technology and economic prosperity in which his only remaining problems would be the use of leisure time.

This twentieth century optimism was temporarily deflated by two world wars and the great economic depression of the early 1930's, but it came surging back in the late 1940's. Franklin Delano Roosevelt said in 1944 that "we shall expand indefinitely," and he was referring to unlimited expansion in terms of prosperity and well - being for all.

A contrary philosophy was expressed by Aldo Leopold(1949)[5], William Vogt(1948)[6] and Fairfield Osborn (1948)[7] which suggested that man was out of balance with his environment and would soon pay the consequences. These men insisted that only strict attention to the principles of ecology and the view that man was part of a sensitive and intricate ecosystem could save us from a programme of self–defeat. Fairfield Osborn stated this philosophy well when he wrote (1948):

The question remains. Are we to continue on the same dusty perilous road once travelled to its dead end by other mighty and splendid nations, or, in our wisdom, are we going to choose the only route that does not lead to the disaster that has already befallen so many other people of the earth? (p. 193)

He concluded his book by stating:

There is only one solution: Man must recognize the necessity of cooperating with nature. He must temper his demands and use and conserve the natural living resources of this earth in a manner that alone can provide for the continuation of civilization. The final answer is to be found only through comprehension of the enduring processes of nature. The time for defiance is at an end.

The fears and warnings of Osborn, Vogt and Leopold seem more pertinent today than when they were first written more than twenty years ago. Nonetheless, these views were not widely accepted by educated people throughout the world. They were held primarily by ecologists and conservationists who have continued in a state of depression over the ecologic condition of the world, and who spend long hours commiserating with each other, basically convinced that the real message of ecology will never get accepted before irreversible harm has been done. The problem is, however, that it is so hard to demonstrate that irreversible harm has been done. In many cases the necessary research has not yet been accomplished, or if it has, the message lies buried in technical reports. In other cases, the problem requires a sense of historical perspective and ecologic outlook that is not often acquired in current educational programmes. It takes more than the written word of popular publications to convince the pragmatic businessman and politician that things are really as bad as ecologists say they are. Man still has great dreams of making the desert bloom and controlling the unruly river with hydro schemes. Each success is quoted far more often than numerous failures.

So the tide of optimism about the power of science and technology to erase man's problems continued to expand. In 1955 the editors of *Fortune* compiled a volume entitled, *The Fabulous Future*, in which they invited prominent business leaders to express their views about the future of man. Most of the essays were clear extensions of the *Baconian Creed*, and most expressed in glowing terms the prospects of the future. David Sarnoff, then Chairman of the board of RCA, stated this creed as follows:

There is no longer any margin for doubt that whatever the mind of man visualizes, the genius of science can turn functioning fact.

Under a section entitled, "Things to come," Mr. Sarnoff envisioned:

Other sources of energy – the sun, the tides, and the winds-are certain to be developed beyond present expectations. New materials by the score - metals, fabrics, woods, glass - will be added to the hundreds of synthetics and plastics already available through our capacity to rearrange the structure of matter.

Fresh water, purified from the briny seas, will enable us to make deserts flourish and to open to human habitation immense surfaces of the globe now sterile or inaccessible.

Mr. Sarnoff emphasized, however, that the big question is man himself. Can he realise his potential l? Can he meet the social ills of modern nations? Sarnoff felt that we could attain a technologically utopian world if social tolerance and mutual understanding were first achieved.

Crawford Greenawalt, President of Dupont Company, indicated a similar optimism based on the caution of a social contingency. "If we are successful in recapturing that atmosphere of freedom, incentive, and self-respect, the future will be boundless indeed." Mr. Greenawalt emphasized personal freedom and the capitalistic system as the great provider. He felt that America's progress was primarily due to our political and economic system, and not to our abundant and relatively virgin natural resources. His conclusion was one of optimism:

Fortunately we do not have to visualize the precise of things to come to be able to predict with confidence another 25 years or more of growth prosperity.

The ecologist would criticize this as being too provincial a view, limited to the United States, and much too limited in its time dimension. Twenty-five years in the history of man is a mere blip on the scanning screen of history.

George Humphrey, Secretary of the Treasury in 1955, limited his predictions to the "free world":

The present and future of the free-world people look good. An America of confidence, prudence and imagination will mean ... a future finer than our minds can even dream.

Henry Luce, Editor-in Chief of Time–Life, Inc., also foresaw a splendid future for man; a life of unlimited prosperity and super–abundance:

Today we can glimpse the end of poverty .... Abundance has become visibly the norm of life in America. Having been achieved in America as a human reality, this economy of abundance is likely to become the global condition of man's life on earth.

Although these preceding statements were from leaders of business and government in mid 1950's, scientists were also expressing similar views of the future. At times they

---

Note : * From *The Challenge of Man's Future* by Harrison Brown, copyright © 1954 by Harrison Brown, reprinted by permission of the Viking press, Inc.

somewhat more guarded by "ifs, ands, and buts," but on the whole optimism shone through. An example would be the writing of the eminent scientist, Harrison brown (1954)[8]:*

It is clear that the nations of the West possess sufficient resources and productive capacity to catalyze a successful world development programme at the present time. Our physical ability to bring about successful transition is not one of the unknowns. We have the ability to do it; whether we have the vision and the will is another matter (p. 248).

I can imagine a world within which machines function solely for man's benefit, turning out those goods which are necessary for his well- being relieving him of the necessity for heavy physical labour and dull, routine, meaningless activity. The world I imagine is one in which people are well fed, well clothed, and well housed. Man in this world, lives in balance with his environment, nourished by nature in harmony with the myriads of other life forms which are beneficial to him. He treats his land wisely, halts erosion and over cropping, and returns all organic waste matter to the soil from which it sprung. He lives efficiently, yet minimizes artificiality. It is not an overcrowded world; people can, if they wish, isolate themselves in the silences of a mountaintop, or they can walk through primeval forests or across wooded plains. In the world of my imagination, there is organization, but it is as decentralized as possible, compatible with the requirements for survival. There is a world government, but it exists solely for the purpose of preventing war and stabilizing population, and its powers are irrevocably restricted. The government exists for man rather than man for the government.

In the world of imagination the various regions are self - sufficient, and the people are free to govern themselves as they choose and to establish their own cultural patterns. All people have a voice in the government, and individuals can move about when and where they please. It is a world where man's creativity is blended with the creativity of nature, and where a moderate degree of organization is blended with a moderate degree of anarchy.

Is such a world impossible of realization? Perhaps it is, but who among us can really say? At least if we try to create such a world there is a chance we will succeed. But if we let the present trend continue it is all too clear that we will lose forever those qualities of mind and spirit which distinguish the human being from the automaton. (p. 258)

Dr. Brown considered unbridled population growth as the most devastating trend standing in the way of achieving a balanced and prosperous world. Although he believed that science and technology could meet most of our physical needs, he shared with Sir Charles Galton Darwin (1853)[9] the fears that human populations might not be stabilized in an orderly way, and will again be controlled someday by high death rates. This ambivalent faith and fear was clearly expressed in the following paragraph from his final chapter.

In our survey of the situation in which man now finds himself, we see that, although our high-grade resources are disappearing, we can live comfortably on low grade resources. We see that, although a large fraction of the world's population is starving, all of humanity can, in principle, be nourished adequately. We see that, although world populations are increasing rapidly, those populations can, in principle, be stabilized. Indeed, it is amply clear that, if man wills it, a world community can be created in which human beings can live comfortably and in peace with each other. But it is equally clear that the achievement of this condition will require the application of intelligence, imagination, courage, unselfish help, planning and prodigious effort. And it is equally clear that the time for decision is the present. With the consumption of each additional barrel of oil and ton of coal, with the addition of each new mouth to be fed, with the loss of each additional inch of topsoil, the situation becomes more inflexible and difficult to resolve. Man is rapidly creating a situation from which he will have difficulty extricating himself. (p. 265)

This viewpoint of guarded optimism represented sound scientific thinking and reasonable philosophy as well. It placed the burden squarely on man and his institutions. It saw in world affairs the potentials of both a tragic and a glorious future for man.

The Onset of Despair

In general, through the 1950's and early 1960's optimism prevailed, and the balance tipped decidedly toward the vision of a marvellous future for man. Economic prosperity was skyrocketing in many countries of the world. America was on the verge of its "New Frontier. The conquest of space was catapulting man's dreams towards distant goals. The world was not yet enmeshed in any Major wars. Medicine was making great strides with the anticipated conquest of malaria, cholera and polio. The future looked bright. The thoughts of Henry Luce in 1955 seemed to be on the verge of realization.

Then the bubbles of bright prospects began to break. The United States gradually became bogged down in the distressing war in Vietnam. The Middle East erupted again into serious military action. America lost three of her outstanding leaders by assassination. Violence erupted in her cities. The War on Poverty became a hollow phrase. India experienced recurring famines. Africa became the scene of tragic wars in some of her most advanced countries. Tension increased throughout the world. A deep and pervading pessimism began to set in. The bright and glorious future of science and technology was tarnished even among the most hopeful and entirely scuttled among many Of the world's people.

This pessimism was clearly expressed his many writings of 1966 and 1967. The editors of the *Johns Hopkins Magazine produced* an issue in 1967 built around the theme, "The War Against Suffering." Its preface contained these stark facts:

Two–thirds of the human races live in the underdeveloped areas of the world.

Most of them drink unsafe water, prepare food dangerously, dispose of waters recklessly, and live in unfit dwellings.

In some parts of the developing world, every living individual is afflicted with intestinal parasites.

In some parts of the developing world, half of the children born never reach their fifth birthday.

Within the developing world at least 400 million people suffer from trachoma, a curable disease that causes progressive loss of sight.

Within the developing world, despite a massive campaign by the World Health Organization to eradicate malaria, 400 million people live in malarias areas where no eradication programme is under way. In some of these areas, most people have the disease.

Schistosomiasis, a debilitating parasitic disease, afflicts 200 million people–more than the population of the United States. In some the chances of escaping the disease are only one in five.

Leprosy afflicts more than 10 million people; fewer than one in five area receiving any kind of treatment. In the countries where leprosy is prevalent, 740 million people area expressed to the risk of infection.

Cholera, a disease on the decline in the 1950's is spreading. The number of reported cases tripled between 1960 and 1964.

Venereal diseases are spreading into the underdeveloped areas of the world, to an extent not yet measured.

This is, in part, the health situation amid two-thirds of the world's people. By the year 2000, if present demographic trends continue, it could be the story of four-fifths of the world's people.

An equally grim picture of the world's condition was drawn in an article on poverty in *Scientific American in the late 1960's* (Simpson, 1968)9. This article pointed out that two–thirds of the world's people live in countries whose annual per capita income is less than $300. The world's largest democracy, India, has a per capita annual income of less than $100. This is less than one–seventh the definition of poverty in the United States. One might say that the cost of living is less in India than in America, but this is a common misconception. Many staples of life, such as rice, flour, salt, and sugar are actually more expensive in India than in the United States. In Kolkata, one of India's most crowded cities, 77 percent of the population has less than 40 square feet of living space per person. In Pakistan, a survey conducted by the NIH Office of International Research, indicated that 46 percent of the households surveyed had an inadequate caloric intake. Simpson concluded that the rich nations and people of the world are getting richer, while the poor got poorer.

A similarly pessimistic view of global trends was composed in December 1966 by a Committee of biologists working under the auspices of the international Biological Programme, sponsored by the National Research Council.

The introduction to their programme statement read as follows:

The gravest problem facing man in a peaceful world is the establishment of a reasonable harmony between a stabilized world population and the environmental resources upon which that population depends.

Man, like other organisms, lives in and depends upon environment. That environment, it is increasingly clear, is both limited and vulnerable. Millions of human beings at present exist with inadequate food. Vast quantities of wastes reduce the quality of our environment.

Mankind is engaged in a programme of self-defeat, Human population increases at an unprecedented rate, and it has proved difficult to stabilize population in those countries where stability is most needed. Technological power is altering environment at an increasing rate, often in ways which are to man's disadvantage - erosion, occupation of prime farm land by housing, atmospheric pollution, and the wide spread use of poisons intended for pests. The product of increase in population and increase in the technological power of that population is an increase in rate of detrimental change in the environment on which man depends.

There is no present reason for confidence that man will succeed in bringing about a harmony between his population and environment. It does not seem that technology alone can produce a long-term solution. Technological progress can increase food production and improve environmental condition, but such benefits are only palliatives if population meanwhile increases. Technological expedients may also produce unforeseen environmental detriment, as in the case of currently increasing pollution problems. Solution of the problems of man's relation to his environment is possible only through difficult, long range decisions on limitation of both population and the technological modification of environment.

References

1. White, L. The historical roots of our ecologic crisis. *Science*, 155: 1203-1207(1967).
2. Anjou, G. *The formation of the Bible*. St. Louis and London: Herder, 1963.
3. Leighly, J. (ed.).*Land and Life. A selection from the writings of Carl Ortwin Sauer*. Berkeley: University of California

Press, 1967.

4. Leopold, A. *The Land Ethic. An essay in a sand country Almanac.* New York: Oxford University Press, 1949, pp. 201-226.
5. Vogt, W. *Road to Survival.* New York: William Sloane Associates, 1948.
6. Osborn, F. *Our Plundered Planet.* Boston: Little Brown, 1948.
7. Brown, H. *The Challenge of Man's future.* New York: Viking Press, 1954.
8. Darwin, C.G. *The next million Years.* New York: Doubleday, 1953.
9. Simpson, D. The Dimensions of World Poverty. *Scientific American, 219: 27-35 (1968).*

5

Theory About War and Destruction Down the Ages

When in doubt about
Ultimate causes go to
The primitives.
(Iain Prattis, anthropologist)

Humanity's propensity for warfare does not originate from a single, simple, reductionistic cause. It stems from several factors interacting over long periods of evolutionary time. These involve genetic strategies, environmental forces, mental development, and the development of culture. Given recent developments in evolutionary biology, socio-biology, anthropology, and cognitive psychology, improved understanding of humanity's propensity for warfare and destruction is at hand. As such, this book aims to develop a reasonably comprehensive theory which takes into account humanity's evolutionary past in order to help explain the present.

A "red line" throughout our theory is that the *evolution* of much contemporary social behaviour has originated during the past 1 to 2 million years when our ancestors lived in small, tight-knit kin groups. We call these groups "nucleus ethnic groups." Numbering approximately 100 individuals at most, a nucleus ethnic group comprised of one's offspring, one's Siblings' offspring, and one's parents and their siblings and their offspring. Plausible ideas are reviewed about how nucleus ethnic groups came into being, how they occupied niches in evolution, and how they came to engage in inter group conflict. Understanding functions and priorities of nucleus ethnic groups forms the basis for deciphering1 how the past and present are linked and2 how forces of the past operate directly/indirectly, overtly/covertly in war faring propensities today. These forces help shape nationalism and patriotism as contemporary expressions of humanity's propensity for warfare.

To put this theory to work, it is applied to radical reinterpretation of[1] causes of coups d' etat in Africa, the role of nationalism as a means of mobilization for conflict in ethnically homogeneous groups and societies, and[3] the role of patriotism as a mobilization devices in multi-ethnic societies. In the case of African coups d' etat, we show that ethnic mobilization-as described by our theory-is often central to understanding conflict and war proneness. In the case of nationalism, it is used to explain the conflicts involving Iran and Iraq, Israel and the Arab countries, and Afghanistan and the USSR, as conflict and war proneness in pre-World War II Japan and South Africa today. In the case of patriotism, we acknowledge that major cultural and sociohistorical preconditions for nationalism (as a mobilizing device for conflict) are simply not available to multiethnic societies. The phenomenon of "patriotism," however, fills the gap. The theory explains why this is so, and how it operates as a mobilization force for out–group enmity and warfare in multi-ethnic societies such as the United States and the Russians until a recent past.

Finally I ask does peace have a chance ? Of one thing the record is clear. Traditional approaches to the study of war–as well as the vehicles for reducing warfare, such as arms negotiations and peace marches - contain little promise. From an evolutionary perspective, these approaches are poorly informed about key variables that perpetuate the process. For example, to understand war it is essential to decipher how one's nucleus ethnicity benefits. To understand how people are mobilized for war, it is important to examine how leaders appeal to nucleus ethnicity. Peace initiatives would have to begin at the grass-roots level of societal formation, cohesion, and mobilization as understood from an evolutionary perspective. At the very least, peace efforts must take into consideration ethnocentrism as it is communicated through school textbooks, nationalistic and patriotic programming, and sate policies fostering links between nucleus ethnicity and general social welfare.

Lest my intentions be misunderstood, it cannot be emphasized too strongly that this theory is most relevant to understanding *central tendencies* in humanity‘s propensity for warfare. It does not presume to explain all wars. It is, however, relevant to understanding war proneness and, therefore, has something to say about the staying power of any society to wage war. A society may wage war for reasons not identified by our theory, but the life expectancy of such a war is likely to be short–lived unless core elements of our theory are present.

It is also important to realize that this theory does not advocate that what is typical of war faring propensities today *ought to be.* Nor does it embrace any form of genetic reductionism. Although it suggests that warfare and destruction propensities are deeply entrenched in human nature, the purpose of this book is to decipher mechanisms involved and provide clues for their possible control.

6

Burdens of Development Consequences of Chemical Disasters

Bhopal MIC Disaster–02 December 1984

The Issue

Developing countries are particularly vulnerable to industrial crises. However, industrial accidents such as Bhopal are not just an Indian or even a Third World problem but are industrial disasters waiting to happen, whether they are in the form of "mini-Bhopals, smaller industrial accidents that occur with disturbing frequency in chemical plants in both developed and developing countries, and "slow-motion Bhopals, unseen chronic poisoning from industrial pollution that causes irreversible pain, suffering, and death (Weir, pp. xi-xii). These are the key issues we face in a world where toxins are used and developed without fully knowing the harm that can come from their use or abuse.

Leading Upto the Events

Developing countries, such as India, are particularly vulnerable as they lack the infrastructure (e.g. communication, training, education etc.) required to maintain technology but are nevertheless, eager to set up and maintain industrial plants. As a result, they compete globally to attract multinational companies for their investment and capital, and in this process, often tend to ignore the safety and health violations that many MNC's engage in. "Developing countries confer upon MNC's a competitive advantage because they offer low-cost labour, access to markets, and lower operating costs. Once there, companies have little incentive to minimize environmental and human risks. Lax environmental and safety regulation, inadequate capital investment in safety equipment, and poor communications between Companies and governments compound the problem" (Cassels, p. 279).

The Bhopal facility was par : of India's Green Revolution aimed to increase the productivity of crops. Considered an essential factor in the effort to achieve self-sufficiency in agricultural production, pesticide use increased dramatically during the late 1960's and early 1970's. The decision to manufacture the pesticides in India, as opposed to relying on imports was based on India's goal of preserving foreign exchange and its policy of industrialization (Cassels, p. 39). In 1969, Union Carbide

(UCC-the parent company) set up a small plant (Union Carbide India Ltd-UCIL) in Bhopal, the capital city of Madhya Pradesh, to synthesise pesticides.

Bhopal was chosen as the site for the Carbide plant because of its central location in India, a railway system that spanned the country, a large lake which provided a reliable source of water, and sufficient electricity and labour to sustain a large scale industrial plant. The MIC facility was located in the existing Carbide plant to the north of the city, adjacent to an existing residential neighbourhood and barely two kilometres from the railway station. Union Carbide claims that the "squatter settlements" around the plant arrived only after it did. However, "all three of the worst-affected communities in the disaster apparently existed before the Union Carbide plant opened" (Weir, p. 36).

Until 1979, the Indian subsidiary of Carbide used to import MIC or methyl isocyanate from the parent company. After 1979, it started to manufacture its own MIC. MIC is one of many "intermediates" used in pesticide production and is a dangerous chemical. It is a little lighter than water but twice as heavy as air, meaning that when it escapes into the atmosphere it remains close to the ground. It has the ability to react with many substances: water acids, metals, and the small deposits of corrosive materials that accumulate in pipes, tanks, and valves. The MIC in Bhopal was used for the production of various pesticides, mainly Sevin brand carbaryl insecticide and Temik brand aldicarb pesticide. All the pesticides produced at UCIL were sold in the Indian market. According to many, Bhopal is the site of the greatest industrial disaster in history. On the night of December 23, 1984, a dangerous chemical reaction occurred in the Union Carbide factory when a large amount of water got into the MIC storage tank # 610. The leak was first detected by workers about 11:30 p.m. when their eyes began to tear and burn. They informed their supervisor who failed to take action until it was too late. At that time, a large amount, about 40 tons of Methyl Isocyanate (MIC), poured out of the tank for nearly two hours and escaped into the air, spreading within eight kilometres downwind, over the city of nearly 900,000.

Thousands of people were killed (estimates ranging as high as 4,000) in their sleep or as they fled in terror, and hundreds of thousands remain injured or affected (estimates range as high as 400,000) to this day. The most seriously affected areas were the densely populated shanty towns immediately surrounding the plant— Jayaprakash Nagar, Kazi Camp, Chola Kenchi, and the Railway Colony. The victims were almost entirely the poorest members of the population.

This poisonous gas, caused death and left the survivors with lingering disability and diseases. Not much is known about the future medical damage of MIC, but according to an international medical commission, the victims suffer from serious health problems that are being misdiagnosed or ignored by local doctors (Lancet, "Round...").

Exposure to MIC has resulted in damage to the eyes and lungs and has caused respiratory ailments such as chronic bronchitis and emphysema, gastrointestinal problems like hyperacidity and chronic gastritis, ophthalmic problems like chronic conjunctivitis and early cataracts, vision problems, neurological disorders such as memory and motor skills, psychiatric problems of various types including varying grades of anxiety and depression, musculoskeletal problems and gynaecological problems among the victims. It is estimated that children born in Bhopal after the disaster face twice the risk of dying as do children elsewhere, partly because parents cannot care for them adequately. Surprisingly enough, despite the serious health problems and the deaths that have occurred, Union Carbide claims that the MIC is merely a "mild throat and ear irritant" (Lancet, "Round..." p. 952).

The Bhopal disaster was the result of a combination of legal, technological, organizational, and human errors. The immediate cause of the chemical reaction was the seepage of water (500 litters) into the MIC storage tank. The results of this reaction were exacerbated by the failure of containment and safety measures and by a complete absence of community information and emergency procedures. The long term effects were made worse by the absence of systems to care for and compensate the victims.

Furthermore, safety standards and maintenance procedures at the plant had been deteriorating and ignored for months. A listing of the defects of the MIC unit runs as follows:

- Gauges measuring temperature and pressure in the various parts of the unit, including the crucial MIC storage tanks, were so notoriously unreliable that workers ignored early signs of trouble (Weir, pp. 41-42).
- The refrigeration unit for keeping MIC at low temperatures (and therefore less likely to undergo overheating and expansion should a contaminant enter the tank) had been shut off for some time (Weir, pp.41-42).
- The gas scrubber, designed to neutralize any escaping MIC, had been shut off for maintenance. Even had it been operative, post-disaster inquiries revealed, the maximum pressure it could handle was only one-quarter that which was actually reached in the accident (Weir, pp. 41-42).

- The flare tower, designed to burn off MIC escaping from the scrubber, was also turned off, waiting for replacement of a corroded piece of pipe. The tower, however, was inadequately designed for its task, as it was capable of handling only a quarter of the Volume of gas released (Weir, pp. 41-42).
- The water curtain, designed to neutralize any remaining gas, was too short to reach the top of the flare tower, from where the MIC was billowing (Weir, pp. 41-42).
- The lack of effective warning systems; the alarm on the storage tank failed to signal the increase in temperature on the night of the disaster (Cassels, p. 19).
- MIC storage tank number 610 was filled beyond recommended capacity; and
- a storage tank which was supposed to be held in reserve for excess MIC already contained the MIC (Cassels, p. 19).

Ironically, in Bhopal, the people living around the Union Carbide plant were warned of potential hazards in a series of local newspaper articles, but residents ignored these warnings because they did not know how to react to them, while local officials dismissed them as sensationalist reporting (Technology Review, p. 73).

Interestingly enough, Carbide tried to hide its poor safety and maintenance record along with the other faults already mentioned, by claiming publicly that the company was the victim of sabotage by a 'disgruntled employee'. Yet, Carbide didn't release the name of this employee or bring charges against him/her. However, there is evidence to the contrary which supports the view that Carbide (both the parent company and its Indian subsidiary) was a negligent company that failed to improve its deteriorating plant. Incidentally, in a report (May 1982) of the Indian subsidiary conducted by a three-member safety team from the Union Carbide headquarters in the U.S., indicated that "a serious potential for sizeable releases of toxic materials in the MIC unit either due to equipment failure, operating problems, or maintenance problems thus requiring various changes to reduce the danger of the plant; there is no evidence the recommendations were ever implemented" (Weir, pp.40-41).

Furthermore, "Carbide persistently shows 'wanton and wilful disregard for the health and safety of its workers and the communities in which it operates'"(New Statesman and Society, "Surviving..." p. 5). Additionally, a scientific report published by two U.S. organizations, the National Toxic Campaign and the international Council on Public Affairs, Union Carbide continues to be " 'a major discharger of toxic substances into the environment, and a major generator of hazardous waste'. In 1988, the company generated more than 300 million pounds of hazardous waste - an increase of 70 million compared with 1987" (New Statesman and Society, "Surviving..." p. 5).

Carbide had dropped the safety standards at the Bhopal plant well below those it maintained at a nearly identical facility in West Virginia. It is also important to note here that Carbide was able to operate its deteriorating plant because industrial safety and environmental laws and regulations were lacking or were not strictly enforced by the state of Madhya Pradesh or the Indian government making them indirectly responsible for the tragedy at Bhopal.

Legality Aspects

This disaster gave rise to the world's largest lawsuit, one that spanned half-way around the world and dragged on for more than seven years. Although the final settlement ($470 million) satisfied the imperatives of the company and the Government of India, it was condemned by the victims (Cassels, preface).

For years after the tragedy, the delay in delivering final compensation to the victims has further propagated the suffering to the victims. Furthermore, other elements of relief ordered by the Indian Supreme Court haven't been implemented. These are the medical surveillance programme, the contingency insurance and the new hospital. There has been much dissent and several organizations have voiced that the settlement with Union Carbide, made on behalf of the victims by the Indian government, should be voided. These petitioners argue that the Indian court had no authority to dismiss criminal charges or grant immunity against future charges, to Union Carbide since pleas bargaining is not permitted under Indian law.

The petitioners also argued that while the settlement amount was based on an estimated 40,000 severely injured victims, medical studies suggest the number may be closer to 400,000 (Forbes, "The ghost..." p.108). Also, many medical experts believe that liability to provide adequate compensation and facilities for the handicapped victims requiring long-term follow up and treatment should rest with Union Carbide Corporation and not with the Indian Government (Lancet, "Round..." p. 952). Moreover, more than 250,000 claims were never documented or classified, making it hard for these victims to obtain compensation. Much to the anger and outrage of these groups and victims and the relief of Union Carbide, on October 1991, the Indian Supreme Court upheld the Bhopal settlement of $470 million dollars. Many feel that this is a clear signal from the Indian government that MNC's investing in the country will receive only a "slap on the wrist" in the event that something like this happens again.

Forum and Scopc

Issues of jurisdiction were central to the legal battle that followed the tragedy. These centred around the relationship of the parent Union Carbide Corporation to its Indian subsidiary and the appropriateness of the place where litigation is being conducted. Union Carbide Corporation maintains that it's subsidiary is separate from the parent company and so it only should be liable instead of the whole corporation. The Indian government's petition argues that in so far as Union Carbide designed, constructed, owned, and operated the plant from which the chemical escaped, the company should be held absolutely liable for all the resulting damage. Second, the company, in undertaking an activity that it knew was ultra-hazardous to the public at large, is strictly liable for the harm that was the material consequence of such activity, regardless of whether the harm that resulted was through fault of another or its own negligence. Third, the company was negligent in designing, constructing, operating and maintaining its plant and thus, failed to exercise its duty of care to protect the public from the dangers inherent in its plant and processes (More house and Subramanian, pp. 81-82).

Lawsuits were filed in both U.S. and Indian courts but ultimately, it was decided that the case should be tried in an Indian court. Lawsuits filed in U.S. courts related to the Bhopal case were refused on the grounds that the immediate location of the accident was in India, the victims were Indian, and he U.S. connection with its Indian affiliate did not appear to give it an unusual degree of control.

Legal Stand

Following the disaster, the Government of India passed the Bhopal Gas Leak Disaster (Processing of Claims) Act, 1985. The Act gave power to the Central Government to represent all claimants in appropriate forums, appoint a Welfare Commissioner and other staff and to discharge duties connected with hearing of the claims and distribution of compensation. Under this Act, in 1985, the Government formulated a scheme known as the Bhopal Gas Leak Disaster Scheme, for the registration, processing, and determination of compensation to each claim and appeals arising from thereon.

Since the tragedy, the victims have waged an "unrequited struggle for justice, but they have been ill-served by the Indian government, which failed to pursue the victims' case aggressively in the Indian courts, opting instead to go easy on Union Carbide and maintain a favourable investment climate" (New Statesman and Society, "Toxin..." p.18). Union Carbide settled out of court for $470 million, thus avoiding any damaging legal precedent or liability. In return, India's Supreme Court ordered the dismissal of all civil and criminal charges against Carbide and its officers, and gave them immunity from future prosecution. The Supreme Court felt that in this case, the victims needed immediate relief, not further legal delay.

International Law at present plays almost no role in a Bhopal scenario. Substantive international law remains weak in the area of pollution, industrial hazards, and multinational business regulation (Weir, p.46). An international treaty is needed under which it would be agreed that, if courts in a signatory country award compensation after due process of law, then the award would automatically be enforced by courts in other signatory countries (Economist, p. 70).

Procedural Measures and Double Standards

With regard to process standards, it is apparent that Union Carbide had double standards when operating its plant in India and in West Virginia. An investigation of both the UCIL plant and its counterpart in Institute, West Virginia revealed that "while the latter plant had computerized warning and monitoring system, the former relied on manual gauges and the human senses to detect gas leaks. The capacity of the storage tanks, gas scrubbers, and flare tower was greater at the Institute plant. Finally, emergency evacuation plans were in place in Institute, but nonexistent in Bhopal" (Cassel, p.19). Also, the manner in which Carbide decided to manufacture MIC was questioned at the design stage when a controversy arose regarding the question of whether substantial storage capacity or nominal storage of MIC would be required. UCC, which provided the basic design of the plant, supervised its engineering, and defined operating procedures to run it, insisted on the former [despite the fact that] UCIL felt that the latter was...inherently safer (More house and Subramanian, p. 3).

Death and Maiming Estimates

Estimates of the number dead and injured vary widely. Poor documentation, mass burials and cremations, and conflicting medical opinions ensure that the precise number will never be known. In addition, death records may not include homeless and transient individuals who perished. The original count of the dead was more than 2,000. By 1987, the official death toll stood at about 3,500 and by 1992, it was over 4,000. Victims' organizations placed the figure many thousands higher. In addition, 30,000 to 40,000 people were maimed and seriously injured, and 200,000 were otherwise affected through minor injury, death of a family member, and economic and social dislocation (Cassels, p. 5).

Environmental Problem Type

Not very much is known about the environmental impacts of the gas leak from the Bhopal plant. The Indian Council of Agricultural Research has issued a preliminary report on damage to crops, vegetables, animals, and fish from the accidents, but these offer few conclusive findings since they were reported in the early stages after the disaster. This report however, did indicate that the impact of whatever toxic substances emerged from the Carbide plants were highly lethal on exposed animals. Large number of cattle (estimates range as high as 4,000), as well as dogs, cats, and birds were killed. Plant life was also severely damaged by exposure to the gas. There was also widespread defoliation of trees, especially in low lying areas (More house and Subramanian, pp. 36-38).

Impediments in Cross Cultural Understanding

There appear to be have been serious communication problems and management gaps between Union Carbide and its Indian operation. This failure to communicate hazards was the result of the parent' companies hands-off approach to its overseas operation, and can be traced to cross-cultural barriers. These can possibly be related to "disruptions and flaws which appear in multinational operations because of "the absence of common values, norms, and expectations among managers in different nations, from tendencies towards ethnocentric attitudes, from psychological impediments to cross-cultural understanding, and from obstructions and deficiencies in the flow of information within the translational system attributable to distance and shared ownership. The fact that the operating manuals at Bhopal were printed only in English is an emblematic example of these problems (Cassels, p. 21).

Human Rights

In mid-July 1985, the government of India Health Minister stated that 36 pregnant women had spontaneously aborted, 21 babies were born with deformities, and there were 27 stillbirths, all suspected to have been caused by the poison gas leak in Bhopal. An examination of 114 women in the field clinics in two of the gas affected slums in Bhopal three months after the disaster revealed that an extremely high proportion of these women had developed gynaecological diseases such as leucorrhoea (90 per cent), pelvic inflammatory disease (79 per cent), cervical erosion and/or endocervicitis (75 per cent), excessive menstrual bleeding since exposure to the gas (31 per cent), and suppression of lactation (59 per cent). Also, there were several thousand pregnant women in the communities that were among the worst affected by the gas. Respiratory complication and the resulting hypozyia were bound to affect the foetuses as much as it did the mothers (More house and Subramanian, pp. 33-34).

CHRONICLE OF CHEMICAL DISASTERS

10 July 1976 Seveso Italy

An explosion at Seveso's Icmesa Chemical plant on 10 July 1976 set off a deadly chain of events that resulted in immediate measurable effects on plants and small animals. In spite of this, the regional government took ten days to declare the area polluted by dioxin and to evacuate the eleven thousand citizens. By this time forty thousand farm and domestic animals were dead from the effects of the poison cloud. More than three hundred houses were demolished and buried with soil trucked in from uncontaminated areas. The heart of seveso was destroyed, perhaps forever.

Over four hundred children suffering from chloracne, a disfiguring dermatological disease manifesting itself in recurring boils and skin eruptions over face and body, were hospitalized. The same number of expectant mothers were aborted and the expectation is that the rate of cancer in the town will increase dramatically.

What is more shocking than the effects of the accident is the inadequate and delayed response of the authorities. No one in Seveso seemed to realize the magnitude of the disaster. Dioxin is seven thousand times more deadly than cyanide and not even the factory workers were fully aware of the toxicity of the chemicals they handled. Furthermore, the industrialists refused to accept responsibility. A leading executive attempted to minimize the catastrophe in a fatuous statement that only added to the enragement of the victims. 'Capitalism means progress', he claimed, 'and progress can sometimes lead to inconvenience'.

This unbelievable insensitivity to the realities of Seveso fuelled an already volatile political situation in Italy and led to the first ecologically motivated assassination. Typically, the company lawyers were able to delay final judgment for ten years, and although five executives were initially given two–and-a-half to five year prison sentences for wilful negligence, by the time the appeals were heard, all but two were acquitted. Neither of these spent more than one year in jail.

6 December 1917- Halifax, Canada

The Belgian relief ship, Imo, grossly overburdened with unstable and outdated explosives, accidentally rammed the French munitions vessel, Mount Blanc in the harbour of Halifax, Nova Scotia. The resulting explosion destroyed half the city. Between 2,000 and 3,000 were killed and 8,000 were seriously injured in the disaster. Railway carriages were hurled hundreds of yards off their tracks. The suburb of Richmond was entirely obliterated. In one freak incident a Halifax man was hurled through the air and landed, uninjured, in a tree over a mile away.

21 September 1921- Oppan, Germany

The biggest chemical explosion in German history occurred in a warehouse in Oppan just south of Frankfurt. Foolishly advised workers use dynamite to blast loose 4,000 tons of ammonium nitrate fertilizer. In the blast, the ammonium nitrate itself converted to an explosive, and the entries load became a massive bomb. The death toil was over 560, with at least 3,000 serious injuries. A large section of Oppan was subsequently demolished.

1931-1935-Hawk's Nest, West Virginia, USA

Under direction of the Union Carbide Company workers constructed a hydroelectric tunnel at Hawk's Nest. Ventilation safety was largely ignored throughout the tunnelling operation resulting in the worst casualty rate through death by silicosis in history. It is believed that between 2,000 and 3,000 workers died from silicosis acquired while building this tunnel.

16 April 1947-Texas City, USA

The freighter *Grand Camp*, anchored in Galveston Bay, caught fire. Unknown to port authorities it contained 1,500 tons of ammonium nitrate fertilizer, the same deadly substance that destroyed Oppan. At 8.00 am the smouldering ship exploded with such force that its impact was registered a hundred miles away. But the disaster did not stop there. Fire engulfed the Monsanto styrene synthetic rubber plant in the harbour, which in turn exploded, spreading fire throughout the town. This fire burned on until the following day, when a second freighter, the *High Flyer*, also loaded with nitrates, caused a third disastrous explosion. The death toll was nearly 600, with approximately 2,000 serious burn victims.

28 July 1948- Ludwigshafen, Germany

At the factory site of the I.G. Farber chemical plant, a railway car containing the highly volatile dimethylethen was carelessly ignited by workers who were not told of its contents. The resulting explosion destroyed the factory and all its workers; it also caused a firestorm in the town, killing 200 and injuring 4,000.

11 July 1978- San Carlos de la Rapita, Spain

An over loaded tanker, carrying combustible propylene gas and travelling too fast, slid out of control on a corner and struck a wall. The result was a raging sheet of flame that engulfed a roadside campsite accommodating nearly 800 tourists. Over 200 campers were burned to death in the inferno.

3 November 1982- Salang Tunnel, Afghanistan

A petrol tank truck exploded inside the two-mile long Salang Tunnel. The Soviet and Afghan military mistook the collision for a guerrilla army attack and sealed off both ends of the tunnel. The result was that fire and carbon monoxide poisoning killed approximately 2,000 people trapped in the tunnel, although some put the figure as high as 2,700.

25 February 1984- Cubato, Brazil

Seepage from a leaking petrol pipeline in the south-east Brazilian town of Cubato was allowed to accumulate, despite complaints of fumes. When the leak was finally ignited, the explosion resulted in a giant fire ball that razed the town to the ground. At least 600 died and 3,000 sustained injuries.,

19 November 1948- Ixhautepec, Mexico

At 5.43 am. the Mexico City shanty town suburb of St Juna Ixhautepec was rocked by a massive explosion that enveloped it in flames. This was the initial blast of an hour–long series of disturbances registering 0.5 on the Richter earthquake scale. Fireballs measuring 300 meters in diameter roared through the streets for nearly two hours, destroying entries blocks of houses and incinerating every form of life in their path.

The reason for the explosion was careless storage of liquefied petroleum gas mostly in the form of propane, at the state-owned Pemex oil Company's gas complex in Ixhautepec. Pemex operations in Mexico had previously been described by inspectors as 'a catastrophe waiting to happen'. In the six months prior to the disaster, there had already been four separate major incidents, resulting in 89 deaths and hundreds of injuries. It was days before the last fires at Ixhautepec were extinguished and the casualties estimated. Well over 1,500 died in the disaster, and at least 7,000 were seriously injured.

12 December 1987- Minedoro Island, Philippines

The greatest ferry peacetime ship disaster in history was caused by the oil tanker Vector when it struck a heavily loaded ferry off Mindoro Island in the Philippines. The Manila ferry Dona Paz, owned by Sulpicio lines, sank rapidly with the loss of between 2,000 and 3,000 passengers. Coastguard reports clearly blamed the disaster on the oil tankers' actions.

2 July 1988- North Sea. UK

The world's worst oil rig disaster occurred on Occidental petroleum's *Piper Alpha* platform in the North Sea. The explosion and fire claimed the lives of 166 oil workers.

In 1980, the Norwegian platform station. *Alexander Kielland*, capsized in the Ekofisk field in the North Sea, killing 123. In November 1986, 45 oil workers were killed just off the Shetlands in a helicopter crash.

While the North Sea has the worst records of any single region for oil field disasters, with a death toll of more than 500, hundreds of oil workers have died in other regions during the last decade. An American oil-drilling ship sank in the South China Sea in October 1981, killing 81. The following year, in September 1982 another American- Owned oil rig, Ocean *Ranger*, keeled over in the North Atlantic and 84 men perished.

Hazardous Chemical Waste at Love Canal

Despite their dramatic impact, large-scale industrial disasters are relatively rare events in the overall theatre of chemical war. It is the secondary disasters, those occurring without immediate effect and without the photographs and body counts, that are the most frightening and difficult to deal with in terms of regulation and control.

The American Environmental Protection Agency (EPA), which came into being in 1970, has labelled toxic waste as 'the most serious environmental problem in the US today'. America alone produces 80 million tones of hazardous waste each year–the equivalent of more than 700 pounds per person. Further, the EPA point out that 90 per cent of all hazardous waste is dumped illegally or in a manner likely to threaten life.

The EPA recognizes some 50,000 hazardous waste sites in the United States, of which at least 2,000 may pose 'significant risks to human health or the environment'. Further, they note, only 200 of these sites were even licensed for disposal of toxic waste.

An EPA official stated the case bluntly: 'every barrel stuck in the ground is a ticking time bomb.' The cost of the clean-up after years of industrial dumping is almost unimaginable. One study estimates that the cost of cleaning up just one thousand of the most dangerous would be 44 billion dollars.

The most infamous and emblematic toxic waste case is that of love Canal near Niagara Falls, New York. Love Canal and its proximity to the natural wonder of the great falls has become a metaphor for the dark side of the American dream. Love Canal was a failed canal project built by William Love in the 1890s. The abandoned, canal trench was some three thousand feet long, sixty feet wide and ten feet deep and for a time become a popular swimming spot. However, during the 1940s the Olin Corporation and Hooker Chemicals, the owners of the site began using the Love Canal to dispose of toxic chemicals. From 1942 to 1952, Hooker dumped some 21,000 tons of toxic chemicals into the canal.

In 1953, in what appeared to be an act of philanthropy, Hooker disposed of the dump site by deeding the land for one dollar to the local Board of Education so that a school could be built there. The company failed to warn the board about the nature of the deadly chemicals in the dump. They did, however, have the forethought to protect themselves by writing a disclaimer into the deed, which transferred liability to the school board or any claims that might arise in connection with the buried toxic waste.

In this way, Hooker was simply unloading responsibility for a toxic waste site on to an unknowing community. Despite the fact that, as early as 1958, there is documentary evidence to show that Hooker was aware that children from the school were being 'burned by material at the old Love Canal property; the company still did not reveal the truth about the site to the school board or those with homes in the area.

It was not until 1976 that the community awoke to the horror of the toxic poisoning. After several years of unusually heavy rains, the water table in the area rose and basements and house foundations began to stink of chemicals. Entire gardens withered, pets died and children developed severe chemical burns on their hands and feet. Surveys soon indicated that air, water and soil pollution in the area was several hundred times above the safe level. Also the population was showing extremely high levels of birth defects, miscarriages, cancers, blood diseases, hyperactivity, asthma, nervous breakdowns and suicides.

Despite overwhelming evidence, spokesmen for the chemical industry attempted to discredit the claims of residents at Love Canal, denying all responsibility and even attempting to blame the victims themselves. In a television interview, the vice-presidents at of the Chemical Manufacturers' Association, took the official industry line and implied that the residents of Love Canal were simply a community of hypochondriacs. At times, even many of the government bodies that were supposed to protect citizens were reluctant to deal with such a troublesome issue. It was only because a strong community- based residents' organization forced the issue that anything was achieved at Love Canal.

In 1979, when only two out of seventeen pregnant women in the community had managed to give birth to healthy children, the New York authorities termed Love Canal an area of 'grave and imminent peril'. The school was closed, more than two hundred houses were demolished and over a thousand families were evacuated at a cost in excess of $100 million.

As nightmarish the situation at Love Canal was, it is one which will recur again and again throughout the industrial world. The EPA claimed 'We Know of 4,000 to 5,000 potential Love Canals right now'. Hugh Kaufman, head of hazardous waste assessment at the EPA, said,' `the only unusual thing about Love Canal is that it was discovered.'

References

"After Bhopal." Lancet, Issue 603. July 16, 1988.

"Bhopal: Absolutely Liable." Economist, Volume 308, Issue 560. July 23, 1988.

"Coping With Disaster." Technology Review, Volume 91, Issue 6. August 1988.

Cassels, Jamie. The Uncertain Promise of Law: Lessons From Bhopal. University Of Toronto Press Incorporated. 1993.

Chakravarty, Subrata N. "The Ghost Returns." Forbes, Volume 146, Issue 13. December 10, 1990.

"Editorial: Toxic Futures". New Statesman and Society. Volume 3, Issue 85. January 26, 1990.

"Freaks of Nature: Errors of Man". World Health. January 1991.

"Fresh Disaster at Bhopal Indian Politics Threaten To Compou". Barron's, Volume 68, Issue 5. February 1, 1988.

Hearing Before the Subcommittee in Asian and Pacific Affairs of the Committee on Foreign Affairs House of Representatives. Ninety-Eight Congress, Second Session. December 12, 1984.

Jasanoff, Sheila. Learning from Disaster: Risk Management After Bhopal. University of Pennsylvania Press, Philadelphia. 1994.

Khera, S.S. The Establishment of the Heavy Electrical Plant At Bhopal. Committee of Case Studies. The Indian Institute of Public Administration, New Delhi. 1963.

Kurzman, Dan. A Killing Wind: Inside Union Carbide and The Bhopal Catastrophe. McGraw Hill Book Company. 1987.

"Land That Time Forgot". Barron's. January 22, 1990.

Lappen, Alyssa A. "Breaking Up Is Hard To Do". Forbes, Volume 146, Issue 13. December 10, 1990.

Morehouse, Ward and Subramanian M. Arun. The Bhopal Tragedy: What Really Happened And What It Means For American Workers And Communities At Risk. Council on International and Public Affairs. 1986.

"Poison Gas, Up Two Bucks". Nation, Volume 248, Issue 9. March 6, 1989.

"Round The World: India—Long Term Effects of MIC". Lancet, Issue 644. April 29, 1989.

"Second Thoughts On Bhopal". Barron's, Volume 69, Issue 8. February 20, 1989.

"Spectrum: Update—Reforestation, Chernobyl, Bhopal". Environment, Volume 30, Issue 5. June 1988.

"Surviving Bhopal". New Statesman And Society, Volume 3, Issue 127. November 16, 1990.

"The Ghosts of Bhopal". Economist, Volume 310, Issue 590. February 18, 1989.

"Toxin Town", New Statesman And Society, Volume 7, Issue 331. December 2, 1994.

Weir, David. The Bhopal Syndrome: Pesticides,

Environment, And Health. Sierra Club Books, San Francisco. 1987.

Kumar, Sanjay "India: The Second Bhopal Tragedy". Lancet, Volume 341, Issue 854, May 8, 1993.

7

Disease and Disaster Burden of Climate Change

Introduction

Extreme climate events are expected to become more frequent as a result of climatic change. Climate extremes can have devastating effects on human societies, and other species. History records widespread disasters, famines and disease outbreaks triggered by droughts and floods. These complex, large-scale disruptions exert their worst effects in poor countries but even the richest industrial societies are not immune. Extreme weather events are, by definition, are stochastic events. There are two categories[1]:

- Extremes based on simple climate statistics, such as very low or very high temperatures;
- More complex, event driven extremes: droughts, floods, or hurricanes - these do not necessarily occur every year at a given location.

With climate change, even if the statistical distribution of simple extreme events remains the same, a shift in the mean will result in a non-linear change in the frequency of extreme events. The detection of change in simple climate extremes is more likely than the detection of changes in event-driven extremes.

Climate variability can be expressed at various temporal Scales (by day, season and year) and is an inherent characteristic of climate, whether or not the climate system is subject to change. Much attention has focused on the influence of EL Nino-Southern Oscillation (ENSO) on weather patterns in many parts of the world. In sensitive regions, ENSO events may cause significant inter-annual perturbations in temperature and /or rainfall within a loose 2-7 year cycle. However, it is important that such perturbations are not confused with climate change. In reality, these fluctuations introduce more noise into the long-term trends, making it more difficult to detect the climate change signal.

The effect of climate change on the frequency and/or amplitude of EL Nino is uncertain. However, even with little or no change in amplitude, climate change is likely to lead to greater extremes of drying and heavy rainfall and increase the risk of droughts and floods that occur with EL Nino in many regions.

A range of physical, ecological and social mechanisms can explain an association between extremes of climate and disease (Figure 7.1, Table 7.1 and Table 7.2). Social mechanisms may be very important but are difficult to quantify: for example, droughts and floods often cause population displacement. Outbreaks of infectious disease are common in refugee populations due to inadequate public health infrastructure, poor water and sanitation, overcrowding and lack of shelter. Climate also can affect infectious diseases that are spread via contaminated water or food. Water-related diseases are a particular problem in poor countries and communities, where water supplies and sanitation often are inadequate. Outbreaks of cholera, typhoid and diarrhoeal diseases can occur after flooding if the floodwaters become contaminated with human or animal waste, while drought reduces the water available for washing and sanitation and also tends to increase the risks of diseases.

There is a web of interactions between ecosystems, climate and human societies, which influences the occurrence of infections. For example, the resurgence of communicable disease in the past few decades is thought to have resulted primarily from social factors including population growth, urbanization, changes in land use and agricultural practices, deforestation, international travel and breakdown in public health infrastructure. From the opposite perspective, major communicable diseases such as malaria also can severely limit social development.

This chapter summarizes what is known about the historical effects of climate extremes on human health. The following section describes studies of infectious diseases and climate extremes related to EL Nino Southern Oscillation. The next considers the impacts of short-term extremes of temperature. The final section contains a discussion of climate-related disasters.

EL Nino and Infectious Diseases

There is a well-studied relationship between rainfall and diseases spread by insect vectors which breed in water, and are therefore dependent on surface water availability. The main species of interest are mosquitoes, which spread malaria and viral diseases such as dengue and yellow fever. There is considerable evidence linking mosquito abundance to rainfall events. Mosquitoes need access to stagnant water in order to breed- conditions that may be favoured by both wet and dry spells. For example, heavy rain can create as well as wash away breeding sites, while in normally wet regions drought conditions can increase breeding sites by causing stagnation of water in rivers. The timing of rainfall in the year and the co-variation of other climatic factors are also important.

The transmission of vector-borne diseases transmission is sensitive to temperature fluctuations. Increases in temperature reduce the time taken for vector populations to breed. Increase in temperature also decrease the incubation period of the pathogen (e.g. malaria parasite, dengue or yellow fever virus) meaning that vectors become infectious more quickly. On the other hand (depending on threshold that are species-specific) hot, dry conditions can reduce the lifetime of mosquitoes. Temperature also may affect the behaviour of the vector and human populations, affecting the probability of transmission. Warmer temperatures tend to increase biting behaviour of the vèctor and produce smaller adults which may require multiple blood meals in order to reproduce.

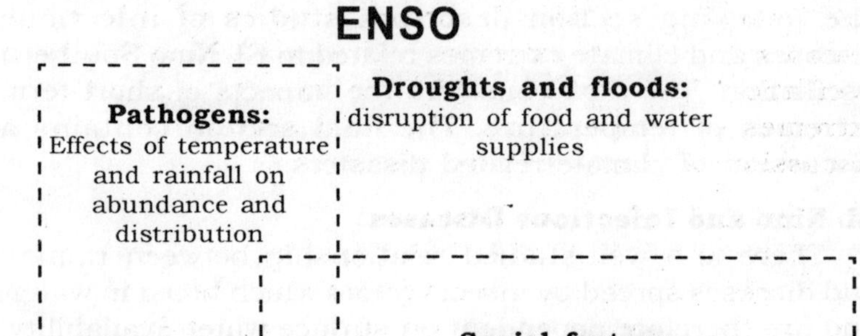

Fig. 7.1. ENSO and disease. ENSO events cause physical effects such as droughts and floods (blue circle). Where these overlap and interact with suitable ecological and socioeconomic conditions (within dotted lines) they may cause disease outbreaks (dark shaded area).

Table 7.1. Mechanisms by which above-average Rainfall can Affect Health

Event	*Type*	*Description*	*Potential health impact*
Heavy Precipitation event	Meteorological	"Extreme event"	Increased or decreased mosquito abundance. (if breeding sites are washed away)
Flood	Hydrological	River/stream tops over its banks	Changes in mos quito abundance contamination of surface water.
Flood	Social	Property or crops damaged	Changes in mos quito abundance contamination of water with faecal matter and rat urine and increased risk of respiratory and diarrhoeal disease deaths (drowning) injuries health effects associated with population displacement loss of food supply psychosocial impacts.

Malaria

Malaria is the world's most important vector–borne disease. Over 2.5 billion people are at risk, and there are estimated to be 0.5 billion cases and more than 1 million deaths from malaria per year. Malaria incidence is influenced by the effectiveness of public health infrastructure, insecticide and drug resistance, human population growth, immunity, travel, land–use change and climate factors.

Table 7.2. Mechanisms by which below-average Rainfall can Affect Health

Event	*Type*	*Description*	*Potential health impact*
Drought	Meteorological	Evaporation exceeds water absorption; soil moisture decreases. Several indices have been developed based on meteorological Variables, e.g., Palmer Drought Severity Index.	Changes in vector abundance if vector breeds in dried up river beds, for example.
Drought	Agricultural	Drier than normal conditions leading to decreased crop production.	Depends on socio economic factors, i.e., other sources of food available and the means to acquire them.
Drought	Social	Reduction in food supply or income, reduction in water supply and quality.	Food shortage, illness, malnutrition (increases risk of infection) Increased risk of disease associated with lack of water for hygiene.
Drought	Food shortage/ famine/ drought disaster	Food shortage leading to deaths > 10 killed, and/or 200 affected, or government call for external assistance.	Deaths (starvation) malnutrition (increases risk of infection) health impacts associated with population displacement.

Very high temperatures are lethal to the mosquitoes and the parasites. In areas where temperatures are close to the physiological tolerance limit of the parasite, a small temperature increase would be lethal to the parasite and malaria transmission would therefore decrease. However at low temperatures a small increase in temperature can greatly increase the risk of malaria transmission.

Malaria's sensitivity to climate is illustrated in desert and highland fringe areas where rainfall and temperature, respectively, are critical parameters for disease transmission. In these regions higher temperatures and/ or rainfall associated with EL Nino may increase transmission of malaria. In areas of unstable malaria in developing countries, populations lack protective immunity and are prone to epidemics when weather conditions facilitate transmission. Across the globe, many such areas experience drought or excessive rainfall during ENSO events.

Drought in the previous year has been identified as a factor contributing to increased malaria mortality. There are several possible reasons for this relationship.

Drought-related malnutrition may increase an individual's susceptibility to infection. Also, drought may reduce malarial transmission resulting in a reduction in herd immunity in the human population. Therefore, in the subsequent years, the size of the vulnerable population is increased[2].

Alternatively, a change in ecology of the natural predators may affect mosquito vector dynamics; mosquito populations recover more quickly than their predator populations following a dry year. Famine conditions may have contributed to excess mortality during historical epidemics of malaria, for example following the

1877 EL Nino in India. Many deaths occurred after the end of the drought; the proximate cause was malaria when drought-breaking rains increased vector abundance, exacerbated by population movement and the concentration of people in feeding camp[3].

Many parts of South America show ENSO-related climate anomalies. Serious epidemics in the northern countries of South America have occurred mainly in the year after EL Nino (year +1). In 1983 following a strong EL Nino event, Ecuador, Peru and Bolivia experienced malaria epidemics. In Venezuela and Colombia, Malaria increased in the post-Nino year (+1). A statistically significant relationship was found between EL Nino and malaria epidemics in Colombia, Guyana, Peru, and Venezuela.

The causal mechanisms are not completely understood. EL Nino is associated with a reduction of the normal high rainfall regime in much of Colombia, as well as an increase in mean temperature, increase in dew point, and decrease in river discharges. These relationships between malaria and ENSO nevertheless can be used to predict high and low-risk years for malaria, giving sufficient time to mobilize resources to reduce the impact of epidemics.

Africa has desert fringe malaria around the Sahara, (e.g., the Sudan). And the Kalahari (Namibia, Botswana). Of these areas, South Africa and a region east of the Sahara show ENSO-related rainfall anomalies. Several recent studies have examined evidence of relationships between climate extremes and malaria in Africa.

The 1997/98 EL Nino was associated with heavy rainfall and flooding in Kenya, after two year of drought. From January to May 1998, a major epidemic of falciparum malaria occurred. Brown et al. reported an attack rate of approximately 40 per cent in the town of Wajir, Kenya. Three districts in Kenya reported a six-fold increase in malaria cases in the first two months of 1998 compared to the same period in 1997. The malaria epidemic was compounded by wide spread food shortages.

Other researchers emphasize the significance of non-climate factors in explaining recent malaria epidemiology in Africa. A resurgence of malaria in the high-lands of Kenya over the past 20 years has been attributed to resistance to antimalarial drugs. Another study did not find a relationship between climate trends and the timing of malaria epidemics in Kenya. Based on a 30 year time series of climate and disease data, it concluded: ..."intrinsic population dynamics offer the most parsimonious explanation for the observed interepidemic period". One study has reported no significant meteorological trends in four high-altitude sites in East Africa where increases in malaria have been reported. This study used spatially averaged climate data that may be unreliable for this purpose. An association between rainfall, temperatures and the number of inpatient malaria cases three to four months later has been reported recently[4].

Dengue

Dengue is the most important arboviral disease of humans, occurring in tropical and subtropical regions worldwide. In recent decades, dengue has become an increasing urban health problem in tropical countries. The disease is thought to have spread mainly as a result of ineffective vector and disease surveillance; inadequate public health infrastructure; population growth; unplanned and uncontrolled urbanization; and increased travel. The main vector of dengue is the domesticated mosquito, *Aedes aegypti that* breeds in urban environments in artificial containers that hold water. Dengue also can be transmitted by *Aedes albopictus,* which can tolerate colder temperatures.

Dengue is seasonal and usually associated with warmer, more humid weather. There is evidence that increased rainfall in many locations can affect the vector density and transmission potential. ENSO may act indirectly by causing changes in water storage practices brought about by disruption of regular supplies. Rainfall may affect the breeding of mosquitoes but this may be less important in urban areas: *Aedes aegypti* breed in small containers, such as plant pots, which often contain water in the absence of rain. The disease has been prevalent in North India, specifically Delhi since 1997 propping up in October and remaining active through November.

Between 1970 and 1995, the annual number of epidemics of dengue in the South Pacific was positively corrclated with the Southern Oscillation Index (SOI). This is plausible since, in this part of the world, high positive values of the SOI (denoting EL Nino conditions) are associated with much warmer and wetter conditions than the average-ideal for breeding of mesquites. In a subsequent study, Hales et al. examined the relationship between ENSO and monthly reports of dengue cases in 14 island nations in the Pacific. There were positive correlations between SOI and dengue in ten countries. In five of these (American Samoa, Nauru, Tokelau, Wallis and Western Samoa) there were positive correlations between SOI and local temperatures and/or rainfall. During EL Nino, these five islands are likely to experience wetter and warmer than normal conditions. Local weather patterns may trigger an increase in transmission in larger, more populated islands where the disease is endemic, but infected people then carry the disease to smaller neighbouring islands. This implies that the effect of climate on vector-borne diseases is not necessarily confined to the region affected by altered climate suggesting that forecasts may need to the take account of regional social and environmental factors too.

A study of dengue in Vietnam, found that the number of cases increased in EL Nino years. In Thailand, which does not have a strong ENSO signal, there was no correlation. Many countries in Asia experienced an unusually high level of dengue and dengue hemorrhagic fever in 1998, some of which may be attributable to EL Nino-related weather. Gagnon et al. reported positive associations between EL Nino and dengue epidemics in French Guyana, Indonesia, Colombia and Surinam, regions that experience warmer temperatures and less rainfall during EL Nino years[5].

These studies do not identify unequivocally the environmental risk factors for increases in dengue cases. Further regional or global scale studies are needed to determine whether EL Nino is associated with a change in dengue activity and if so, what climatic parameters (temperature, rainfall, humidity, sea level of wind velocity) are primarily responsible.

Rodent-borne Diseases

Rodent act as reservoirs for a number of diseases whether as intermediate infected hosts or as hosts for arthropod vectors such as ticks. Certain rodent-borne diseases are associated with flooding including leptospirosis, tularaemia and viral haemorrhagic diseases. Other diseases associated with rodents and ticks include plague, Lyme disease, tick borne encephalitis (TBE) and hanta virus pulmonary syndrome (HPS).

Rodent populations have been shown to increase in temperate regions following mild wet winters. One study found that human plague cases in New Mexico occurred more frequently following winter-spring periods with above average precipitation. These conditions may increase food sources for rodents and promote breeding of flea populations. Ticks also are climate sensitive.

Infection by hantaviruses mainly occurs from inhalation of airborne particles from rodent excreta. The emergence of the disease hantavirus pulmonary syndrome in the early 1990s in the southern United States has been linked to changes in local rodent density. Drought conditions had reduced populations of the rodents' natural predators; subsequent high rainfall increased food availability in the form of insects and nuts. These combined effects lead to a ten fold increase in the population of deer mice from 1992 to 1993. In 1998, an increase in cases of hantavirus was linked to increased rodent populations which in turn, were attributed to two wet relatively warm winters in the southern United States associated with 1997/98 EL Nino. A comprehensive study by Engelthaler et al. in the Four Corners region, USA, concluded that above average precipitation during the winter and spring of 1992-1993 may have increased rodent populations and thereby increased contact between rodents and humans and viral transmission[6].

Diarrhoeal Illness

Many enteric diseases show a seasonal pattern, suggesting sensitivity to climate. In the tropics diarrhoeal diseases typically peak during the rainy season. Floods and droughts are each associated with an increased risk of diarrhoeal diseases, although much of the evidence for this is anecdotal. The suggestion is plausible, however, since heavy rainfall can wash contaminants into water supplies, while draught conditions can reduce the availability of fresh water leading to an increase in hygiene-related diseases.

Major causes of diarrhoea linked to contaminated water supplies are: cholera, cryptosporidium, *E. coli,* giardia, shigella, typhoid, and viruses such as hepatitis A. Outbreaks of cryptosporidiosis, giardiasis, leptospirosis and other infections have been shown to be associated with heavy rainfall events in countries with a regulated public water supply.

An association between drinking water turbidity and gastrointestinal illness has been reported. This was one of the first studies to apply time series methods to the analysis of water-related diseases. A study of waterborne disease outbreaks in the United States has shown that about half were significantly associated with extreme rainfall. Outbreak locations from an Environmental Protection Agency database were assigned to watersheds. The rainfall in the months of the outbreak and in previous months was estimated from climate records: for outbreaks associated with surface water the association was strongest for rainfall events in the same month as the outbreak.

Transmission of enteric diseases may be increased by high temperatures, via a direct effect on the growth of disease organisms in the environment. In 1997 a markedly greater number of patients with diarrhoea and dehydration were admitted to a dehydration unit in Lima, Peru, when temperatures were higher than normal during an EL Nino event. A time series analysis of daily data from the hospital confirmed an effect of temperature on diarrhoea admissions, with an estimated 8 per cent increase in admissions per 1°c increase in temperature[7].

Analysis of average diarrhoea reports in the Pacific Islands (1978-1986) suggested a positive association with average temperature and an inverse association with estimated water availability. Time series analysis of diarrhoea reports in the islands of Fiji (1978-1992) confirmed a statistically significant effect of monthly temperature changes (an estimated 3 per cent increase in diarrhoea reports per 1°c increase in temperature). Extremes of rainfall also were associated with increases in diarrhoea.

In summary, there is good evidence of associations between several important communicable diseases and climate on several temporal and geographical scales. This is true of vector--borne diseases, many enteric illnesses and certain water related diseases. These associations are not found every where-hardly surprising given the complexity of the causal pathways involved. Relationships between year to year variations in climate and communicable diseases are most evident where these climate variations are marked, and in vulnerable populations in poor countries. Major scientific reviews agree that EL Nino can provide a partial analogue for the effects of global climate change on communicable diseases. However the intergovernmental Panel on Climate Change (IPCC) cautions:

"Policymakers should appreciate that although our scientific capacity to foresee and model these various health outcomes of climate change continues to evolve, it is not possible to make precise and localized projections for many health outcomes..."

Temperature Extremes: Heat Waves and Cold Spells

In recent years there has been a great increase in interest in time series studies of temperature and mortality. These are seen as the most satisfactory method for quantifying the short-term associations between ambient temperatures and daily mortality. Any long-term patterns in the series, (e.g., seasonal cycles) are removed. The effect of a hot day is apparent only for a few days in the mortality series; in contrast, a cold day has an effect that lasts up to two weeks. In many temperate countries mortality rates in winter are 10-25 per cent higher than death rates in summer but the causes of this winter excess are not well understood.

It is likely that different mechanisms are involved in heat and cold related mortality; cold related mortality in temperate countries is related in part to the occurrence of seasonal respiratory infections. High temperatures cause some well-described clinical syndromes such as heatstroke. Very few deaths are reported as attributed directly to heat. Exposure to high temperatures increases blood viscosity and it is plausible that heat stress may trigger a vascular event such as heart attack or stroke. Studies have shown that elderly people have impaired temperature regulation. Physiological studies in the elderly indicate that low temperatures are associated with increased blood pressure and fibrinogen levels[8].

The Impact of Heat Wave Events on Mortality

Heat waves can kill. In July 1995 a heat wave in Chicago, USA, caused 514 heat related deaths (12 per 100000 population) and 3300 excess emergency admissions. The morgues were full and bodies had to be stored in refrigerated trucks. From 12 to 20 July, daily temperatures ranged from 34-40 0c, with the highest temperatures on 13 July. The maximum number of deaths occurred on 15 July[9].

During heat waves, excess mortality is greatest in the elderly and those with pre-existing illness. Much of this excess mortality is due to cardiovascular, cerebrovascular and respiratory diseases. The mortality impact of a heat-wave is uncertain in terms of the amount of life lost: a proportion of the deaths occur in susceptible persons who were likely to have died in the near future. Nevertheless, there is a high level of certainty that an increase in the frequency and intensity of heat waves would increase the numbers of additional deaths due to hot weather.

There is no standard international definition of a heat wave. Operational definitions are needed for meteorological services. As meteorological agencies are becoming more commercialized they are keen to develop practical applications of their forecasts and tailor them to use needs.

The Netherlands meteorological bureau uses the following definition to trigger advance warnings in the media and directly, to health services: at least 5 days with maximum temperature above 25°c of which at least 3 days with maximum temperature above 30°c. The evidence on which this is based is not clear. In the United States, the National Weather Service suggest that a heat advisory(early warning) be issued when the daytime heat index reaches 40.6°c and a night time minimum temperature of 26.7°c persists for at least 48 hours. Local definitions are used: in Dallas the medical examiners office define a heat wave as three consecutive days of temperature over 37.8°c.

It is surprisingly difficult to define a heat wave as responses to very high temperatures vary between populations and within the same population over time 1987 heat wave in Athens resulted in 926 deaths classified as heat-related, although the attributable excess mortality was estimated to be more than 2000. A subsequent heat wave in 1988 was associated with a much smaller excess mortality. This has been observed also in Chicago following the 1995 heat wave.

Few analyses have looked at the impacts of heat waves in developing countries and the evidence is largely anecdotal. A heat wave in India in June 1998 was estimated to have caused 2600 deaths over 10 weeks of high temperatures. In Ores, the temperature rose 49.5°c was reported to have caused 1300 deaths. The high temperatures were exacerbated by recurrent power failures that affected cooling systems and hospital services in Delhi.

Important behavioural factors may be specific to certain countries: in Japan, young children are often affected when left in motor vehicles. Not all heat related deaths are due to weather conditions. For example, in the United States in 1994, 221 heat related deaths were recorded, but only 101(46 per cent) were due to ambient weather conditions. The rest were due to overexertion during exercise, for example. During the period 1979-1994, heat-related mortality due to weather conditions was 2.7-3.7 Per million populations in the four highest reporting states (Arizona, Arkansas, Kansas, and Missouri).

Most of these deaths occurred in the over 55 age group. Overall the impact of mortality is underestimated because death rates from other diseases increase during heat waves. This is true in all populations where it has been investigated.

Rooney et al. estimated the excess mortality associated with the 1995 heat wave in thc United Kingdom. An estimated 619 extra deaths (8.9 per cent increases) were observed relative to the expected number of deaths, based on the 31 day moving average for that period. Excess deaths were apparent in all age groups but most marked in females and for deaths from respiratory and cerebrovascular diseases. A heat wave in Belgium in 1994 was associated with excess mortality. Part of the excess was due to mortality displacement, since there was a deficit in deaths in the elderly following the heat wave (no deficit was apparent for age group 0-64 years)[10].

Vulnerability to Temperature-related Mortality

Indicators of vulnerability to heat and cold that have been investigated include:

- Age and disease profile
- Socioeconomic status
- Housing conditions
- Prevalence of air conditioning
- Behaviour (e.g. clothing).

These factors also have counterparts in individuals as risk factors for heat related mortality of morbidity, such as presence of air conditioning at time of death.

Both individual and population level studies provide strong and consistent evidence that age is a risk factor for heat-related mortality. Studies vary on the age at which the vulnerability is increased. There are physiological reasons why the elderly are more vulnerable.

An important study was undertaken following the Chicago heat wave in 1995. Semenza et al. interviewed the relatives of those who died during the heat wave and control who lived near the case, matched for age and neighbourhood. Individual risk factors for dying in the heat wave were identified: chronic illness; confined to bed; unable to care for themselves; isolated; without air conditioning. A comparison of mortality rates in three Illinois heat waves (1966) by age group, sex and ethnic group (white vs. other) found that women and white people were at a greater risk[11].

Winter Mortality

In many temperate countries there is a clear seasonal variation in mortality. Death rates during winter being 10-25% higher than those in summer. The major causes of winter death are cardiovascular, cerebrovascular, circulatory and respiratory diseases.

Annual outbreaks of winter diseases such as influenza, which have a large effect on winter mortality rates, are not strongly associated with monthly winter temperatures. Social and behavioural adaptations to cold play an important role in preventing winter deaths in high latitude countries.

Sensitivity to cold weather (measured as the percentage increase in mortality per 1 0c change in temperature) is greater in warmer regions. Mortality increases to a greater extent with a given fall in temperature in regions with warmer winters, in populations with less home heating and where people wear lighter clothes[12].

The elderly (aged 75 and over) are particularly vulnerable to winter death, having a winter excess of around 30%. This vulnerability is not yet well understood but may arise through a combination of physiological susceptibility, behavioural factors and socioeconomic disadvantage. Excess winter mortality is an important problem in the United Kingdom where there has been much debate about the role of poor housing, fuel poverty and other socioeconomic issues for the elderly population. Several studies have linked routine mortality data at ward or enumeration district level with small-area indictors of housing and deprivation.

A study of ischemic heart disease mortality in Stockport found higher winter excess in the higher social class groups although a clear gradient was not observed. A small area study found that inadequate home heating and socioeconomic deprivations were the strongest independent predictors of ward-level variation in excess winter death in England and Wales. In general, however, studies have found only weak or absent relationship between excess winter mortality and deprivation[13].

The Potential Impact of Climate Change on Temperature Related Mortality

Global climate change is likely to be accompanied by an increase in frequency and intensity of heat waves, as well as warmer summers and milder winters. Extreme heat of summer has an impact on human health, may be exacerbated by increase in humidity. There has been significant warmings in most regions in the last 25 years, some of which, the IPCC has attributed to human activities. However, it is not clear that the frequency of heat waves has been increasing, although few studies have analysed daily temperature data to confirm this. There is much regional variation in the trends observed. Gaffen and Ross looked at data from 1961-1990 for 113 weather stations in the United States and found that the annual frequency of days exceeding a heat stress threshold increased at most station.

Predictive modelling studies use climate scenarios to estimate future temperature related mortality. Those studies which use the empirical statistical model (based on coefficients derived from linear regression of the temperature mortality relationship) find that reductions in winter deaths are greater than increases in summer deaths in temperate countries. However, other methods indicate a more significant increase in summer deaths. Kalkstein and Green estimated future excess mortality under climate change in cities of United State. Excess summer mortality attributable to climate change, and assuming acclimatization, was estimated to be between 500-1000 for New York and 100-250 for Detroit by 2050.

Populations can be expected to adapt to changes in climate via a range of physiological, behavioural and technological changes. These will tend to reduce the impacts of future increases in heat-waves. The initial physiological acclimatization to hot environments can occur over a few days but behavioural and technological changes, such as changes to the built environment, may take many years.

While it is well established that summer heat waves are associated with short term increases in mortality, the extent of winter associated mortality directly attributable to stressful weather is difficult to determine and currently being debated. Limited evidences indicate that, in at least some temperate countries, reduced winter deaths would outnumber increased summer deaths. The net impact on mortality rates will vary between populations. There are no clear implications of climate change for non- fatal outcomes as there is a lack of relevant studies.

Natural Disasters

The health effects of disasters are difficult to quantify because secondary effects and delayed consequences are poorly reported and communicated. Information on natural disasters generally is gathered by the organizations and bodies directly involved in disaster relief and reconstruction. As a result, information usually is collected for specific operational purposes not as a database; figures are estimated, not measured directly. This is especially true of flood events and windstorms where the actual deaths and injuries directly caused by the event are small compared to the problems that arise as a result, including deaths from communicable diseases and the economic losses sustained[14].

EL Nino has an effect on the total number of persons affected by natural disasters. Worldwide, disasters triggered by droughts are twice as frequent during the year after the onset of EL Nino than other years. This risk is concentrated in southern Africa and south-east Asia.

The EL Nino effect on disasters is strong enough to be apparent at the global level. In an average EL Nino year, around 35 per 1000 persons are affected by a natural disasters. This is over four times greater than the rate in non EL Nino years, based on analysis of data from 1963 to 1992. This difference in risk is much stronger for famine disasters; EL Nino's global disaster footprint is largely determined by the consequences of drought.

In 1997/98 Kenya was particularly hard hit by flooding and excess rainfall. Ecuador and northern Peru experienced severe flooding and mudslides along the coastal regions which severely damaged the local infrastructure. In Peru, 9.5 per cent of health facilities were damaged, including 2 per cent of hospitals and 10 per cent of other health centres. At the other extreme, Guyana, Indonesia and Papua New Guinea were severely affected by drought. Although not all natural disasters in 1997/98 should be attributed to the EL Nino event, global estimates of the impact vary from 21000 to 24000 deaths[15].

Trends in Weather Disasters

Globally, there is an increasing trend in natural disaster impacts. An analysis by the reinsurance company Munich Re found a three-fold increase in the number of natural catastrophes in the last ten years, compared to the 1960s. This is primarily from global trends affecting population vulnerability rather than changes in the frequency of climatologically triggers.

Developing countries are poorly equipped to deal with

weather extremes. The number of people killed, injured or made homeless by natural disasters has increased alarmingly. This is due partly to population growth and the concentration of population in high-risk areas like coastal zones and cities. Large shanty-towns with flimsy habitations often are located on land subject to frequent flooding. In many areas the only land available to poor communities may be that with few natural defences against weather extremes. Direct hits of extreme events on towns and cities tend to cause large losses. In recent decades there has been a large migration towards the cities and more than half the population of the world now lives in urban areas. Such migration and increasing vulnerability means that even without increasing numbers of extreme events, losses attributable to each event will tend to increase[16].

There are several sources of information but the largest, most used and most reliable is a database created in 1988 with support from the World Health Organization and the Belgium Government (EM-DAT). The objective or EM-DAT is:

"*... to serve the purposes of humanitarian action at national and international levels. It is an initiative aimed to rationalize decision-making for disaster preparedness as well as providing an objective base for vulnerability assessment and priority setting.*"

The Centre for Research on the Epidemiology of Disasters CRED) records events where at least 10 people were reported killed; 100 people were reported affected; there was a call for international assistance; or declaration of a state of emergency. There are increasing trends of economic and insured losses from disaster events, and economic annual losses have increased ten-fold since the 1950s. However, much of the upward trend in economic losses probably is due to societal shifts and increasing vulnerability to weather and climate extremes[17].

Data for the 1980s and 1990s are shown in Table 7.3. This shows the numbers of events, people killed and people affected by weather-related natural disasters in each decade, by region of the world. Some regions are more severely affected than others. Although some show a decreases in the number of people killed (Africa and eastern Mediterranean) and the number of people affected (Africa, Americas and south- East Asia).

Reasons for the observed increases include:

- Increasing concentration of people and property in urban areas.
- Settlement in exposed or high risk areas (e.g. flood plains, coastal zones).
- Changes in environmental conditions (e.g. deforestation can increase flood risk).

Recently there has been an apparent increase in the number of disasters but little change in the number of people killed. In 2000 there were over 400 disasters, with 250 million people affected. This paradox may be explained by technological advances in the construction of buildings and infrastructure alongwith advancements in early warning systems, especially in more developed regions. Although there are pronounced year–to–year fluctuations in the numbers of deaths due to disasters, a trend towards increased numbers of deaths and numbers of people affected has been observed in recent decades.

The Health Impacts of Disasters

Extreme weather events directly cause death and injury and have substantial indirect health impacts. These indirect impacts occur as a result of damage to the Local infrastructure, population displacement and ecological changes. Direct and indirect impacts can lead to impairment of the public health infrastructure, psychological and social effects, and reduced access to health care services. The health impacts of natural disasters include[18].

- Physical injury;
- Decreases in nutritional status, especially in children;
- Increases in respiratory and diarrhoeal diseases due to crowding of survivors, often with limited shelter and access to potable water;
- Impacts on mental health which may be long lasting in some cases;
- Increased risk of water-related and infectious diseases due to disruption of water supply or sewage systems, population displacement and overcrowding;

Table 7.3. Number of events, people killed and affected, by region of the world for the 1980s and 1990s

Region	*1980s*			*1990s*		
	Events	*Killed*	*Affected*	*Events*	*Killed*	*Affected*
Africa	243	416851	137758905	247	10414	104269095
Eastern Europe	66	2019	129345	150	5110	12356266
Eastern Mediterranean	94	161632	17808555	139	14391	36095503
Latin America & Caribbean	265	11768	54110634	298	59347	30711952
South East Asia	242	53853	850496448	286	458002	427413756
Western Pacific	375	35523	273089761	381	48337	1199768618
Developed	563	10211	2791688	577	5618	40832653
Total	1848	691857	1336185336	2078	601219	1851447843

- Release and dissemination of dangerous chemicals from storage sites and waste disposal sites into flood waters.

Table 7.4. Theoretical risk of acquiring communicable diseases, by type of disaster

Type	*Person to person*	*Water borne*	*Food borne*	*Vector borne*
Earthquake	M	M	M	L
Volcano	M	M	M	L
Hurricane	M	H	M	H
Tornado	L	L	L	L
Heat wave	L	L	L	L
Cold wave	L	L	L	L
Flood	M	H	M	H
Famine	H	H	M	M
Fire	L	L	L	L

H=High, M=Medium, L=Low.

(*Source*: Reproduced from reference 106.)

Floods

Floods are associated with particular dangers to human populations. Immediate effects are largely death and injuries from drowning and being swept against hard objects. Local infrastructure can be affected severely during a natural disaster. EL Nino related damage may include: flood bring damage to buildings and equipments, including materials and supplies; flood damage roads and transport; problems with drainage and sewerage; and damage water supply systems.

During and following both catastrophic and non-catastrophic flooding, there is a risk to health if thc floodwaters become contaminated with human or animal waste. A study in populations displaced by catastrophic floods in Bangladesh in 1988 found that diarrhoea was the most common illness, followed by respiratory infection. Watery diarrhoea was the most common cause of death for all age groups under 45. In both rural Bangladesh and Khartoum, Sudan, the proportion of severely malnourished children increased after flooding. In developed countries, both physical and disease risk from flooding are greatly reduced by a well maintained flood control and sanitation infrastructure and public health measures, such as monitoring and surveillance activities to detect and control outbreaks of infectious diseases. However, the recent experience of flooding in Central Europe, in which over 100 per people died, showed that floods can have a major impact on health and welfare in industrialized countries too[19].

Floods also cause psychological morbidity. Following flooding in Bristol, UK, primary care attendance rose by 53% and referrals and admissions to hospitals more than doubled. Similar psychological effects were found following floods in Brisbane, Australia, in 1974. An increase in psychological symptoms and post-traumatic stress disorder, including 50 flood-linked suicides, were reported in the two months following the major floods in Poland in 1997.

A number of studies have established a link between dampness in the home including occasional flooding, with a variety of respiratory symptoms. For example, a Canadian study found that flooding was linked significantly to childhood experience, of cough, wheeze, Asthma, bronchitis, chest illness, upper respiratory symptoms, eye irritation and non-respiratory symptoms.

Windstorms and Tropical Cyclones

Impoverished and high–density populations in low-lying and environmentally degraded areas are particularly vulnerable to tropical cyclones, the majority of deaths caused by drowning in the storm surge.

Bangladesh has experienced some of the most serious impacts of tropical cyclones this century, due to a combination of meteorological and topographical conditions and the inherent vulnerability of a low-income, poorly resourced population. Improved, early warning systems have decreased the impacts in recent years. However, the experience of Hurricane Mitch demonstrated the destructive power of an extreme event on such a region[20].

Droughts

A drought can be defined as "a period of abnormally dry weather persists long enough to produce a serious hydrologic imbalance," or as a "period of deficiency of moisture in the soil such that there is inadequate water available for plants, animals and human beings. There are four general types of drought, all which have impact on humans, in different ways:

1. Meteorological: measured precipitation is unusually low for a particular region;
2. Agricultural: amount of moisture in the soil is no longer sufficient for crops under cultivation;
3. Hydrological: surface water and groundwater supplies are below normal;
4. Socioeconomic; lack of water affects the economic capacity of people to survive, i.e., affects non-agriculture production.

The health impacts on population occur primarily on food production. Famine often occurs when a pre–existing situation of malnutrition worsens: the health consequences of drought include diseases resulting from malnutrition. In addition to adverse environmental conditions political, environmental or economic crises can trigger a collapse in the food marketing systems.

The major food emergency in Sudan during 1998 illustrates the interrelationship between climatic triggers of famine and conflict.

In times of shortage, water is used for cooking rather than hygiene. This increases the risk of diarrhoeal diseases (due to faecal contamination) and water washed diseases (trachoma, scabies). Outbreaks of malaria can occur due to changes in vector breeding sites and malnutrition increases susceptibility to infection.

Forest fires

The direct effects of fires on human health are burns and smoke inhalation. Loss of vegetation on slopes may lead to soil erosion and increased risk of landslides often exacerbated when an urban population expands into surrounding hilly and wooded areas.

Air pollution is linked to increased mortality and morbidity in susceptible persons, and increased risk of hospital and emergency admissions. Assessments are being undertaken of the short-term impacts on mortality and morbidity associated with the 1997 EL Nino episode. However, such assessments often are limited by lack of baseline data. WHO has published health guidelines for episodic vegetation fires[21].

Conclusions

The increasing trend in natural disasters partly is due to more complete reporting, as well as increasing vulnerability of populations. Poverty, population growth and migration are major contributory factors affecting this vulnerability. Particularly in poor countries, the impacts of major vector-borne diseases and disasters can be limited or even reverse improvements in social development; even under favourable conditions recovery from major disasters can take decades.

References

1. WHO reports on climate change 2003, WHO Geneva.
2. Bouma, M.J. & Dye. C. Cycles of the malaria associated with El Nino in Venezuela. *Journal of the American medical association 278:1772-1774 (1997).*
3. Diaz, H. F. et al. Climate and human health linkages on multiple timescales. *Climate and climatic impacts through the last 1000 years.* Jones. P.D. et al. Cambridge, UK Cambridge University Press 2000.
4. Githeko, A.K & Ndegwa, W Predicting malaria epidemics in the Kenyan highlands using climate data: a tool for decision makers. *Global Change and Human Health 2:54-63(2001).*
5. Gagnon, A.S. et al Dengue epidemics and the EL Nino Southern Oscillation. *Climate Research* 19(1): 35-43 (2001).
6. Engelthaler, D.M. et al. Climate and environmental patterns associated with hantavirus pulmonary syndrome, Four Corners region, United States. *Emerging Infectious Diseases* 5:87-94 (1999).
7. Checkly. W. et al. Effects of El Nino and ambient temperature on hospital admissions for diarrhoeal diseases in Peruvian children. *Lancet* 355 (2000).
8. Woodhouse, P.R. et al. Seasonal variation of blood pressure and its relationship to ambient temperature in an early population. *Journal of Hypertension 11(11): 1267-1274 (1993).*

9. Dematte, J.E. et al. Near-fatal heat stroke during the 1995 heat-wave in Chicago. *Annals of Internal Medicine 29:173-181 (1998).*
10. Sartor, F. et al. Temperature, ambient ozone levels and mortality during summer 1994 heat-wave in Belgium. *Environmental Research* 70(2):105-113 (1995).
11. Bridger, C.A & Helfand, L.A Mortality from heat during July 1966 in Illinois. *International Journal of Biometeorology* 12:51-70 (1968).
12. Donaldson, G.C et al. Outdoor clothing and it relationship to geography, climate, behaviour and cold related mortality. *International Journal of Biometeorology* 45:45-51 (2001).
13. Mitchell, R Short days – Shorter lives: studying winter mortality to get solutions. *International Journal of Epidemiology 30:1116-1118 (2001).*
14. Glantz, M & Jamison, D.T. Societal response to Hurricane Mitch and intra-versus intergenerational equity issues: whose norms should apply? *Risk Analysis 20(6):869-882 (2000).*
15. National Oceanic and Atmospheric Administration (NOAA). *An experiment in the application of climate forecasts: NOAA-OGP activities related to the 1997-98 EL Nino event. Boulder, US, Office of Global Programs, US Dept of Commerce 1999.*
16. Guha-Sapir, D Rapid assessment of health needs in mass emergencies: review of current concepts and methods. *World Health Statistics Quarterly 44:171-181 (1991).*
17. Changnon, S.A et al. Human factors explain the increased losses from weather and climate extremes. *Bulletin of the American Meteorological Society* 81 (3):437-442 (2000).
18. Noji, E.N. *The public health consequences of disasters.* New York, US, Oxford University Press 1997.
19. Red Cross. *Death toll rise in central Europe's epic floods* (2002). http://www.redcross.org/news/in/flood/020819europe.html
20. Pan American Health Organization (PAHO). The devastating path of Hurricane Mitch in Central

America. *Disasters: Preparedness and mitigation in the Americas (supplement 1):* S1-S4 (1999a).

21. Institute of Environmental Epidemiology (IEE). *Health guidelines for vegetation fire events. Schwela, D.H et al. eds.* Singapore, Singapore: Institute of Environmental Epidemiology 1999.

8

Dimensions of Road Traffic Disasters

Introduction

In road traffic, risk is a function of four elements. The first is the exposure- the amount of movement or travel within the system by different users or a given population density. The second is the underlying probability of a crash, given a particular exposure. The third is the probability of injury, given a crash. The fourth element is the outcome of injury. This situation is summarized in Figure 8.1.

Risk arises largely as a result of various factors, that include[1].

- Human error within the traffic system;
- The size and nature of the kinetic energy of the impact to which people in the system are exposed as a result of errors;
- The tolerance of the individual to this impact;
- The quality and availability of emergency services and acute trauma care.

The human operator often adapts to changing conditions in ways that do not always serve safety. A single error can have life or death consequences. Behind road-user errors, there are natural limitations. These include vision in night traffic, the detection of targets in the periphery of the eye, the estimation of speed and distance, the processing of information by the brain, and other physiological factors associated with age and sex that have a bearing on crash risk. Influencing the human error are external factors such as the design of the road, the design of the vehicle, traffic rules and the enforcement of traffic rules. Sophisticated and quality-assured systems that combine human beings and machines, therefore, need to have an in-built tolerance of human error.

The tolerance of the human body to the physical forces released in crashes is limited. Injury is broadly related to the kinetic energy applied to the human frame. The energy involved in a collision varies as the square of the velocity, so that small increases in speed result in major increases in the risk of injury.

Fig. 8.1

The main risk factors for road traffic injuries.

Factors influencing exposure to risk

- Economic factors, including social deprivation.
- Demographic factors.
- Land use planning practices which influence the length of a trip or travel mode choice.
- Mixture of high-speed motorized traffic with vulnerable road users.
- Insufficient attention to integration of road function with decisions about speed limits, road layout and design.

Risk factors influencing crash involvement

- Inappropriate or excessive speed.
- Presence of alcohol, medicinal or recreational drugs.
- Fatigue.
- Being a young male.
- Being a vulnerable road user in urban and residential areas.
- Travelling in darkness.
- Vehicle factors-such as braking, handling and maintenance.
- Defects in road design, layout and maintenance which can also lead to unsafe road user behaviour.
- Inadequate visibility due to environmental factors. (making it hard to detect vehicles and other road

users).

- Poor road user eyesight.

Risk factors influencing crash severity

- Human tolerance factors.
- Inappropriate or excessive speed.
- Seat-belts and child restraints not used.
- Crash helmets not worn by users of two-wheeled vehicles.
- Roadside objects not crash protective.
- Insufficient vehicle crash protection for occupants and for those hit by vehicles.
- Presence of alcohol and other drugs.

Risk factors influencing severity of post-crash injuries

- Delay in detecting crash.
- Presence of fire resulting from collision.
- Leakage of hazardous materials.
- Presence of alcohol and other drugs.
- Difficulty rescuing and extracting people from vehicles.
- Difficulty evacuating people from buses and coaches involved in crash.
- Lack of appropriate pre-hospital care.
- Lack of appropriate care in the hospital emergency rooms.

The relationship between impact forces in crashes and the injuries that are sustained is known for a number of parts of the body and type of injury for different categories of road users, as well as for different age groups. Biomechanical thresholds associated with age, sex and speed are reliable predictors of crash injury. For example, impact forces that produce a moderate injury in a robust 25-year-old male will result in a life-threatening injury if applied to a 65-year-old infirm female[2].

The main road injury problems are being sustained worldwide by people who make similar mistakes, share the same human tolerance to injury limits and have the same inherent behavioural limitations. While the problems are different both qualitatively and quantitatively, the main risk factors appear to be the same worldwide.

Traditionally, analysis of risk has examined the road user, vehicle and road environment separately. In this report, a systems framework, where interactions between different components are taken into account, is used. Such as systems-oriented approach has been necessary for significant progress in tackling road trauma to be made.

Factors Influencing Exposure to Risk

Risk in road traffic arises out of a need to travel-to have access to work, for instance, or for education or leisure pursuits. A range of factors determines who uses different parts of the transport system, how it is used and why, and at what times.

While in practical terms it may not be possible completely to eliminate all risks, it is possible to reduce the exposure to risk of severe injury and to minimize its intensity and consequences.

Rapid Motorization

Motor vehicles

One of the main factors contributing to the increase in global road crash injury is the growing number of motor vehicles. Since 1949, when Smeed[3] first demonstrated a relationship between fatality rates and motorization, several studies have shown a correlation between motor vehicle growth and the number of road crashes and injuries. While the motor vehicle and subsequent growth in the number of motor vehicles and road infrastructure has brought societal benefits, it has also led to a societal cost to which road traffic injury contributes significantly.

This explains why a number of studies are drawing attention to the need for careful consideration and planning of transport and mobility in view of the increasing motorization in different parts of the world.

Periods of economic prosperity tend to be associated with increasing mobility and demand for transport services. On the other hand, periods of economic decline lead to low generation of movement. In times of economic growth, traffic volumes increase, along with the number of crashes and injuries, and there are generally reductions in walking and cycling. Reductions in alcohol-related crashes have also been observed to coincide with periods of economic recession[4].

Motorization rate rises with rising income. In wealthier countries, there has been dramatic growth in the numbers of cars, but in many poorer countries the increases have been principally in motorcycles and minibuses. Some 80% of all cars are owned by 15% of the world's population, situated in North America, Western Europe and Japan.

In China, where the economy is experiencing rapid growth, the number of vehicles has more than quadrupled since 1990, to over 55 million. In Thailand, between 1987 and 1997, there was an almost four–fold increase in the number of registered motor vehicles, from 4.9 million to 17.7 million. In India, the number of four-wheeled motor vehicles increased by 23 % to 4.5 million between 1990 and 1993. All of these figures are far below the rates of car ownership per capita in high income countries. It is predicted that the motor vehicle numbers for countries of the Organization for Economic Co-operation and Development (OECD) could increase up to 62% by the year 2015, to a total of 705 million[5].

Motor vehicle growth in low-income countries is taking place against a background of associated problems. Only a small number of people in these countries can afford cars, while the costs of road, parking spaces, air pollution and road traffic injuries are borne by the whole society. Despite the rapid growth in motorized traffic, most families in low income and middle-income countries are unlikely to own a car within the next 25 years.

In terms of exposure to risk, the main modes of travel in these countries in the foreseeable future are likely to remain walking, cycling and using public transport. This emphasizes the importance of planning for the needs of these road users, who bear a high proportion of the burden of road traffic injuries.

Traffic volume is a particularly important risk factor for injuries among child pedestrians. Roberts et al. have shown that when traffic volumes fall there is a reduction in child pedestrian death rates.

Buses and trucks are a major mode of travel in low income and middle-income countries. High volumes of passengers being transported have an impact on the safety, not only of the passengers themselves, but also on vulnerable road users. In New Delhi, buses and trucks are involved in almost two thirds of crashes involving vulnerable road users, and these people make up over 75% of all road traffic deaths[6].

Motorized two- wheeled vehicles

Although the greatest growth rate in the number of motor vehicles is expected in Asian countries, most of the increase in vehicle fleets is likely to be in motorized two-wheeled vehicles and three-wheelers. In many such places, it is estimated that motorized two-wheelers will comprise between 40% and 70% of the total vehicle fleet.

In south-east Asia, there are several countries with a large proportion of two–wheeled and three-wheeled vehicles whose growth in numbers has been associated with a large rise in road traffic injuries. Examples are Çambodia (where 75% of all vehicles are motorized two-wheelers or motorized three-wheelers), the Lao People's Democratic Republic (79%), Malaysia (51%) and Vietnam (95%). In Vietnam, the number of motorcycles grew by 29% during 2001; at the same time road deaths rose by 37%. An increase in use of motorized two-wheelers in China, Province of Taiwan, where such vehicles comprise 65% of all registered motor vehicles, was also associated with increasing deaths and injuries[7].

Like other motor vehicles, motorized two-wheelers also cause injuries to other road users. In low-income countries, where the majority of pedestrian impacts are with buses and cars, one hospital-based study in New Delhi found that 16% of injured pedestrians had been struck by motorized two-wheelers[8].

Non-Motorised Traffic

Non-motorized vehicles predominate in both rural and urban areas in some low-income and middle-income countries. In these countries, the proportion of road traffic injuries from non-motorized forms of travel varies according to the way motorized and non-motorized modes of travel are split. In Asia, however, motorcycles are dominant, which partly explains the high proportion of motorcycle fatalities and injuries. Generally speaking in developing countries, pedestrian and cyclist traffic has grown without accompanying improvements in facilities for these road users. The high numbers of pedestrian and cyclist casualties in these countries reflects not only their inherent vulnerability but also insufficient attention to their needs in policy–making[8].

Demographic Factors

Different group of people have different exposures to risks. As populations change over time, so does the overall exposure of that population. Fluctuations in the relative sizes of different population groups will have a strong effect on the road traffic toll. For instance, in industrialized countries, young drivers and riders-at increased risk of involvement in road crashes-are currently overrepresented in casualty figures. Demographic changes, though, in these countries over the next 20-30 years will result in road users over 65 years of age becoming the largest group of road users. Their physical vulnerability, though, places them at high risk of fatal and serious injuries. In low-income countries, the expected demographic evolution suggests that younger road users will continue to be the predominant group involved in road crashes.

In some high-income countries, more than 20% of the population will be 65 years or above by 2030. Despite the rise in number of older people holding driving licences in such countries, their declining driving ability as well as possible financial constraints will mean that many of them will have to give up driving. In many low-income countries, older people may never have driven in the first place. Worldwide, a large proportion of older people will still be dependent on public transport or will walk. This illustrates the importance of providing safer and shorter pedestrian routes and safe and convenient public transport.

Transport, Land Use and Road Network Planning

Planning decisions regarding transport, land use and road networks have significant effects on public health-as they affect the amount of air pollution by vehicles, the degree of physical exercise undertaken by individuals, and the volume of road traffic crashes and injuries.

The development of a network of roads-or indeed of other forms of transport, such as railways-has a profound effect on communities and individuals. It influences such things as economic activity, property prices, air and noise pollution, social deprivation and crime-in addition to health. Long commuting times degrade the quality of life and therefore health. Sedentary travel directly and adversely affects health[9].

In the absence of proper land–use planning, residential commercial and industrial activity will evolve in a haphazard pattern, and road traffic will evolve similarly to meet the needs of tnese various activities. This is like to produce heavy flows of traffic through residential areas, vehicles capable of high speed mixing with pedestrians, and heavy, long–distance commercial traffic in using route not designed for such vehicles. The consequent exposure to traffic injury can be high for car occupants, and even more so for vulnerable road users, such as pedestrians, cyclists and motorized two-wheeler users.

The mixed nature of road traffic in many low-income and middle–income countries-with pedestrians, bicycles, handcarts, mopeds, motorcycles, vans, cars, trucks and buses in different proportions-mean that many of the technical aspects of planning, highway design, traffic engineering and traffic management need to be worked out locally rather than being imported. For example, in many Asian cities, with some notable exceptions, the road network is used by at least seven categories of motorized and non-motorized vehicles, of varying widths and speeds, all sharing the road space. There is generally no effective channelling or segregation of the different categories or speed control.

Where planning of land use does take place, it is often done with a view to create efficient flows of traffic, resulting in major arterial, high-speed routes that cut of different urban sections, to the disadvantage of local residents. Environmental criteria–such as reduction in noise, pollution and visual intrusion-are also often employed in planning. Safety considerations are brought in much less often. When safety criteria are applied to land use planning, though, there is ample evidence of significant reductions in exposure to traffic injury[10].

Increased Need for Travel

All growing urban areas experience a movement of residents from the inner districts to the suburbs. Socioeconomic changes in many places are leading to a profusion of out-of-town supermarkets and shopping malls, with a consequent loss of local shops. Both these phenomena generate increased traffic, less opportunity for travel by public transport, and increased exposure to risk.

These factors need to be better recognized and evaluated in planning processes. This applies not only to developed countries but also to developing countries, some of which contain rapidly-growing mega cities, with their significant but undocumented changes in patterns of wealth and living space.

Choice of Less Safe Forms of Travel

Of the four main modes of travel, road travel scores by far the highest risk in most countries-using almost any measures of exposure-compared with rail, air and marine travel.

Within the mode of road travel, major variations in risk exist among pedestrians, cyclists, riders of motorized two-wheelers, car occupants, and bus and truck passengers. The risks for these road users also vary greatly according to the traffic mix and hence vary greatly from country to country. In general, in high-income countries, riders of motorized two-wheelers have the highest levels of risk.

In European Union countries, the risk of death for motorized two-wheeled users is 20 times that of car occupants. Travelling by car is some 7-9 times safer than cycling or walking, but car occupants are still 10 times less safe than bus occupants. All these relative risks are calculated on the basis of distance travelled. Even when the risks of walking or cycling before or after a train or bus trip are taken into account, travel by public transport is still safer than car travel, when the collective safety of all users is considered[11].

The choice of mode of travel is greatly influenced by the climate. Extremes of temperature severely limit cycling and walking. As Table 8.2 shows, the traffic crash cost of injuries among motorized two-wheeler users is also higher than for any other mode.

The level and mix of motorized two-wheeler use have long been volatile features of road use. Both for urban commuting and for rural recreation. In this context, if the number of road injuries is to be minimized, care should be taken to avoid the adoption of policies which could encourage the growth of motorized two-wheeler traffic by giving advantages to motorized two-wheeled users.

A recent report by the Transport organization for London stated that one reason for providing motorized two-wheelers with exemption from the city's congestion charge scheme was their smaller contribution to congestion in central London. Transport for London suggested that there could be a small increase in motorized two-wheeler activity as a consequence of the new scheme, though it stated that distinguishing such a change from background trends could be difficult. When compared against trends over recent years for all other vehicle types, though, the relative share of trips undertaken by motorized two-wheeler was already increasing, and motorized two-wheeler users are a leading casualty group in the United Kingdom. By the end of 2002, deaths and serious injuries among motorized two-wheeled users in London were 31% above the 1994-1998 average. Thus, if present trends continue, it seems unlikely that the target of a 40% reduction in motorcycle deaths by 2010 will be achieved.

Risk Factors Influencing Crash Involvement

Speed

The speed of motor vehicles is at the core of the road injury problem. Speed influences both crash risk and crash consequence. "Excess speed" is defined as a vehicle exceeding the relevant speed limit; "inappropriate speed" refers to a vehicle travelling at a speed unsuitable for the prevailing road and traffic conditions. While speed limits only declare higher speeds to be illegal it remains for each driver and rider to decide the appropriate speed within the limit.

The speed drivers choose to travel at is influenced by many factors (see Table 8.3). Modern cars have high rates of acceleration and can easily reach very high speeds in short distance. The physical layout of the road and its surroundings can both encourage and discourage speed. Crash risk increases as speed increases, especially at road junctions and while overtaking-as road users underestimate the speed, and overestimate the distance, of an approaching vehicle[12].

Table 8.1
Deaths per 100 million passenger-kilometres versus passenger-travel hours in European Union countries for the period 2001-2002

	Deaths per 100 Million passenger kilometres [a]	*Deaths per 100 Million passenger travel hours* [b]
Roads (total)	0.95	28
Powered two-wheelers	13.8	440
Foot	6.4	75
Cycle	5.4	25
Car	0.7	25
Bus and coach	0.07	2
Ferry	0.25	16
Air(civil aviation)	0.035	8
Rail	0.035	2

[a] Passenger-kilometres is the total distance covered by all the individuals travelling on that mode.

[b] Passenger-travel hours is the total time spent by all the individuals travelling on that mode.

Source: reproduced from reference 10.

Table 8.2
Traffic crash cost per passenger-kilometres

Mode of transport	*Cost per passenger- km (in US$)*
Commercial aviation	0.01
Rail	0.06
Bus	0.23
Car	0.28
General aviation	0.39
Motorcycle	1.52

Source: reproduced from reference 11.

Crash Risk

There is a large amount of evidence of a significant relationship between mean speed and crash risk:

- The probability of a crash involving an injury is proportional to the square of the speed. The probability of a serious crash is proportional to the cube of the speed. The probability of a fatal crash is related to the fourth power of the speed[13].

Table 8.3
Examples of factors affecting driver's choice of speed

Road and vehicle related	*Traffic and environment related*	*Driver related*
Road	Traffic	Age
Width	Density	Sex
Gradient	Composition	Reaction time
Alignment	Prevailing speed	Attitudes
Surroundings	Environment	Trill-seeking
Layout	Weather	Risk acceptance
Markings	Surface condition	Hazard perception
Surface quality	Natural light	Alcohol level
Vehicle	Road lighting	Ownership of vehicle
Type	Signs	Circumstances of
Power/weight ratio	Speed limit	Journey
Maximum speed	Enforcement	Occupancy of
comfort		vehicle

- Empirical evidence from speed studies in various countries has shown that an increase of 1 km/h in mean traffic speed typically results in a 3% increase in the incidence of injury crashes (or an increase of 4 - 5% for fatal crashes), and a decrease of 1km/h in mean traffic speed will result in a 3% decrease in the incidence of injury crashes (or a decrease of 4 - 5% for fatal crashes)[14].
- Taylor et al.[15] In their study on different types of roads in the United Kingdom, concluded that for every 1 mile/h (1.6 km/h) reduction in average traffic speed, the highest reduction achievable in the volume of crashes was 6% (in the case of urban roads with low average speeds). These are typically busy main roads in town with high levels of pedestrian activity, wide variations in speeds and high

frequencies of crashes.

- A meta- analysis of 36 studies on speed limit changes showed, at levels above 50km/h, a decrease of 2% in the number of crashes for every 1 km/h reduction in the average speed[16].
- A variation in speeds between different vehicles travelling at different speeds within the traffic stream is also associated with crash occurrence.
- A study of crashes within rural 60km/h zones involving injuries to car occupants found that the relative risk of crash involvement doubles, or more, for each increase of 5 km/h of travelling speed above 60km/h[17] (see Table 3.4). Travelling at 5 km/h above a road speed limit of 60km/h results in an increase in the relative risk of being involved a casualty crash that is comparable with having a blood alcohol concentration (BAC) of 0.5 gram per decilitre (g/d1)[18].

Table 8.4

Relative risks of involvement in a casualty crash for speed and alcohol

Speed(km/ h)	*Speed (relative risk [a])*	*Blood alcohol Concentration (g/d1)*	*Blood alcohol Concentration (relative risk [b])*
60	1.0	0.00	1.0
65	2.0	0.05	1.8
70	4.2	0.08	3.2
75	10.6	0.12	7.1
80	31.8	0.21	30.4

[a] Relative to a sober driver travelling at the speed limit of 60 km/h.
[b] Relative to driving with a zero blood alcohol concentration.

Source: reproduced from reference 13.

Severity of Crash Injuries

Speed has an exponentially detrimental effect on safety. As speeds increase so do the number and severity of injuries. Studies show that the higher the impact speed, the greater the likelihood of serious and fatal injury:

- For car occupants, the severity of crash injury depends on the change of speed during the impact, usually denoted as ?v. As ?v increases from about

20 km/h to 100km/h, the probability of fatal injuries increases from close to zero to almost 100%.

- The probability of serious injury for belted front-seat occupants is three times as great at 30 miles/h (48 km/h) and four times as great at 40 miles/h (6 km/h) and, compared with the risk at 20 miles/h (32 km/h).
- For car occupants in a crash with an impact speed of 50 miles/h (80 km/h), the likelihood of death is 20 times what it would have been at an impact speed of 20 miles/h (32 km/h).
- Pedestrians have a 90 per cent chance of surviving car crashes at 30 km/h or below, but less than a 50% chance of surviving impacts at 45 km/h or above[19].
- The probability of a pedestrian being killed rises by a factor of eight as the impact speed of the car increases from 30 km/h to 50 km/h.
- Older pedestrians are even more physically vulnerable as speeds increase.
- Excess and inappropriate speed contributes to around 30 per cent of fatal crashes in high-income countries[20].

Pedestrians and Cyclists

A disproportionately large number of pedestrian crashes and cyclist crashes occur in low-income countries. Pedestrian casualties also represented a huge cost to society in industrialized nations, where the risks (measured in distances travelled or time spent travelling) are many more times higher for pedestrians and cyclists than for car users[21].

The crash risks incurred by pedestrians and cyclists result from a complex mix of factors. A fundamental factor in high-income countries is thc fact that the modern traffic system is designed largely from the respective of a motor vehicle user. Provision for pedestrians and cyclists in low-income countries is rudimentary or even non-existent.

The principal risk factor for unprotected road users is the mixing of unprotected people with motor vehicles capable of high speeds. The survival of unprotected users depends upon ensuring either that they are separated from the high speeds of motor vehicles or–in the more common situation of shared use of the road–that the vehicle speed at the point of collision is low enough to prevent serious injury on impact with crash-protective safer car fronts. The absence of adequate separate pedestrian and cyclist facilities, such as footpaths or cycle tracks, creates a high risk for these road users.

If separation is not possible, road management and vehicle speed management are essential. At low speeds, drivers have more time to react to unexpected events and to avoid collisions. At speeds of less than 30 km/h, pedestrians and cyclists can mix with motor vehicles in relative safety. Poor provision at crossings and junctions is also a feature of unsafe shared use. In urban areas, most fatal or serious cyclist crashes occur at junctions[22].

Other risk factors for pedestrians and cyclists include:

- poor street visibility;
- poor understanding on the part of pedestrians of road safety; in a study in Jordan, nearly half of children crossing a road did not check for oncoming traffic even once before or while crossing;
- alcohol impairment on the part of the cyclists or pedestrians;
- poor design of the fronts of cars[23].

Young Drivers and Riders

Globally, road crash injury is a leading cause of death for young drivers and riders. Both young age and inexperience contribute to the high risk of these drivers and riders. Young drivers have a higher crash risk than older drivers. Being a young male is also predictive of crash involvement as a driver, it has been established in industrialized countries that men, especially young men in their first few years of driving, have higher rates of crash involvement than women, even when corrected for exposure factors[24].

In a study of injuries in Australia, Japan, Malaysia and Singapore, the highest injury risk was found among motorcyclists with a provisional licence, followed by those in their first year of riding.

The crash risks for teenage drivers are greater than

those for any other comparable age group, with 16-year-old and 17-year-old–drivers being at particular risk. Studies in developed countries indicate that the risks were particularly high during the 12 months after a full licence had been issued. The factors behind the elevated risk include:

- Mobility patterns and vehicle characteristics (e.g. the vehicle is often borrowed);
- Psychological characteristics, such as thrill seeking and over–confidence;
- less tolerance of alcohol compared with older people;
- excess or inappropriate speed, the most common error among young drivers and riders.

Late-night driving is also a predictive factor for serious crashes among young drivers. For 16-year-old drivers, the late-night risk is three times the daytime risk. While the night-time risks are greater for the youngest drivers, it is among drivers aged 20-44 years that the ratio of night-time driving risk to daytime risk is greatest- by a factor of four.

The risk for young drivers increases exponentially as the number of passengers increases. One case-control study indicated that a third of all crashes involving young drivers might have been prevented if young drivers had been restricted to driving with no more than one passenger.

Alcohol

Crash Risk

A case–control study carried out in Michigan, United States, in 1964, known as the Grand Rapids study, showed that drivers who had consumed alcohol had a higher risk of involvement in crashes than those with a zero BAC and that this risk increased rapidly with BAC. These results provided the basis for the future setting of legal blood alcohol limits and breath content limits in many counties around the world, typically at 0.08 g/dl.

In 1981, an Australian study found that the risk of crash involvement was 1.83 times greater at a BAC of 0.05 g/dl than at a BAC of zero. Re-analysis of the Grand Rapids data by Hurst et al. also concluded that the risks associated with lower BAC levels were greater than originally thought. This information, together with findings from behavioural and experimental studies. Provided a justification for many countries to reduce their legal BAC limits to 0.05g/dl. An Australian study of alcohol and motorcycle crashes found that having a BAC level greater than zero was associated with five times the risk relative to a zero BAC.

Age of Drivers

The risk of a crash with alcohol varies with age and drinking experience. Zador estimated that crash rates of male drivers aged 16-20 years were at least three times the estimated crash rate of male drivers aged 25 years and above, for every BAC level. With few exceptions, the relative risk of being fatally injured in a single- vehicle crash was found to decrease with increasing driver age for every BAC level, for both men and women.

A study on drivers killed in road crashes estimated that teenage drivers had more than five times the risk of a crash compared with drivers aged 30 and above, at all levels of BAC. Driver in the 20-29 years age group were estimated to have a threc times higher risk than drivers aged 30 years and above, at all BAC levels. Teenage drivers with a BAC of 0.03 g/d1 carrying two or more passengers were 34 times more at risk of a crash than drivers aged 30 years or more, with zero BAC, driving with one passenger.

Severity of Crashes

A study in the United States of relative fatality risks at different BAC levels indicated that for single-vehicle crashes, each 0.02% increase in BAC level approximately doubled the risk of involvement in fatal crash A similar finding was reported in a New Zealand study that used a sample of crashes involving mainly single vehicles. The study calculated the risk for a driver of a fatal injury during the night-time, according to the number of passengers in the vehicle, the driver's age, the driver's BAC level.

The frequency of drinking and driving varies considerably around the world. Despite that, and despite the fact that there have been few studies in low-income countries, research indicates that the phenomenon countries to be a major risk factor in traffic crashes. After many years of decline, the rate of road traffic deaths involving alcohol has begun rising in several high-income countries. A review of surveys of drinking and driving levels in traffic in European Union countries found that alcohol was present in between 1% and 3% of drivers. Roadside surveys taken in Croatia indicated that over 4% of drivers were intoxicated. A Ghanaian study found that over 7% of drivers in a random breath test had BAC levels above 0.08g/dL. In New Delhi, India, a study showed that a third of motorized two-wheeler riders taken to hospital admitted to driving under the influence of alcohol.

Driver Fatigue

Fatigue or sleepiness is associated with a range of factors[23] (see Table 7.5) including long-distance driving, sleep deprivation and the disruption of circadian rhythms. Three high-risk groups have been identified:

- Young people, particularly males, aged 16-29 years;
- shift workers whose sleep is disrupted by working at night or working long, irregular hours;
- people with un-treated sleep apnoea syndrome of narcolepsy.

Surveys of commercial and public road transport in developing countries have revealed that transport owners, in pursuit of increased profits, frequently force their drivers to drive at excessive speeds, to work unduly long hours and to work when exhausted.

Peak levels of fatigue-related crashes at night are often 10 times higher than daytime levels. Research in France on the working hours and habits of truck drivers showed that their risk of crashes related to fatigue increased when:

- they were driving at night;
- the length of their working day had increased;
- they were working irregular hours

Hand–held Mobile Telephones

The number of hand-held mobile telephones has increased rapidly in many high-income countries-in the United States, for example, from 500000 in 1985 to over 120 million in 2001. Europe has also seen sharp increases in their number.

The use of hand–held mobile telephones can adversely affect driver behaviour - as regards physical as well as

Table 8.5. Factors that predispose a driver to fatigue

Drivers at risk of fatigue	*Temporal factors causing fatigue fatigue*	*Environmental factors in*	*Sleep-related factors*
Young drivers (up to 25 years)	Driving between 02.00 and 05.00	Driving in remote areas with featureless terrain	Driving with sleep debt
Drivers over 50 years	More than 16 hours of wakefulness before trip	Monotonous roads	Driving with a sleep-related condition
Males	Long work period before trip	Main arterial roads	Driving when normally
Shift workers	Long times since start of trip	Long-haul driving	Drivers disposed to
Those for whom driving is part of job	Irregular shift work before trip	Unexpected demands, break down, etc.	Driving after poor-quality sleep
Those with medical conditions(such as narcolepsy)	Driving after successive nights of shift work	Extreme climate conditions	
After consuming alcohol Driving after inadequate rest and sleep	Driving under time pressure Some drivers are drowsy in the afternoon	Driving an unfamiliar route.	

Source: reproduced from reference 23.

perceptual and decision-making tasks. The process of dialling influences a driver's ability to keep to the course on the road. Results of studies on distraction and mental load show that driver reaction times area increased by 0.5-1.5 seconds when talking into a mobile telephone.

Conclusion

Analysis of available crash data and other road traffic research show that while the main road safety problems experienced in various parts of the world often differ in quality and quantity, they have many characteristics in common. The dominant, common characteristics of the risks associated with road traffic are as follows:

- Unnecessary travel, the choice of less safe travel modes and routes, and unsafe mixes of traffic all lead to increased risk.
- The design of roads and road networks is an important factor. Exposure to risk is increased significantly by road networks failing to route heavy traffic around populated areas or to separate pedestrians from motorized traffic.
- Excess and inappropriate speed is widespread and may contribute to around 30 per cent of road traffic crashes and deaths. In collision at 80 km/h, car occupants run a 20 times higher risk of being killed than at 30 km/h. Pedestrians have a 90 per cent chance of surviving car crashes at 30 km/h or below, but less than a 50 per cent chance of surviving impacts at 45 km/h or above.
- Impairment by alcohol countries to contribute to crash injury and increases the risk. All non-zero BAC levels carry more risk than zero BAC, and crash risk starts to rise sharply at levels of 0.04 g/dl. Legal BAC limits set at 0.10 g/dl allow three times more risk than limits set at 0.05 g/dl; at 0.08 g/dl, the risk is twice as much as that at 0.05 g/dl.
- Young novice drivers are at increased risk of crash injury; the risk among teenage drivers is higher than among any other comparable age group. Excess or inappropriate speed is a common contributory factor in crashes involving young drivers.

- Pedestrians, cyclists and motorized two-wheeler users bear a disproportionate share of the global road injury burden and are all at high risk of crash injury.
- For all road users, the risk of crash injury is increased by failing to see and failing to be seen. If daytime running lights were fitted and used, almost a third of all motorized two-wheeler crashes involving lack of visibility could be avoided; in the case of cars, more than 10% of such crashes could be avoided.
- The non-use of seat-belts and child restraints more than doubles the risk of serious and fatal injury, as does the non-use of bicycle helmets. Similarly, the non-use of crash helmets by motorized two-wheeler users almost doubles their risk of serious or fatal head injury.
- Crash analysis shows that the majority of pedestrian fatalities involve impact with unproductive car fronts. If all cars were designed to provide protection equivalent to that of the best car in the same class, an estimated half of all fatal and disabling injuries to car occupants would be avoided. Roadside design and the positioning of roadside objects play key roles in determining crash injury, as well as influencing the behaviour of road users.
- Inadequate post-crash care is a major problem in many places. The availability and quality of such care has a substantial effect on whether road traffic injuries leads to subsequent death or disability.

The availability in low-income countries of data on road traffic crashes is often basic. For a proper understanding of the risk factors predominating in local settings, more investment for systematic, independent and high-quality research is needed, particularly from high-income countries. Such worldwide research into the causes of crashes and crash injury is essential for achieving safer traffic systems.

References

1. Tingvall C. The Zero vision. In: van Holst H, Nigren A, Thord R, eds. *Transportation, traffic safety and health: the new mobility. Proceedings of the 1st international conference, Guthenburg, Sweeden, 1995.* Berlin, Springer –Verlag, 1995: 35-57.
2. Mackay GM. Some features of road trauma in developing countries. In: *Proceedings of the International Association for Accident and Traffic Medicine Conference, Maxico, DF, September 1983.* Stockholm, International Association for Accident and Traffic Medicine 1983: 21-25.
3. Smeed R. Some statistical aspects of road safety research. *Journal of the Royal Statistical Society,* 1949.112 (Series A):1-34.
4. Sweedler BM. The worldwide decline in drinking and driving. In: Kloeden CN, Mclean AJ, eds. *Proceedings of the 13th International Conference on Alcohol, Drugs and Traffic Safety, Adelaide,*13-*18 August* 1995. Adelaide, Road Accident Research Unit, 1995.
5. Kopits E, Cropper M. *Traffic fatalities and economic growth.* Washington, DC, the World Bank, 2003 (Policy Research Working Paper No. 3035).
6. Mohan D, Tiwari G. Road safety in low income countries: Issues and concerns regarding technology transfer from high income countries. In: *Reflections on the transfer of traffic safety knowledge to motorizing nations.* Melbourne, global Traffic safety trust, 1998: 27-56.
7. Chiu W et al. The effect of the Taiwan motor cycle helmet use law on head injuries. *American Journal of Public Health, 2000.90:793-796.*
8. Varghese M Analysis of 198 medical-legal records of road traffic accident victims treated in a Delhi hospital. *Journal of Traffic Medicine 1990,* 18:280.
9. Litman T. *If health matters integrating public health objectives in transportation planning.* Victoria, BC, Victoria Transport Policy Institute, 2003.
10. Koornstra MK, ed. *Transport safety performance in the EU.* Brussels, European Transport Safety Council, Transport Accident Statistics Working Party. 2003

(http://www.etsc.be/rep.htm, accussed 17 November 2003).

11. *Miller T et al.* Is it safe to travel by bicycle, car or big truck ? Journal of Crash Prevention and Injury Control, 1999, 1:25-34.
12. Nilsson G. *The effects of speed limits on traffic accidents in Sweden.* Sartryck, Swedish National Road and Transport Research Institute, 1982.
13. Finch DJ et al. *Speed, speed limits and accidents.* Crowthorne, Transport Research Laboratory 1994 (Project Report 58).
14. Mackey M, Hassan AM. Age and gender effects on injury outcome for restrained occupants in frontal crashes. In: *Proceedings of the Association for the Advancement of Automotive Medicine Conference.* Chicago, IL, Association for the Advancement of Automotive Medicine 2000:75-92.
15. Hobbes CA, Mills PJ. *Injury probability for car occupants in frontal and side impacts.* Crownthorne, Transport Research Laboratory, 1984 (TRL Report 1124).
16. Allosp RE, ed. *Safety of pedestrians and cyclists in urban areas.* Brussels, European Transport Safety Council, 1999 (http://www,etsc.be/rep.htm, accessed 17 Nov. 2003).
17. Rodriguez DY, Fernandez FJ, Velasquez HA. Road traffic injuries in Colombia. *Injury Control and Safety Promotion, 2003, 10:29-35.*
18. Cerrelli E. *Crash data and rates for age–sex groups of drivers, 1996* Washington, DC, National Centre for Statistics and Analysis, 1998 (NHTSA Research Note).
19. Lam LT et al. Passenger carriage and car crash injury: a comparison between younger and older drivers. *Accident Analysis and Prevention, 2003, 35:861-867.*
20. Haworth NL. Alcohol in motorcycle crashes. In: Laurell H, Schlyter F, eds. *Proceedings of the 15th International Conference on Alcohol, Drugs and Traffic Safety, Stockholm, 22-26 May 2000.* Stockholm, Swedish National Road Administration, 2000 (http://www.vv.se/trf-sak/t2000/316.pdf, accessed 17 November 2003).
21. Zador PL, Krawchuk SA, Voas RB. *Relative risk of fatal crash involvement by BAC, age, and gender.* Washington,

DC, National Highway Traffic Safety Administration, 2000 (DOT HS-809-050).

22. Mishra BK, Banerji AK, Mohan D. Two wheeler injuries in Delhi, India: A study of crash victims hospitalized in a Neuro-surgery ward. *Accident analysis and prevention, 1984, 16:407-416.*
23. Mock C, Amegashi J, Darteh K. Role of commercial drivers in motor vehicle related injuries in Ghana. *Injury Prevention, 1999, 5:267-271.*
24. Brown ID Tickner AH, Simonds DCV. Interference between concurrent tasks of driving and telephoning. *Journal of applied Psychology, 1969, 53:419-424.*

9

Disaster Management – Philosophy and Trigger Mechanism

"Disasters are the ultimate test of human behaviour, bringing out what is normally hidden – the best and the worst in people, the abilities normal life does not tap and the dark motives we all repress."[1]

Introduction

Man has struggled against the elemental forces of nature ever since the beginning of life itself. History is replete with numerous incidents of disasters that have struck mankind. Wind, water and tectonic forces have wrecked havoc in the past and continue to cause large-scale loss of life and damage and destruction of property and living environment. Although science and technology have made tremendous strides in the present century, the struggle of mankind against the evil forces of nature has not ceased altogether and large regions of the world continue to remain susceptible to natural disasters and are becoming increasingly vulnerable. Evidence has been documented to show that disasters have been increasing in frequency as well as severity in the last century. The number of disasters resulting from natural hazards was three times higher world wide in the past ten years than in the 1960s and economic losses were eight times higher increasing in US to $ 60 billion a year.[2] For the three- year period 1993-95 the United States Sub Committee on Natural Disasters Reduction estimated that annual losses from natural disasters in the country averaged one billion dollars per week.

Most of the world's natural disasters occur in the countries in Asia and the Pacific. The geographic position of Asia in general and south Asia in particular render it vulnerable to a number of natural hazards such as cyclones, floods, droughts, earthquakes and landslides.[3] It has been estimated that almost three million people have perished in natural disasters in the past three decades while tens of millions have suffered hardships.

Things appear to be getting worse in two ways – on the one hand natural disasters appear to be becoming more frequent and on the other, their effects are becoming more severe. Table below shows the global impact of disasters in the last decade. Asia appears to be the worst sufferer in terms of human lives lost, population affected and damage to the property etc.

Global Impact of Disasters in the Last Decade

Effect	*Africa*	*Americas*	*Asia*	*Europe*	*Oceania*	*Total*
Human Lives Lost	85551	81058	406199	16115	3614	592,537
Affected population (in million)	10.4	5.7	176	1.9	1.9	195.9
Estimated Damage (in billion US $)	25	178	401	148	11	741

Source – World Disaster Report, 2000.

India is a 'land of disasters'[4] with almost every type of disaster having struck the nation in the last century including one of the worst cyclones towards the end of the twentieth century (Super Cyclone in Orissa in October 1999) and one of the worst earthquakes at the dawn of the new millennium (Gujarat Earthquake in January 2001). Be it an 'act of God' or an 'act of Man', a mind-boggling spectrum of disasters wreak havoc in the Indian sub-continent year after year. The unique geo-physical setting of the sub-continent makes it highly vulnerable to natural disasters like drought, floods, cyclones, earthquakes etc. With over one billion population living in a very high-density environment; with one of the poorest infrastructures of this world in terms of transportation and communication and with the barest of the amenities that the citizens expect in the 21st century, India is and likely to remain prone to disasters and a Disaster Manager's nightmare. In fact the frequency of all kinds of disasters, varying from epidemics to road accidents and perennial droughts and floods, is escalating resulting in a multi-fold increase of injuries, disabilities and deaths, disrupting life-supporting systems and adding to the health, social and economic burden of an already impoverished people.[5] According to the latest estimates, 22 out of 27 states (85 per cent of the country's area) are vulnerable to one or the other type of disasters and 57 per cent area lies in high seismic zone including the national capital.[6] It has been rightly assessed that, 'in this part of the world, disasters occur with amazing frequency'.[7] Table shows human lives lost due to natural disasters in India in the last decade.

Another aspect of disasters in the last century is that more and more disasters are taking place not only due to natural but increasingly as a result of man-made causes which involve either interference in natural processes resulting in disturbed environment, or due to sheer disregard to basic safety parameters and procedures while undertaking development activities such as urbanisation and industrialisation. The impact of disasters does not depend only on the force with which it strikes, but also on the way it is received and felt. Low-income communities are the worst sufferers of disasters and the poorest of the poor generally the worst hit. Frequent incidence of disasters

Human Lives Lost due to Natural Disasters in India in the Last Decade

Year	*Floods*	*Cyclones*	*Hailstorms*	*Earthquakes*	*Total*
1990-91	1320	979	-	-	2299
1991-92	1185	304	-	768	2257
1992-93	1193	497	-	-	1690
1993-94	1690	318	-	7938	9946
1994-95	2038	247	59	-	2344
1995-96	2072	361	31	-	2664
1996-97	2069	1719	40	-	3828
1998-99	2567	1292	-	106	3965
1999-2000	2117	10,457	-	-	12,574
Total					

(*Source* : Ministry of Agriculture, Govt of India).

in a particular region of the world/country exerts ever-increasing pressure on the economic condition of the people of that region as repeated disasters weaken the natural resources of the region and its capacity to support the population.

Systematic Approach to Disaster Management

There is no ready-made solution to disaster problems. Many developed countries such as USA and Japan have also suffered from severe disasters in the past and continue to do so even now. But through a systems and integrated approach to Disaster Management, including preparedness and mitigation techniques and by actively involving the community, these countries have succeeded in reducing the impact of disasters on the people to a large extent. It took several years for these countries to collect data and information, its analysis and investigation before evolving the required response for training and educating the people. These countries continue to strengthen their disaster management capabilities through continued research and database collection.

The Disaster Management scenario in India is currently in its inception stage with the importance of the subject having been recognised only recently, i.e., in 1999 at the National Level when a High Power Committee (HPC) was constituted under the chairmanship of Shri J.C. Pant in August 1999. The aim of the HPC was to 'look into Disaster Management Planning at National, State and district levels holistically and take into consideration both – natural and man-made disasters.'[8] The terms of reference of the HPC were :

- Review of existing arrangements for preparedness and mitigation against natural and man-made disasters including *existing system of response in the wake of disasters and to minimise response time through effective communication and measures to ensure efficacy of relief operations.*
- Recommendations for strengthening existing organisational structures.
- Preparation of model disaster management plans at national, state and district levels.

THEORETICAL CONSIDERATIONS

An essential prerequisite for understanding Disaster Management and developing crisis management strategy is comparative inquiry, ideally a comparative inquiry that is intensive rather than extensive.[9] An objective examination of previous disaster management processes and subsequent training and evaluation benchmarked to the theory of Systems Approach as applicable in Business Management theory and practice seeking for comparative applicability in the local context, should logically lead to the desired structures required for effective Disaster Management doctrine.

What are Disasters ?

What is a disaster? The term 'disaster' owes its origin to French desastre, Italian disastro and Latin Astrum (star). The term *des* mcans bad and *aster* means star. Thus, disaster would mean bad or evil star. The Oxford Dictionary defines disaster as 'an event that causes much suffering or loss and as a sudden or great loss or misfortune'.[10] However, this definition does not convey the full implications of the term for those who have to deal with disasters, as a sudden or great misfortune affecting an individual or a family does not normally concern the authorities.

The term disaster often suggests images such as earthquakes, tidal waves, floods, cyclones and explosions and yet it is difficult to define a disaster by physical characteristics alone. Is the flooding of an uncultivated and uninhabited plain a disaster ? What about a landslide in an uninhabited mountainous region. In general, for to be considered disasters, these events have to affect an area of human development. Often even this is not enough. An earthquake might cause little damage in Los Angeles because the target area has relatively earthquake-resistant buildings. But the same amount of seismic activity in Delhi might result in a catastrophe due to a virtual absence of earthquake safety measures in its buildings. Hence an ideal definition of disaster must include consideration of hazardous event's effect on the target population.

The World Health Organisation (WHO) defines disaster as 'an occurrence that causes damage, economic destruction, loss of life and deterioration in health and health services on a scale sufficient to warrant an extraordinary response from the affected community or area.[11]

P.C. Sinha, an acknowledged Indian disaster management expert defines disaster as 'an occurrence arising with little or no warning, which causes or threatens serious disruption of life and perhaps death or injury to large number of people, and requires therefore, a mobilisation of effort in excess of that normally provided by the statutory emergency services.'[12]

Another relevant definition has been given by the High Powered Committee (HPC) constituted by the Government of India in 1999. According to the HPC, disaster is 'an event triggered by natural or man-made causes that lead to sudden disruption of normalcy within society causing widespread damage to life and property to such an extent that normal social and economic mechanisms available are not adequate to restore normalcy.'[13]

Perhaps the most appropriate definition is the one given by USA's Federal Emergency Management Agency (FEMA) which defines disaster as 'an occurrence of a severity and magnitude that normally results in deaths, injuries and property damage and that cannot be managed through the routine procedures and resources of government. It usually develops suddenly and unexpectedly and requires immediate, coordinated and effective response by multiple government and private sector organizations to meet human needs and speedy recovery.[14]

Having analysed the available definitions of disaster, it is clear that for an event to be categorized as a disaster, it must have most of the following attributes :-

- It has be an unusual event of sufficient magnitude and severity.
- It should develop suddenly and perhaps unexpectedly.
- It should result in widespread damage to property and disrupt normal life and routine functioning of the affected community.

- It could generally be accompanied by high casualty figures in the affected population.
- It would require immediate, coordinated and effective response by multiple government and private sector organisations.
- The response mechanism must address immediate human needs and facilitate speedy recovery.

Hazards and Vulnerability

A disaster is the product of a hazard such as earthquake, flood or windstorm coinciding with a vulnerable situation, which might include communities, cities or villages. Without vulnerability or hazard there is no disaster.

Hazards are defined as "Phenomena that pose a threat to people, structures or economic assets and which may cause a disaster. They could be either man-made or naturally occurring in our environment".

Vulnerability is defined as "the extent to which a community, structure, service, or geographic area is likely to be damaged or disrupted by the impact of particular hazard, on account of their nature, construction and proximity to hazardous terrain or a disaster prone area."

This relationship can be written as an equation :

Disaster Risk = Hazard + Vulnerability

Types of Disasters

Disasters can be broadly classified into natural and man-made. But this classification is too simplistic from the point of view of their management in the holistic interpretation of the term as will be discussed later in this chapter. Hence, a more functional classification of disasters is called for. One classification given out by the British doctrine on Disaster Management[15] is as under:-

- ***Environmental*** :These are the most common and universal disasters such as hurricanes, earthquakes, floods, etc.
- ***Ordinary*** : Disasters such as rail/road accidents, sinking of a ship, crashing of an airliner are ordinary disasters because the risk perception by the passengers is comparatively low or non-existent altogether.

- ***Technological***: Disasters which are a result of high technology or lack of it such as the Bhopal Gas Tragedy, Chernobyl nuclear disaster, etc.
- ***Industrial*** : Where the workers know their job to be hazardous such as mining disasters.
- ***Social*** : There are the results of social/ethnic upheavals in the society such as the on-going insurgency in J&K, Northern Ireland etc.
- ***Hybrid*** : Those which spread across time and space and disasters within disasters.

The classification given out by the HPC on Disaster Management to the Government of India is very relevant. The HPC has identified 30 odd disasters and categorized them in five types from the point of view of their management as follows:-[16]

- ***Water and Climate Related Disasters*** : Such as cyclones, flood, droughts etc.
- ***Geologically Related Disasters*** : Such as earthquakes, landslides etc.
- ***Chemical,Industrial and Nuclear Related Disasters*** : Such as the Bhopal Gas Tragedy.
- ***Accident Related Disasters*** : Such as the Purushottam Express accident near Tundla in 1996, the Delhi Uphaar Cinema tragedy of 1997 and the Patna Boeing crash of July, 2000 and.
- **Biologically Related Disasters :** Such as the Surat Plague scare of September, 1994.

Another classification given by the Ministry of Home Affairs, the nodal ministry of disaster management in India, is given as under :

- Disasters which are neither anticipated nor expected.
- Disasters which are anticipated but not expected.
- Disasters which are anticipated and also expected.

Management

Definition : Management is a widely applied and universally understood term in the present day environment and does not, therefore, require much elaboration. Management has been defined in numerous manners but the definition given by the Australian Army's Glossary of Military Terms is most appropriate. It defines management as a 'process of establishing and attaining objectives to carry out responsibilities. Management consists of those continuing actions of planning, organizing, directing, coordinating, controlling and evaluating the use of men, money, materials, and facilities to accomplish tasks.[17]

Disaster Management : After having fully understood 'the terms disaster and management and also how disasters occur and affect a community, we are now in a position to analyse Disaster Management as a subject.

A working definition of disaster management has been provided by Indian Institute of Public Administration, New Delhi. It defines disaster management as, *a collective term which encompasses all aspects of planning for and responding to emergencies and disasters, including both pre- and post-disaster activities and involves the management of both the risk and the consequences of the event.*[18]

Chronology of a Disaster : Most disasters follow a definite sequence in so far as their occurrence is concerned. These events are listed in a chronological order below :-[19]

- ***Initial Beliefs and Norms of the Community* :** In most societies, the affected community would be apathetic to a disaster before it actually occurs as a result of its attitudes, beliefs and value systems. For example, in India people believe in fatalism and karma and are generally averse to taking precautionary or strict safety measures in all spheres of their daily routine and when a disaster strikes they view it as an act of god to be taken in their stride.
- ***Incubation Period* :** The incubation period for a disaster may be from short to indefinite during which a potential hazard is allowed to grow till its impact becomes so large that it precipitates a disaster. To cite the Gujarat earthquake again, the

incubation period for the event was more than a decade, during which the building activity of unsafe multi-storey structures continued unabated.

- ***Precipitation of the Event*** **:** The event precipitates almost without warning although cyclones and floods can now be predicted across the world with advancement in weather forecasting techniques.
- ***Rescue and Relief*** **:** Rescue and relief is the initial and urgent response from the administrative authorities responsible for managing disasters in any community. All humanitarian assistance such as provision of food and shelter, evacuation of casualties, provision of medical aid, disposal of the dead, reconstruction activity and community welfare programmes, which may last from days to a few months, are all within the ambit of rescue and relief operations.
- ***Full Cultural Re-adjustment*** **:** The full cultural adjustment of the affected population including their physical, social, economic and psychological rehabilitation is a comparatively longer process and may require years of continued efforts on the part of the Government as well as community groups.

The Disaster Management Cycle **:** The disaster management cycle which can be diagrammatically represented, consists of following six stages divided into three phases as follows :-

- ***The Before –Disaster Phase***
  - Prevention.
  - Mitigation.
  - Preparedness.
- ***The During–Disaster Phase.*** Response (Rescue and Relief)

(c) ***The After-Disaster Phase***
  - Rehabilitation.
  - Reconstruction.

The Disaster Management Cycle

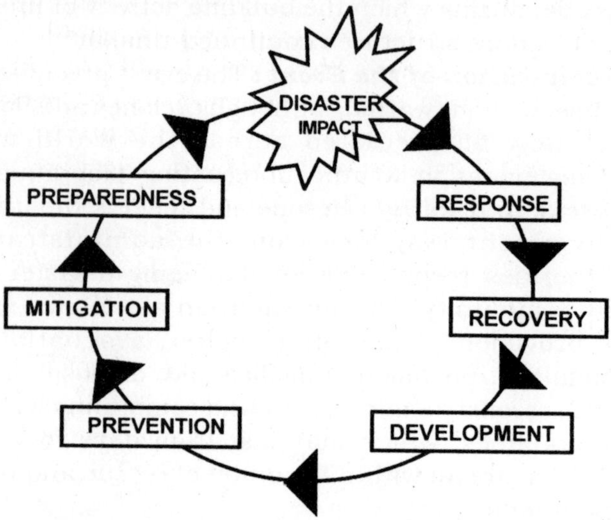

Attributes of an Effective Disaster Management Process

When the Disaster Management Cycle is viewed in the light of chronology of disasters and phases of intervention and costs of disasters, it becomes clear that disaster management is a vast subject dealing with a host of issues and problems requiring a very high degree of expertise in each of them. An effective disaster management process needs to have the following elements:

- A well structured strategic framework so as to enable completion of complex group tasks in time.
- An efficient tactical capability to ensure completion of individual agency tasks in time.
- A creative environment to permit the people to devote their energies to completion of their task with the expectation and confidence that it will make a difference.
- Risk culture to enable a team process to integrate many people's inputs and ideas.
- A comprehensive database to give valid raw material for strategic and tactical debate and to base the strategies and plans upon.

- Accountability and measurable performance objectives by which success and failures can be measured and incentives can be devised.
- Strong organizational knitting to create the environment for intuition and 'gut-feeling' so as to provide the elusive but vital 'human factor'.
- A clearly defined chain of command for clear and unambiguous issuance and compliance of orders and instructions.

Desirable Attributes of Effective Disaster Management

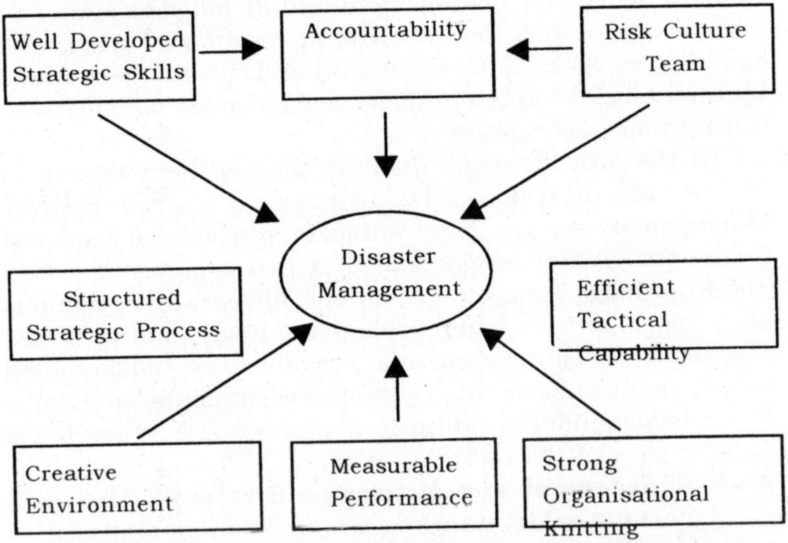

Strategic Aspects of Disaster Management : The business definition of strategy is, 'it is the direction and scope of an organization which ideally matches its resources to a changing environment and in particular so as to meet the stake holders expectations.' In case of disaster management, the organization is the government and the stakeholders are the public.

Risk Management : The start point of effective disaster management is Risk Management and includes prevention and mitigation – the first two stages of disaster management cycle. It also suggests organizations, systems networks and plans for effective prevention and mitigation.

Knowledge Management : This involves making maximum use of available technology for designing effective communications, procedures and programmes to train stakeholders for reducing the risk of disasters as well as for mitigation of disaster impacts.

Situation Management : This deals with the monitoring, warning and preparedness aspects of disaster management cycle and includes effective communication network for the same.

Response Management : This deals with the active element of disaster management and includes alerting and mobilising the agencies involved in rescue and relief, and establishing an effective command and control mechanism for their efficient functioning as well as media management during these operations.

Of the four strategic disaster management described above, the last two viz., Situation and Response Management are the focal subjects and will be analysed further in greater detail. The first two aspects viz., Risk and Knowledge Management are the subjects for specialists such as scientists, meteorologists, town planners and engineers whose recommendations are to be implemented by the politicians during normal developmental activities. Their basic understanding is a prerequisite of having a holistic view of the entire subject.

Risk Management and Mitigation Strategy : The most important understanding which has emerged out of global studies on disasters and their mitigation in recent times is that "disasters occur when hazards and threats of hazards, natural and human, impact on the vulnerabilities of an area/region and its people."[20] Klaus Weirsing, a German sociologist has carried out pioneering work on Risk Management and Mitigation Strategy. A summary of what his concept for risk management and mitigation strategy is given in the subsequent paragraphs.[21]

Mitigation : All measures to reduce loss of life,

livelihood and property caused by natural disasters, either by reducing vulnerability or by modifying,. where possible, the hazard.

Mitigation Strategy : As the definition indicates, the aim of mitigation strategy is to reduce the losses in the event of a future occurrence of a disaster. The primary aim is to reduce the number of deaths and injuries to the affected population while the secondary aim includes reducing damage and economic losses likely to be inflicted on the community as a whole. Increasing awareness amongst the people about potential hazards and required safety measures to reduce the risks from a potential hazard form an integral part of mitigation strategy. However, while all governments commit themselves in principle to an effective mitigation strategy against disasters, only a few translate the commitment to actual practice. Lack of political will and budgetary constraints are the principle reasons for inadequate action on the ground in most cases. The Japanese government is known to spend over $ 2 billion a year on disaster mitigation and preparedness, which obviously cannot be the case with a developing country like India. However, there cannot be a justification for lack of political will even in India which has a vibrant and functioning democracy with the required institutional and legal framework as well as a sound technological base and trained manpower. The essential conditions for successful implementation of mitigation strategy are:

- Political Will and Commitment.
- Resources in terms of Funds and Technology.
- Leadership, Management and Coordination.
- Public Awareness.
- Community Participation.
- Effective Training and Education programmes.
- A long-term Research and Legal framework.
- Cash Incentives for voluntary participation.

TRIGGER MECHANISM

Trigger mechanism is an emergency quick response mechanism like ignition switch which when energized spontaneously sets the vehicle of management into motion

Hazard Evaluation Flow Diagram

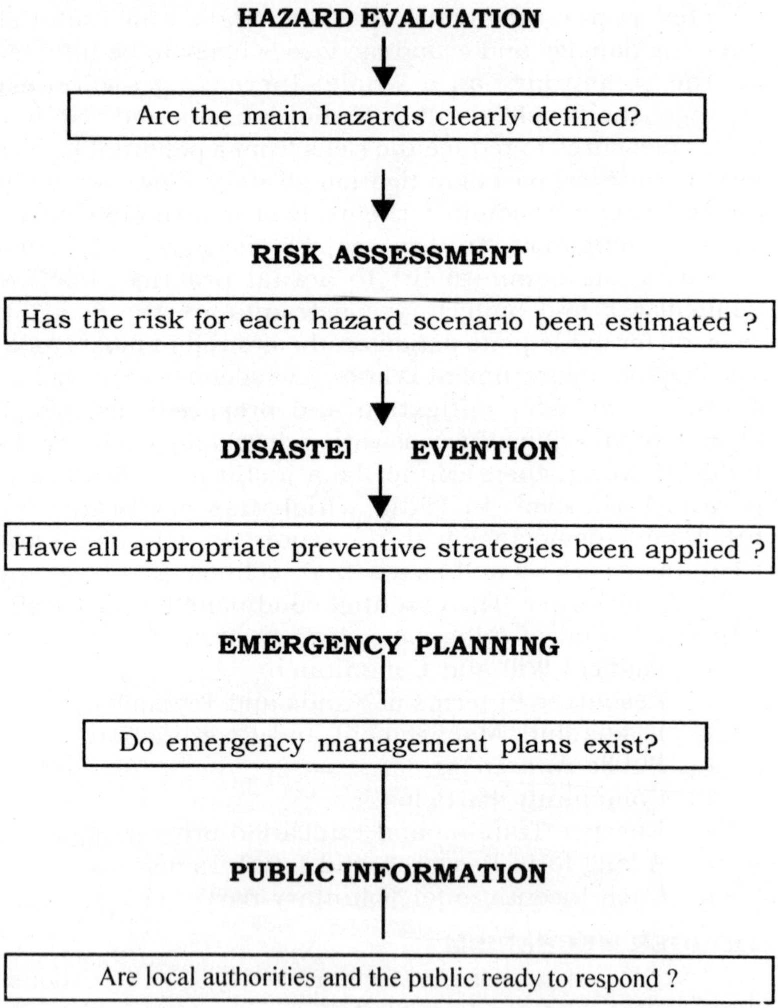

on the road of disaster mitigation process.

Trigger Mechanism Network

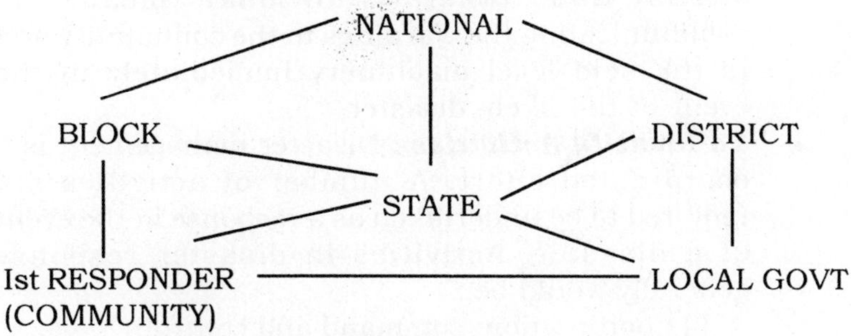

The Trigger mechanism, therefore, envisages that on receiving signals of a disaster happening or likely to happen, all activities required for the mitigation process are energized and activated simultaneously without loss of time and the management of the event is visible on the ground. The primary objective of the trigger mechanism is to undertake immediate rescue and relief operations and stabilize the mitigation process as quickly as possible.

Trigger mechanism requires planners :

- ***To Identify the Disasters and their Probability*** **:** The response managers and planners should identify the disasters to which the area of their concern is prone to and there is a likelihood of such a happening. This would mean identification of the hazards and the vulnerability of area to such hazards. In other words, a profile of the district or the State or the area of concern is required to be prepared which will include vulnerability assessment, past history, the geographical features and the impact and intensity as also the damages of the past disasters.
- ***To Evolve Signal/Warning Mechanism*** **:** After having identified likely disasters and their probability, the next step would be to evolve signal/ warning mechanism which is required to be in place. This mechanism will include the use of

technology, the existing signal warning systems of the India Meteorological Department and the Central Water Commission, use of All India Radio, TV, local sirens and other traditional means of communicating the warnings to the community and to the field level machinery immediately in the event of the likely disaster.

- ***To Identify Activities :*** Disaster management is a coordinated effort. A number of activities are required to be undertaken as a response in the event of a disaster. Activities in disaster response generally would be :
  - (i) Coordination, command and control.
  - (ii) Rapid assessment of damage.
  - (iii) Restoration of Power.
  - (iv) Restoration of Tele-communication.
  - (v) Restoration of surface transport.
  - (vi) Deployment of search and rescue teams.
  - (vii) Deployment of medical and para medical teams.
  - (viii) Supply of food material.
  - (ix) Supply of medicines.
  - (x) Arrangements for drinking water.
  - (xi) Setting up of temporary shelters.
  - (xii) Sanitation and hygiene.
  - (xiii) Transportation of men and material.
  - (xiv) Identification of resources, i.e., man, material and money.
  - (xv) Earmarking of resources, i.e., man, material and money.
  - (xvi) Maintenance of law and order, etc.
- ***To Identify Sub-Activities :*** Having listed out the likely activities which would be needed in specific terms, it would be necessary to determine the sub-activities under each of the activity identified. In fact, each activity comprises of 3 to 4 sub-activities for actual performance on the ground.
- ***To Define the Level of Response :*** The level of response will depend keeping on the magnitude of the disaster in terms of intensity and impact. If the magnitude of a disaster is less, the level of activity

would also be low. In other words, the arrangements needed would be at a lower scale. If the magnitude of a disaster is very severe then the same activity would be required to be undertaken at a much larger scale.

- ***To Specify Authorities*** **:** Each activity is required to be assigned to a specific authority. Since a number of Departments/Organisations would be involved in the response, details like name, designation, telephone/fax nos., mobile no., e-mail addresses of each specified authority for each activity should, therefore, be listed out. As an alternative, similar details of the second in command authority should also be listed for each activity. Similarly there will be number of sub-activities to be undertaken in giving effect to many activities.
- ***To Determine the Response Time*** **:** In an emergency response, one should not forget that time is the essence. Therefore, each specified authority should work out the response time needed for operationalising the activity and the sub-activity. This response time will be graded as lesser time will be required for operationalising the activity and sub-activity at a lower scale and obviously more time would be needed if the activity to be operationalised at much higher scale.
- ***To Work out Individual Activity Plans*** **:** Having identified and defined the activities and sub-activities and the scale at which these will require to be operationalised with reference to the pre-determined response time, it would now be the time to work out the individual activity plan by the specified authority and sub-authorities in the context of the assessment of probable disasters and their likely intensity and impact carried out earlier. These plans will lay down a functional mechanism of coordination in both horizontal and vertical manner. These plans need to identify the resources, i.e., money, man, material and equipment needed

for each activity and its sub-activities for undertaking the operations as also earmarking of these resources. The identification and earmarking of resources would be both in terms of quantity and availability and also functionality.

- ***To Have Quick Response Teams (QRTs)* :** By now it is clear that what will be required to be done by each authority and sub-authority in the context of their activity and sub-activities. The job to be undertaken is now known in advance and the process of planning and organization has been completed. Therefore, at this stage, a Quick Response Team should be constituted for each activity. The team members should know each other and should know their task specific to them for their individual activity as also totality of the task assigned to the team. The specified authority and sub-authorities should have complete details of Quick Response Team members to ensure their availability and proper communication at the time of response.
- ***To Undergo Preparedness Drills* :** Quick Response Teams should undergo preparedness drills and carry out mock exercises so as to resolve any functional hiccups or restrains which are experienced while putting their plan functional on ground. On the basis of the field experience or the lessons learnt from previous disasters, the team should update their functional methodology to be more effective both in terms of time and delivery.
- ***To Provide Appropriate Delegations* :** The performance of Quick Response Teams will depend on availability of resources at their command. It would, therefore, be necessary to provide for the appropriate administrative, financial, and legislative delegations in advance so that the response mechanism becomes functionally viable and sustainable. The delegation to different authorities and sub-authorities should be well defined and clearly laid down. In fact, the Standard Operating Procedures (SOPs) should be laid down in advance

so that one knows what to respond and how to respond.

- ***To Have Alternative Plans*** **:** In emergency response to a disaster, one has to prepare for zero level of failures. It, therefore, needs to be emphasized that alternative plans and contingency measures would also required to be thought of in advance, so that the response mechanism does not get stuck up till the mitigation process is stabilized.

Trigger Authority

The trigger mechanism has thus two important components. These are the Trigger Authority and the coordination, command and control activity. The Trigger Authority would generally be the authority in charge of the disaster response in the district which may be the District Magistrate or the Relief Commissioner or the Central Relief Commissioner or any other officer designated for the purpose.

The Trigger mechanism in fact is a *preparedness plan* in which all the participating managers know in advance the task assigned to them and the manner in which they have prepared themselves to respond. As such the organization and planning has already been taken care of. The resources are identified including manpower, material and equipment. The performers have adequate delegation of financial and administrative powers and have the mandate for accomplishing the task.

The success of the Trigger mechanism depends on the *vision* and *perception* of the planners. They are required to anticipate the likely activities with reference to the nature of the disaster and its impact. In fact the Trigger mechanism can also be called the Standard Operating Procedures (SOPs) where the implementation of the efforts on ground are well laid down.

All the major activities, which are generally common in all types of disasters, will require sub-division and preparation of sub-action plans by each specified authority. They will be required to list all the requirements and their availability within the prescribed response time.

Conclusion

Earlier natural phenomena were feared and hence termed as "Wrath of God". Modern science and technology have however, helped in understanding the mechanisms and computations, which result in such catastrophic events and in devising means by which their effect can be minimized. In the era of advance satellite based predictability and remote sensing techniques, the magnitude of damages wrought by natural calamities can be considerably minimized by recourse to a "Culture of Prevention" through awareness, dissemination of proper knowledge and use of appropriate technologies. While elimination of such occurrence may be beyond our keen, mitigatory actions have to be taken to reduce their impact. Hence the goals of successful Disaster Management can be summarized as follows :-

- Prevent.
- Prepare.
- Respond Immediately and Effectively.
- Recover Quickly.

Ethnic Riot

Is a ethnic riot, which we are now familiar are more familiar as communal riot, a disaster. Yes, if we go by the first full scale, comparative study of the deadly ethnic riot – an intense, sudden, lethal attack by civilian members of one ethnic group on another ethnic group. (Donald Horourity in his book, *The Deadly Ethnic Riot*).

Ethnic riots are probably the most common form of collective violence,[22] by some estimates the form that took more lives than any other in the twentieth century.[23] By world standards, an ethnic riot in which 100 people are killed is a very serious disorder.[24] It also produces refugees, likely requirement of curfews and all manners of inconvenience, indignity and outrage. The figures on refugee provides a more revealing picture of the impact of a disorder. The India –Pakistan partition riots, with a death toll between 100,000 and 200,000, produced an estimated 10 million refugees.[25] On the basis of these and similar figures, it is a reasonable conjuncture that the ratio of refugees to officially reported details in ethnic violence averages at least 100 to one.

References

1. Centre of Excellence for Disaster Management and Humanitarian Assistance; Disaster Response; Hawaii USA; p. 2.
2. UN Report on Natural Disasters, 1997.
3. Report of the HPC on Disaster Management; p. 62.
4. *Ibid.,* 13.
5. *Ibid.,* 14.
6. *Ibid.,* 15.
7. Aroon Purie in *India Today,* 07 Sep. 78; p.1.
8. India Disasters Report, 2000; pp. 3-4.
9. National Centre for Disaster Management; Report of High Powered Committee to the Govt. of India; New Delhi, 2001; p. 38.
10. Sinha, Anil; 'Disaster Management : Lessons Drawn and Strategies for the Future'; In *Training Document on Disaster Management*; IIPA – UP Regional Branch, 2001; pp. 2.9.
11. *Ibid.,* 22.
12. *Ibid.,* 15, pp. 67-68.
13. British Disaster Management Pamphlet 'Disaster Management – A Business Systems Approach'.
14. *The Concise Oxford Dictionary*; Bombay: Oxford University Press, 1989; p. 272.
15. Singh, Mendel and Graham; *Disaster Response in India* (2000), p.13.
16. Sinha, P.C.; *Encyclopedia of Disaster Management* – Vol. 1, New Delhi, 1998; p.1.
17. Report of the HPC on Disaster Management, 2001; pp. 35.
18. *Ibid.,* 27.
19. *Ibid.,* 28.
20. *Ibid.,* 29.
21. Report of the HPC on Disaster Management, 2000, pp. 71.
22. R.P. Richardson, "An Analysis of Recent Conflicts" (mimes, Arlington, 1970) pp. 43-44.
23. Harold Issacs, "Power and Identity : Tribalism in World Politics," Headline series of the Foreign Policy Association, No. 246 (October 1979) : 11-12.

24. Lewis F Richardson, *Statistics of Deadly Quarrels* (Pittsburgh: Box word Press, 1960) Ch. 2.
25. *Ibid.*, p. 43.

10

Types of Disasters and Their Assessment

Types of Disasters

Introduction

The term 'disaster' evokes extraordinary response from outside their community or affected area. The disaster agent is a catalyst which has a potential to create or produce disasters. For example, earthquake, cyclones, floods are disaster agents. Disaster is basically about vulnerability, susceptibility of a potential victim to the life threatening impact of disaster agent, as brought out earlier.

Broad Classification

A wide variety of forces can cause disasters. These forces may be either natural or artificial or a combination of both.

Man-made Disasters

Within this category of disasters, there are variety of conditions resulting in a disaster: -

- ***Civil Disturbances*:** Riots, e.g., Bombay Riots of 1993.
- ***Warfare*:** Conventional, NBC warfare, LICO terrorism-mass movement of people from one place to another.

- ***Refugees*** : Forced movements of large numbers of people usually across frontiers, for example, refugees of *Rwanda,* in *Zaire,* Bangladesh and Afghanistan.
- ***Accidents*** : Collapse of buildings, mine disasters, for example, Bhopal Gas Tragedy of 1984 in India.

Natural Disasters

Within this category of disasters, a variety of forces that may result in disaster :-

- ***Meteorological Disasters*** : Cyclones, hurricanes, cold wave, heat wave and droughts (possibly causing famines).
- ***Topological Disasters*** : Earthquakes, avalanches, landslides and floods.
- ***Biological Disasters*** : Epidemics of communicable diseases for example, Surat Plague.

The division between natural and man-made is to some extent an over simplification, as many disasters are actually caused by more than one or combination of various forces. Some disasters set a chain reaction of disaster. For example, Cyclone can be followed by a flood, which may eventually result in an epidemic of cholera.

Some of the worst disasters have been caused by the cumulative effects of several of these factors. For example, in November 1970, a cyclone was followed by one of the worst tidal waves which led to death of 50,000 people. The occurrence of this natural disaster came at a time of civil strife, followed by Indo-Pak war of 1971 leading to liberation of Bangladesh. It forced ten million people to flee to India, entailing another relief operation. The combined natural and man-made disasters resulted in one of the biggest relief operations since World War II. The long-term perspective will reveal to us that disaster is an interaction of combination of political, social, economic and environment factors. There is no wonder if disasters appear more frequently in developing world than developed ones.

It is difficult to predict precisely where and when a man-made disaster will occur, therefore, it is more difficult to prepare for one. It is possible however, with varying degrees of accuracy to predict the occurrence of a natural disaster.

Keeping all above in mind, let us now focus on natural

disasters and weapons of mass destruction and their effects in India.

Earthquakes

It may seem something of a revelation that the plates of the earth's crust are in slow but constant motion and innumerable earthquakes are registered around the world on the seismographs everyday. However, the tremors are generally so small that they pass without being noticed. It is only when the magnitude is 5.0 or more on the Richter Scale that it is noticeable. With magnitude around 6.0 or more and hitting densely populated areas, these tremors assume apocalyptic proportions both on account of the suddenness of the shock and their mass destructive potential.

India has witnessed some of the most devastating earthquakes during this century like the one in Kangra (1905) in which 20,000 people were killed. In the recent past, earthquakes have caused havoc in Uttarkashi (1991), Latur (1993), Jabalpur (1997) and in Chamoli (1999) with more than 7500 dead, the Latur earthquake was the worst in terms of lives lost, though as a result thereof, much more attention has since been focused on preparatory and mitigation measures for meeting such contingencies.

A massive earthquake measuring 6.9 on the Richter Scale struck Bhuj on 26th January 2001. The earthquake has caused incalculable damages to Bhuj as well as all the other towns of this district and to about 500 villages out of the total of 900 villages. The reported damage to property in Gujarat is about Rs. 21,000 crore and the figure of dead is placed at 17,000-20,000. More than 500 dead has been reported from Ahmedabad which is situated at a distance of 400 Km from Bhuj, where approx. 150 odd multistoried buildings have crumbled down. Damage has also been reported even from far-off places like Surat. After extensive rescue and relief operations reconstruction and rehabilitation was another major exercise and Government of India had already promised assistance of Rs. 5,170 crores.

Causes of Earthquakes

The earth's crust is not one piece but consists of portions

called plates, of varying sizes. These plates are not stable but move with three distinctive types of movements along the boundaries of the plates.

(a) ***Convergent Boundaries*** : Where plates push each other and one plate slides down the other one.

(b) ***Divergent Boundaries*** : Where plates pull away from each other.

(c) ***Transformed Boundaries*** : Where plates slides past each other.

Due to continuous movement of the plates, stress and accumulation takes place at the boundaries of these plates. When the stress accumulation reaches a point of maximum supportive strain, a rupture takes place generating an earthquake. The earthquakes generated this way are most damaging. Approximately 95 per cent of the earthquake activities occur at the plate boundaries. Some earthquake, however, do occur in the middle of the plates, possibly indicating where earlier plate boundaries might have been. The point of rupture is called the focus.

The intensity of shaking at any place is related to the amount of energy released, the focal depth, distance of the place from the focus and the structural properties of the rock or soil on the surface. Some earthquakes are associated with volcanic activities as well.

Types

The three major types of earthquakes are Volcanic, Plutonic and Tectonic Attributes of these are :-

- ***Volcanic*** : It is attributable to volcanic activity usually centred near the volcano. Damage usually is limited and local.
- ***Plutonic*** : These are deep focused quakes to be caused by explosion as deep as 435 miles within the interior of the earth. Though felt on the earth surface, little damage results except perhaps in a limited area directly above the explosion.
- ***Tectonic*** : These earthquakes are most common and most destructive of all quakes. They are caused by slippage along faults in the earth's crust. The grating or rubbing together the sides of faults sets up earthquake waves.

In most earthquakes the earths crust cracks like porcelain. They generally occur on the so-called plate boundaries where moving plates are pulled apart, slide past or converge. The earth-quakes are usually preceded by foreshocks and followed by after shocks. Earth-quakes strike without warning and there is no time for last minute preparation and therefore speedy emergency relief is of utmost importance. Although earthquakes may occur anywhere on the earth's surface, including bottom of the sea, approximately 65 per cent occur in certain seismic area. The Latur and Koyna (Maharashtra) aseismic areas have experienced earthquakes, perhaps due to rift that exist in these areas.

Flood

A flood is defined as a body of water rising, swelling and overflowing land areas. Most river floods result from natural causes, such as excessive rainfall, melting snow or ice jams. In general, floods are classified as either regular or flash floods. Regular floods can be predicted.

'India has always been visited by floods' This is a seasonal and endemic term of disaster which causes great havoc and devastation each year. The primary cause of all floods in India is heavy and concentrated rainfall, June to September is the rainiest period of the year. Rainfall also occurs from October to December in East Coast of Southern Peninsula due to North-East Monsoons. Since preparatory and warning period is adequate, floods can be tackled satisfactorily.

The country receives an annual precipitation of 400 million-hectare metres. Of the annual rainfall, 75 per cent is received during four months of monsoon (June-September) and, as a result, almost all the rivers carry heavy discharge during this period. The flood hazard is compounded by the problems of sedimentation, drainage congestion and synchronization of river floods with sea tides in the coastal plains. The area vulnerable to floods is 40 million-hectare and the average area affected by floods annually is about 8 million hectares. The average annual total damage to crops, house, and public utilities during the period 1953-1995 was about Rs. 9720 million.

Causes of Floods

(a) Flooding may occur due to :-
   (i) Rivers in spate
   (ii) Snowmelt
   (iii) Storm surges
   (iv) Short intense storms causing flash floods

(b) *Flooding in rivers is mainly caused by :*
   (i) Inadequate capacity within the banks of the river to contain high flows.
   (ii) River bank erosion and silting of riverbeds.
   (iii) Landslides leading to obstruction of flow and change in the river course.
   (iv) Synchronisation of flood in the main rivers and tributaries.
   (v) Flow retardation due to tidal and backwater effects.
   (vi) Poor natural drainage.
   (vii) Cyclone and heavy rainfall.

Types of floods. These are :-

(a) Snow Melt Floods.
(b) Storm surge.
(c) Flash floods.

Tropical Cyclones

A Cyclone, is a violent windstorm, usually accompanied by much rain, thunder and lightning. Cyclones take form of very large revolving and moving form (200-300 miles per day), accompanied by lashing winds (80 to 100 miles per day), high tidal waves (10 to 12 feet). These are also known as hurricanes or typhoons. In the Bay of Bengal these normally occur from December to March. The coastal area and areas up to few hundred kilometres inland are more vulnerable to cyclones particularly the coasts of Orissa, Andhra Pradesh and Tamil Nadu.

Characteristics of Tropical Cyclones. These are :-

Destructive Winds **:** The strong winds that blow counter-clockwise in the Northern Hemisphere, while spiraling inwards and increasing toward the cyclone centre are highly destructive. Wind speeds progressively increase towards the core. As the eye arrives, winds decrease to become almost calm but rise again just as quickly as the eye passes and are replaced by hurricane force winds from a direction nearly the reverse of those previously blowing.

Storm Surges **:** The storm surge defined as the rise in sea level about normally predicted astronomical tide, is frequently a key or overriding factor in a tropical disaster. The major factors include.

(i) A fall in the atmospheric pressure over the sea surface.
(ii) The effect of the wind.
(iii) The influence of the sea bed.
(iv) The funneling effect.
(v) The angle and speed at which the storm approaches the coast.
(vi) The tides.

Exceptional Rainfall Occurrences : The world's highest rainfall spread over one or two days has occurred during tropical cyclones. The very high specific humidity condenses into exceptionally large raindrops and giant cumulus clouds, resulting in high precipitation rates. When a cyclone makes landfall, the rain rapidly saturates the catchment area and the rapid runoff may extensively flood the usual water sources or create new ones.

Drought

Drought is a temporary reduction in water or moisture availability significantly below the normal or expected amount for a specific period. This condition occurs either due to inadequacy of rainfall, or lack of irrigation facilities, under exploitation or deficient availability for meeting the normal crop requirement the context of the agro-climatic conditions prevailing in any particular area. This has been scientifically computed as Moisture Index (MI). Drought, in this context can be defined as adverse MI or adverse water balance which may be also due to such other factors as excessive evapo-transpirational losses, high temperature, low soil holding capacity etc. The inadequacy is with reference to the prevailing agro-climatic conditions in any particular area. Therefore there is a drought in Jaisalmer (Average rainfall 200 mm) if rainfall is not sufficient to grow grass and paltry coarse grains, whereas in Bolangir or Koraput (Orissa-rainfall above 1000 mm) there is a drought if there is not enough rainfall for bringing the paddy crop to maturity.

Types of Drought : There are three types of drought :-

- ***Meteorological Drought*** : It describes a situation where there is a reduction in a rainfall for a specific period (days, months, season or year) below a specific amount (long-term average for a specific time).
- ***Hydrological Drought*** : It involves a reduction in water resources (Stream flow lake level, ground water, underground aquifers) below a specified level for a given period of time.
- ***Agricultural Drought*** : It is the impact of meteorological/hydrological drought on crop yield.
- The three drought types are completely different and not synonymous.

Landslides

Landslides are defined as the mass movement of rock, debris or earth down a slope and have come to include a broad range of motions whereby falling, sliding and flowing under the influence of gravity dislodges earth material. They often take place in conjunction with earthquakes, floods and volcanoes. At times, prolonged rainfall causing heavy landslides block the flow of river for quite some time. The formation of river blocks can cause havoc to the settlements downstream on its bursting.

In the hilly terrain of India including the Himalayas, landslides have been a major and widely spread natural disaster that often strike life and property and occupy a position of major concern.

One of the worst, tragedies took place at Malpa in Uttarakhand (present Uttaranchal) on 11th and 17th August 1998, when nearly 380 people were killed when massive landslides washed away the entire village. This included 60 pilgrims going to Lake Mansarovar in Tibet. Consequently various land reform measure have been initiated as mitigation measures.

The two regions most vulnerable to landslides are the Himalayas and the Western Ghats. Studies carried out by Central Road Research Institute indicate a high to very high rate of incidence of landslides in the Himalayas and a high rate in the Western Ghats. The Himalayan mountain belt comprise of tectonically unstable younger geological formations subjected to severe seismic activity. The Western Ghats and Nilgiris are geologically stable but have uplifted plateau margins influenced by neo-tectonic activity. Thus, the two regions have different geological settings leading to characteristic types of landslides. Compared to the Western Ghats region, the slides in the Himalayan region are huge and massive and in most cases the overburden along with the underlying lithology is displaced during sliding, particularly due to the seismic factor. In contrast landslide events in the Western Ghats are confined to the over burden without affecting the bedrock beneath and are generally in the nature of debris flows occurring mainly during monsoons. The effect, of course, is felt much more acutely because of a comparatively higher density of population.

Broadly the country has been divided into the following regions in term of incidence and severity of landslides.

Table 10.1 Incidences of Landslides in India

Region	*Incidences of Landslides*
Himalayas	High to very high
North-eastern Hills	High
Western Ghats and the Nilgiris	Moderate to high
Eastern Ghats	Low
Vindhayachal Low	

Forest Fires

Forests face many hazards but the most common hazard is fire. Forests fires are as old as the forests themselves.

They pose a threat not only to the forest wealth but also to the entire regime of fauna and flora seriously disturbing the bio-diversity, ecology and environment of a region.

During summer, when there is no rain for months, the forests become littered with dry senescent leaves and twigs, which could burst into flames ignited by the slightest spark. The Himalayan forests particularly Garhwal Himalayas have been burning regularly during the last few summers, with colossal loss of vegetation cover of that region.

Causes of Forest Fire

Forest fires are caused by:

Natural causes **:** Many forest fires start from natural causes such as lightning which set trees on fire. Periodic lightning-induced fires have been recorded throughout history from India, South Eastern and Central United States, Australia, Finland and Eastern and Southern Africa. However, rain extinguishes such fires without causing much damage. High atmospheric temperatures and dryness (low humidity) offer favourable circumstances for a fire to start.

Man-made causes **:** Fires are caused when a source of fire like naked flame, cigarette or bidi, electric spark or any other source of ignition comes into contact with inflammable material.

Classification of Forest Fire. Forest fires can broadly be classified into three categories:

- Natural or controlled fires.
- Forest fires caused by heat generated in the litter and other biomes in summer through carelessness of people (human neglect).
- Forest fires purposely caused by local inhabitants.

Types of Forest Fire. There are two types of forest fire:-

- Surface Fire and
- Crown Fire

Surface Fire **:** A forest fire may burn primarily as a surface fire, spreading along the ground as the surface litter (senescent leaves and twigs and dry grasses etc.) on the forest floor are engulfed by the spreading flames.

Crown Fire **:** The other type of forest fire is a crown fire in which the crown of trees and shrubs burn, often sustained by a surface fire. A crown fire is particularly very dangerous in a coniferous forest because resinous material given off by burning logs burn furiously. On hill slopes, if the fire starts downhill, it spreads up fast as heated air adjacent to a slope tends to flow up the slope spreading flames along with it. If the fire starts uphill, there is less likelihood of it spreading downwards.

Avalanches

General Concept **:** Snow cover on a slope tends to slide down the slope because of gravity. Conditions affecting stability include the gravitational force component of the snow and resisting forces, such as the frictional resistance of the slope or the anchoring effect of shrubs. In general, avalanches are caused when this balance is lost and when the forces exceed the resistance. Avalanches are rarely observed closely since they normally occur during a short time period of one or two minutes.

Major Causes **:** Major causes of avalanches can be classified into fixed (prime factors) and variable factors (exciting factors), such as weather conditions and the weight of the snow cover. Avalanches occur when these factors are combined. The types and scale of avalanches can differ depending on the combination of these various factors and their scale.

Pest Infestation

Food losses due to pests, disease, wild animals, insects and weeds are considerable. It is estimated that 35 per cent of world crop production is lost in spite of pesticide and other control programmes. The primary pests are insects, disease and weeds. Losses due to birds and wild animals are low compared to these.

A pest may be defined as any living organism or plant causing harm or damage to people, their animals, crops or possessions. The important pests are those which lead to loss in crop yield or quality resulting in loss of profits to the farmers and reduced stocks for subsistence or export.

Causes of Pest Infestation : Insect outbreaks are

usually the result of a combination of ecological factors. These are :-

- **Temperature**. Often the most important factor that governs insect development is temperature.
- **Mono-culture of Crops.** Generally crop mono-cultures are more vulnerable to pest because there is less resistance and fewer natural enemies of the specific pests attacking the crop.
- **Introduction of plants to new locations**. Some pest problems occurs when crops are introduced into new biological communities.
- **Weather pattern.** For flying insects such as locusts, the prevailing winds are important in determining where they will fly and whether they will survive.
- **Migration**. Movement to a different area with more favourable conditions, allows some pests species to escape control and increase in number.

Characteristics of Pest Infestation : The hazards of pest infestation can be described, as the damage done when the part of the plant attacked is the part to be harvested. Biting insects may damage plants as follows:-

- Reduce the amount of leaf and photosynthetic area, hindering plant growth.
- Tunnel in the stem and interrupt sap flow.
- Destroy buds or growing points and cause subsequent distortion.
- Cause premature fruit fall.
- Attack flowers and reduce seed production.
- Injure or destroy seeds completely or reduce germination.
- Attack roots and cause loss of water and nutrient absorbing tissue.
- Remove stored food in tuber.

Insects with piercing and sucking mouth-parts damage plants are follows :-

- Cause loss of plant vigour by removing excessive quantities of sap.
- Damage floral organs and reduce seed production.
- Cause premature leaf falls.
- Inject toxins into the plant.

- Provide entry points for pathogenic fungi and bacteria.
- Reduce photosynthetic area on leaf surface.
- Transfer plant pathogens.

Disaster Prone Gujarat

A large number of medium and small-scale chemical industries are located in the industrial estates of Vapi, Ankleshwar, Panoli, Nandesari, Vatva and Naroda, which produce numerous organic chemicals for consumption in the country and for exports.

Gujarat has 1600 kilometres of coastline, which is being developed for ports. Considering the infrastructure proposed in the coastal areas, it is expected that port-based mega-chemical industrial estate would be developed.

In addition to the manufacturing industries, there are several infrastructure related projects including pipelines, storages and installations for Hydrocarbons and chemicals. India's first major in-land cross-country gas pipeline named the Hazira-Bijapur-Jagdishpur (HBJ) pipeline originates from Hazira. It traverses the states of Madhya Pradesh, Rajasthan and Uttar Pradesh. The main trunk of the HBJ pipelines consists of carbon steel pipeline ranging from 450 to 900 mm in diameter. Although, originally, 1,700 km. of pipeline was laid, subsequent extensions and spur lines were added increasing the length to over 2,300 km. There is a hydrocarbon supply pipeline from Kandla to Bhatinda, which crosses Rajasthan and other states.Gujarat State Petroleum Corporation and Gujarat Gas have proposed a pipeline network of more than 1200 kilometres in the State. The 73 km. Hazira-Ankleshwar pipeline was recently commissioned.

Gas Authority of India has Jamnagar-Loni pipeline for carrying LPG. Major LNG terminals are proposed at Pipvav, Dahej and Hazira, which would necessitate laying of long cross-country pipelines for carrying natural gas. More than 50 per cent of country's imported crude oil is being handled by the ports of Gujarat. The crude oil carrying pipelines include Salaya-Mathura, Viramgam-Vadodara, and those proposed from Mundra to Punjab. The petroleum products carrying pipelines include Vadodara-Sabarmati, Kandla-Bhatinda and Jamnagar-Kandla (off-shore).

There are several port-based installations for petroleum products, petrochemicals products, solvents and other hazardous chemicals at Kandla, Mundra, Vadinar, Porbandar, Dahej, Pipavav and Hazira. Some of these locations are in earthquakes/and cyclone prone zones. There are isolated storages in different regions, including petroleum storages and LPG bottling plants at Vadodara, Kheda, Sanand, Bavla, Rajkot and Bhavnagar.

Location-wise Classification of Hazardous Industries

The Government of Gujarat has categorized its districts on the basis of chemical and industrial hazardousness. The districts have been classified as follows :-

Sl. No.	*Category*	*Districts*
1.	AA Category (Highly Hazardous)	Bharuch and Vadodara
2.	A Category (Less Hazardous)	Ahmedabad, Jamnagar, Kutch, Rajkot, Surat and Valsad.
3.	B Category (Less Hazardous)	Anand, Bhavnagar, Gandhinagar, Kheda, Mehsana, Panch-mahals and Porbandar
4.	C Category (Much less Amreli, Hazardous)	Banaskantha, Dahod, Dangs, Junagadh, Narmada, Navsari, Patan, Sabarkantha and Surendranagar.

Industrial concentration : The district-wise details of Major Accident Hazard (MAH) factories of Gujarat state are as follows. Details of factories district-wise are given as under:

Name of District	*Total MAH Factories*
Ahmedabad	73
Amreli	01
Anand	07
Bharuch	86
Bhavnagar	04
Gandhinagar	07
Jamnagar	06
Junagadh	03
Kheda	11
Kutch	24
Mehsana	08
Navsari	01
Panchamahals	09
Rajkot	09
Sabarkantha	01
Surat	32
Surendranagar	03
Vadodara	85
Valsad	46
Total	416

The Gujarat Industrial Development Corporation (GIDC) has a total of 83 industrial estates distributed across all the districts of Gujarat. The major ones are as follows :-

Sl. No.	*Industrial Estate*	*Districts*
1.	Ankleshwar	Bharuch
2.	Dahej	Bharuch
3.	Jhagadia	Bharuch
4.	Nandesari	Vadodara

Contd.

Sl. No.	Industrial Estate	Districts
5.	Naroda	Ahmedabad
6.	Odhav	Ahmedabad
7.	Panoli	Bharuch
8.	Petrochemical Complex	Vadodara
9.	Ranoli	Vadodara
10.	Sachin	Surat
11.	Sarigam	Valsad
12.	Vapi	Valsad
13.	Vatva	Ahmedabad

These two lists suggest that Ahmedabad, Bharuch, Vadodara, Valsad, Surat and Kutch have maximum number of chemical and hazardous industries, and hence these districts are vunerable to chemicals hazards. All the districts except Kutch are situated along a north-south alignment and therefore, it is feasible to develop a response plan centred on this geographical region.

Classification of chemical/nuclear disaster : Disasters differ by a number of characteristics including the following:-

- Intensity.
- Number impacted.
- Number of injuries/deaths.
- Role of entities.
- Resource requirement.

Weapons of Mass Destruction

"As dual-use technology and expertise continues to spread internationally the prospects of chemical, biological and radiological terrorism increase. The relative ease of production increases our concern these weapons are attractive to terrorists".

Though WMD terrorist attacks have not caused widespread devastation so far. Dr Oehler's warning is resounding throughout the world. The latest 11 Sep. 2001 terrorist attacks in the USA, the chemical gas attack in

Tokyo sub-way a few years ago and the proliferation and ease of availability/production of chemical and biological agents, warrants that we are adequately prepared in tackling WMD terrorist attacks and disasters. A proper response mechanism will also ensure that the vital interest of our country can be safeguarded even during a war.

Threat of WMD Terrorism/Disasters

Motivational factors for this could be: -

Based on deep-rooted ideological bias and religious fanaticism, the basic 'sadistically homicidal' instinct is to kill or maim as many people as possible in a single strike. WMD weapons provide Quantitative advantage over equivalent amount of conventional explosives to produce an unimaginable degree of mass destruction.

Possession of a credible WMD device/agent may motivate a terrorist organization to resort to blackmail. Terrorist groups will then be able to negotiate from a position of unsurpassed strength. In such an eventuality, the terrorist group may have to undertake a demonstration strike to prove that it actually possesses a WMD device.

Some terrorist groups may prefer to remain anonymous/unseen in order to create greater psychological impact, panic or protect their identity. They may use biological attacks, which manifest themselves after some time. Possible scenarios could be, deliberately causing a Surat (1997) type plague/undiagnosed viral disease like in Siliguri (West Bengal – Feb. 01) or even pollution of water supply system of a major metropolis. Such attacks may also be carried out to cause economic and social damage by targeting livestock and agricultural sector.

Another possibility of use of WMD device with the assistance of state sponsorship from adversarial States (facilitated by the likes of Osama Bin Laden or the underworld) does exist.

Threat of Nuclear Terrorism/Disasters

Damaging a nuclear plant by an attack with explosives or sabotage to engineer a radioactive release.

Attack on a nuclear storage site.

Takeover/theft of nuclear weapons by renegade commanders, scientists or personnel.

Hold up of key nuclear scientists 'off site'

Fabrication of crude nuclear bomb from stolen materials by disgruntled or disloyal scientists.

Radiological Devices. In the opinion of some authorities, theft of a nuclear device or building a nuclear device or building a nuclear bomb however crude, are the least probable courses of action for a prospective nuclear terrorist. Far more likely is the dispersal of radiological material in an effort to contaminate a target population or distinct geographical area. Material such as Cesium 137, Iridium 192, Cobalt 60, and nuclear waste stored at nuclear plants and radiological medical isotopes are available in hospitals and research labs. Besides, the materials from which a 'dirty nuke' is made is stored in every nuclear facility worldwide at differing levels of security management. There are over 400 nuclear reactors other than special research reactors and nuclear labs in all the Nuclear Weapons states. In South Asia alone there are at least seven known research reactors and 16 nuclear power reactors that not only lend themselves to clandestine procurement of nuclear materials but are also potential targets for a terrorist attack with the consequent release of toxic and radiological fumes. Terrorists could use radiological weapons in the following ways :-

Theft of special nuclear materials for radioactive release through radioactivity dispersal devices using highly toxic Plutonium.

Granulate the radioactive substance, mix with an explosive and explode the device near the target area. The bigger the explosion, the larger the dispersal and lesser the density of contamination. The smaller the explosion, the more concentrated the contamination.

Pulverize the radiological material into fine powder and disperse the same through an aerosol. In this case because of the high density of radioactive material, the dispersal has to be from above the target area using a balloon, Unarmed Aerial Vehicle, aircraft or detonation on top of a multi-storey building. This will ensure that the dust settles down over the area and contaminates the target.

Radioactive material can be used to contaminate food stocks, livestock, harvest and crops. This would also ensure that the area is rendered unfit for agriculture and farming for years to come.

A radiological device can be used as a force multiplier during a conventional explosive attack. For example, had the terrorists who blew up the World Trade Tower in New York in 1998, used radiological material along with conventional explosives, one of the most important area of the city would still be uninhabitable and thousands would still be suffering from radiation sickness.

As far as radioactive mass contamination of water is concerned, most analysts feel that the huge quantities of radioactive material required would discourage most terrorist groups. Also many radioactive agents are insoluble in water and so make this option impractical.

Chemical Terrorism

A small vial of the nerve agent VX which was being produced in Khartoum, Sudan, would have been sufficient to bring the complete London, underground ralways system to a halt in addition to causing thousands of deaths. Tear gas and other gases being used for crowd control can also be used in a chemical attack. Fluid Thiodiglycol used in ballpoint inks can be converted into mustard gas agents by chlorination. If a solution of plutonium nitrate is dried, packed as crystals into two stainless steel bowls and surrounded by ordinary blocks of TNT an explosion will occur if the critical mass is calculated correctly.

Types of Threat. In contrast to nuclear terrorism, which remains a problematic and complex matter and is therefore still largely theoretical, chemical terrorism is more concrete and practical and in several instances has already been used. Accordingly, chemical threat may be found in two forms:-

- Attacks meant to cause mass devastation. In these cases, the terrorist organisation releases a toxin in congested population centres, bodies of water, and unventilated area in order to create as many victims as possible.
- Chemical attacks meant primarily to terrorise, blackmail, or cause economic damage. By a specific attack in a particular product (particularly a food product, mainly by introducing a toxic chemical agent into the product itself).

Easy Accessibility of Chemical Agents : For the organizations involved, chemical terrorism has several clear-cut advantages over conventional or nuclear terrorism. First of all, chemical substances are more accessible and available. They can be manufactured using simple chemical processes known to any university student. The components are usually simple products that can be obtained in the free market without restrictions. A chemical attack can be perpetrated using off-the-shelf pesticides sold in grocery stores.

If this were not enough, many countries (including Third World countries and known supporters of terrorist organizations) have large arsenals of chemical materials. Therefore, one must reckon with the possibility of transfer of chemical agents (unlike unclear weapons) from one of these countries, (particularly those that have not flinched from using chemical weapons against their own citizens and in their wars with neighbouring countries) to a terrorist organization in order to perpetrate attacks.

Inexpensive and Easy to Move : Chemical terrorism does not require extensive facilities. Because toxic chemical substances are ordinarily quite inexpensive to purchase or manufacture (at least when compared with nuclear substances) resource starved organizations can obtain and use them very easily. Whereas nuclear bomb, which is large and cumbersome and requires special vehicles and security in transport, small amounts of chemicals suffice for a chemical attack. For example a jar containing several hundred grams of a chemical substance may cause mass mortality and can be moved about easily, with no need for special preparations or security.

Field of Impact : A massive chemical terrorist attack a very wide field of impact. The dispersion of a chemical substance in a congested/covered area may cause many casualties. However, beyond the grave physical damage caused by exposure to the chemical substance, an attack of this kind may cause many additional casualties because of panic and attempts to flee the disaster site. Moreover, a chemical terrorist attack, for the very reason that it involves a non-conventional weapon, will inevitably trigger a serious crisis of morale and undermine the personal security of the citizens of the country attacked.

Difficult to Detect. In this context, it should be borne in mind that most chemical weapons are colourless, odourless, and devoid of any other identifying factor. Therefore, they cannot be detected until the moment citizens are exposed and experience symptoms. Furthermore, it is difficult to protect civil population from chemical substances. This aggravates the morale problem. Terrorist organizations throughout the world could adopt chemical weapons such as those used in the Tokyo subway attack.

Biological Terrorism

Biological terrorism is, 'the use and dissemination of biological weapons (various kinds of microbes) in population centres, by various means, in order to cause morbidity and numerous casualties'. Characteristics are as under :-

- Biological weapons compare favourably with nuclear weapons with respect to their destructive potential. A mere 100 grams of Anthrax released over a major city may cause up to 3 million casualties.
- Minimum infrastructure and expertise required for manufacture.
- Advances in biotechnology have made it easier to manufacture such weapons.
- Monitoring is difficult.

- Existing BWC (1972) is ineffective and lacks verification measures.

Delayed Results and Difficult to Detect. Unlike the tools of chemical terrorism, biological weapons were not designed and ordinarily cannot be used for pinpoint attacks, their principle purpose is mass devastation. The results of a biological attack are not immediate, they become apparent several hours or days later (after some of the victims have left the site of the attack). This may make it harder to detect the perpetrator and target of the attack.

NATO has identified 30 bio agents as potential bio weapons. US has short listed six, namely—Anthrax, Plague, Botulinum Toxin, and Haemorrhagic fevers.

Scientific Advancement. Genetic engineering opens up startling possibilities for the use of bio-weapons by terrorists and rogue states. It has been reported by the latest issue of British science magazine *Nature*, that, 'small changes in DNA of well known bacteria and viruses could turn these agents into mass killers—making subtle genetic alterations to existing pathogens to increase their virulence or durability in the environment or to make them harder to detect or to treat them with drugs is within the limits of today's technology'. Thus, by genetic manipulation on small pox, an unstoppable killer could be unleashed that will be resistant to antibiotics.

Effects of Disaster

General. While each disaster has its own characteristics, it is possible to determine a common base of disaster effect. This is necessary to evolve common disaster relief operations to combat their effects.

Effects.

Extensive Deaths and Danger to Life.

Destruction and Damage to Buildings.

Lack of water Food and Essential Requirement. Need provision and distribution of survival requirements like water, food, fodder, blankets and so on.

Disruption of Communication : This complicates assessment of damage and deployment of relief efforts.

Outbreak or Danger of Epidemics : Preventive

measures should include inoculation, vaccination, water treatment and sanitation as part of disaster relief.

Threat to Crops, Vital Installations, Public Utilities or Fire Hazards : Suitable damage control measures like crop spraying, reinforcements or demolitions and fire services are required.

Special Features of Disaster Relief

Special features of disaster relief are as follows :-

Lack of Early Warning and Information : This results in delayed response due to lack of relief intelligence.

Inadequate Resources : Mobilisation of resources in men and material from multiple sources is a critical planning and organizational problem.

Varying Requirements : Each disaster situation requires separate consideration, planning and expertise to deal with its specified problems.

ASSESSMENT

Introduction

Purpose of Assessment : The overall purpose of an assessment is to assist the state and Central Government, and the Resident/Humanitarian Coordinator in identifying needs for international disaster relief assistance and to facilitate a timely, appropriate response by the international community. The assessment is not meant to supplant specialist assessment teams but to fill gaps in information collection. In particular, the team assists in an on-site assessment of :-

- The nature of the disaster.
- Damage, including secondary threats.
- Effects on the population.
- Ongoing relief activities and local response capacity.
- Needs for international assistance.
- Means of delivering international assistance.
- Expected developments.

Types of Assessment : The different types of assessment are:

Initial or Rapid Assessments : Initial assessment comprises both situation and needs assessment in the early, critical stage of a disaster to determine the type of relief needed for immediate response. Initial assessment aim to :-

- Identify the impact a disaster has had on a society and its infrastructure, and the ability of that society to cope.
- Identify the most vulnerable segments of the population that need to be targeted for assistance.
- Identify the level of response by the affected country and its internal capacity to cope with the situation.
- Identify the most urgent relief needs and potential methods of providing them most effectively.
- Make recommendations which define and set priorities on the actions and resources needed for immediate response.
- Highlight special concerns regarding the development of the situation.
- Draw attention to geographical area/substantive sectors needing in-depth assessment.

Situation/Disaster Assessment : Situation/disaster assessment refers to the process of collecting information on the magnitude of the disaster and the extent of its impact on both the population and infrastructure of the society. This type of information is usually first available to an assessment team.

Needs Assessment : Needs assessment aims to define the level and type of assistance required for the affected population. The initial needs assessment identifies resources and services for immediate emergency measures to save and sustain the lives of the affected population. It is conducted at the site of a disaster or at the location of a displaced population. It may also identify the need for continued monitoring and reassessment of the unfolding disaster.

In-depth or Sectoral Assessment : In-depth assessment may refer to both situation and needs assessment. An in-depth assessment usually starts after the initial surveys and will cover critical sectors that have to be addressed for medium and longer term relief as well as rehabilitation and reconstruction assistance. In-depth assessment are carried out by specialists in the sectors concerned. An assessment should help determine the extent of a disaster and its impact on the population as well as needs for international assistance during immediate relief or survival phase. During this phase, exceptional measures have to be taken to meet the basic needs of survivors with regard to search and rescue, medical assistance, water supply, immediate food needs, shelter and sanitation.

Assessment Recommendations and their Impact on Recovery

It is important that the recommendations of the team do not have a counter-productive effect on the long-term recovery efforts of an affected country. Relief programmes can set the stage for rapid recovery or prolong the length of the recovery period. Every action in an emergency response will have a direct effect on the manner and cost of reconstruction.

Many common relief programmes can create dependencies and severely reduce the survivors ability to cope with the next disaster. For example, food commodities brought into a disaster area without consideration for the local agricultural system can destroy the local market and cause future food shortage where self-sufficiency had been the norm. Another example is when relief supplies, equipment or technology are sent in that cannot be sustained by the survivors. When this assistance wears out or is used up, the survivors may be left in the same conditions as immediately following the disaster.

Reconstruction should be simple, support the use of local materials and systems and be sustainable by the affected state.

Methodology and Planning

The factors that contribute to the design of a successful and accurate assessment are :-

- Identify information that is vital for users.
- Apply standards and indicators to the presentation

of data so that key relationships can be quickly noted.

- Timing of the Assessment.
- Determine the best places to obtain accurate information.
- Use recognized terminology standards and procedures.
- Distinguish between emergency and Chronic Needs.
- Consider state specific sensitivities.

Assessment Process

An accurate assessment depends on thorough planning, design and preparation. Most information needs can be identified in advance. A plan of action should be established as a result of the planning phase. The objectives it is intended to achieve must be enumerated. Various points to be taken into consideration are :-

- In the *Planning stage*, the following points have to be taken into consideration:
  - Specific task of the team.
  - Initial size and composition of team and therefore a consideration of its abilities and limitations.
- *Disaster situation* :
  - Type/occurrence.
  - Possible future developments of the disaster.
- Date and information available (reliability)
- Stricken area (size, topography, accessibility, population density, urban/rural etc).
- In country logistics (means of transport communication, mission support-food, medical, etc). Access and security levels to be checked with appropriate authorities.
- Time available.
- Possible information sources in the area.
- Local cultural and other social factors.
- Political situation (security, freedom of movement, other restrictions).
- In-country UN presence in the affected area (many UN Agencies have programmes with national staff who may be in the affected area. Consider using

their help).

- Presence of any other international relief teams, e.g., military etc.

Taking into account the different methods of data collection, a choice of appropriate methods and information sources has to be made, the participative tools and methods most frequently used are :-

- Focus Groups
- Semi structured interviews
- Open questions
- Walk through a village
- Wealth ranking
- Gender activity profiles
- Time-line needs
- Use of rapid assessment checklist is usually the best way to ensure that all information is reported in a uniform way.
- Members may also study assessment conducted by others, try to inform themselves of the approach used and then use this material, as appropriate, in their reporting. In this case, the source should always be indicated.
- Equipment for the field trip.
- Personal
- Announcement of itinerary and contact points.
- Regional/local authorities
- Central Government (letter of reference)
- UN agencies/missions in the area/NGOs, other international teams, e.g., DART teams.

  In an initial assessment, the gathering of information must proceed rapidly. Assessors should look for patterns and indicators of potential problems. Sources of all information should be identified. Example include whether it was observed, reported by a key informant in a discussion, collated through a checklist, etc. The information will be more meaningful to those interpreting it (especially with conflicting reports) if a source is indicated.

  The following list outlines some of the most common ways of collecting data in emergencies. As the team carries out an initial assessment, it will not normally have an opportunity to use all of these methods in a truly scientific manner. The knowledge of these methods may, however, help to apply a more objective approach and may also be useful in judging the reliability and validity of assessments carried out by others.

- Automatic, initial self-assessment and local assessment, e.g., staff of 'lifeline' system.
  This can involve pre-planned damage reporting by emergency management authorities or authorities involved in the emergency response.
- Visual inspection, semi-structured interviews and focus groups by specialists. Methods can include over flight and checklists. Do remember to interview women to get a gender balanced review of the situation to achieve rapid appraisal of area damage.
- The following actions are to be taken while conducting a rapid assessment in the field.
  * Meet with the local authority, state who you are.
  * Walk through area as much as you can
  * Visit markets, schools, community centres
  * Listen to people
  * Ask questions
  * Triangulate information with a different group of people.
- 'Sentinel' surveillance. This is a method widely used in emergency health monitoring,where professional staff establish a reporting system which detects early signs of particular problems at specific sites. The method can be applied to a variety of other problems where early warning is particularly important.

An assessment should not be seen as an end in itself, but rather as one part of a continuing process of re-assessing the needs and appropriateness of responses to the disaster situation. In general, monitoring, following an assessment, should be carried out by the government.

Principles for Assessment

The following must be assessed carefully :-

- Health
- Shelter and Personal Household Needs
- *Water and Sanitation*
  - Displaced population situation
  - Water system Disruption
  - Sanitation-Displaced Population Situation
  - Sanitation-Non-displaced Population situation
- *Food and Nutrition*
  - Baseline Data
  - Effect of the Event on Food
  - Food Availability
  - Social and Market Impact of Food Aid
  - Agriculture
  - Baseline Data
  - Effect of the Event on Agriculture
  - Agricultural Production Capabilities
  - Other
  - Nutrition
  - Affected Population Profile.
- Displaced Persons Camps, site selection, Planning and Shelter.
- Urban Search and Rescue (SAR)
- Communications
- Electric Power
- Water/Sewage
- Hydro Facilities (Hydroelectric, Irrigation)
- Roads and Bridges.

Conclusion

Prevention of disaster is a longest term strategy to eliminate occurrence of disaster. Preparedness covers short term measures and is designed to include actions necessary during the approach of possible disaster, during the emergency situations and ensuring period to relief and rehabilitation. Prevention is the combination of means discussed in reducing the loss, i.e., land zone planning, engineering control, prediction and warning system. Prevention is financially demanding and takes long time to implement.

Therefore, concurrently with preventive measures, there should be a action programme for dealing with disaster once they occur. It is basically a readiness to cope with disaster situations which cannot be avoided. This involves :

- Forecasting and warning.
- Operational plan of action along with organization to manage that action.
- Training of personnels in rescue and relief techniques.
- Earmarking of funds and stock pilling of supplies, shelters for evacuees.
- Promotion of public awareness.

11

Disaster Management Response Structures at International (UN), National, State and NGO's Level

Introduction

As the modern world witnesses an unprecedented progress in the fields of technology, correspondingly it has also witnessed an increase in the frequency and magnitude of natural disasters, suffering three times as many disasters in 1990s as in the 1960s. In the last decade, an annual average of 211 million people were killed, injured or displaced by natural disasters – seven times as many as those affected by bilateral conflicts.

Natural hazards themselves – earthquakes, volcanoes, hurricanes – do not necessarily lead to disasters. Rather, hazards become disasters when they impact the people and assets that are susceptible to their destructive effects. Factors such as inappropriate land use, poorly designed buildings and infrastructure and an increasingly degraded environment put populations at risk. And though these hazards happen in both developed and developing countries, they often impact developing countries more severely, and sometimes repeatedly, leaving large populations chronically vulnerable.

The immediate effects of such calamities are obvious, thousands are injured or killed. But the humanitarian toll reaches even further. Thousands of people can be driven from their homes, losing their possessions and even their self-respect. Water supplies may become contaminated. Food can become scarce, leading to malnutrition and disease. Some victims cross borders and become refugees; others seek refuge within their own country, joining the worlds thousands of internally displaced. Families become separated and communities are weakened. Related environmental and technological disasters, such as fire or oil spills, may cause permanent damage to ecosystems, water supplies and air quality.

Gentlemen, we need to understand that both complex emergencies and natural disasters have become more frequent, intense and costly. The response to these disasters however efficient can never be adequate. The needs of people in distress are immense and emotions even deeper. Therefore, the need to carry out immediate response at international, national, state and NGOs level. Today we shall have a look at these mechanisms at various levels and try to understand them in order to have a understanding of the holistic response structure at international level.

At the time of an emergency the response can be triggered in the following ways:-

- International response at UN and international organisations level.
- Country level response at national and state level.
- Bilateral donors response.
- NGOs.

Common Elements of Response

Before discussing these response structures and their functioning, let us have a look at some common elements of response which remain universal for all the mechanisms.

- **Immediacy :** In the event of a natural disaster, such as an earthquake, thousands of lives are put at immediate risk. Many can be lost within hours or days of the incident when search and rescue and other life-saving efforts are delayed.

- ***Duration*** : The relief stage that follows a natural disaster response may be over within a matter of days or weeks, notwithstanding the reconstruction efforts that may follow. Response mechanisms therefore need to be automated to allow rapid deployment and provision of staff and relief materials.
- ***Scope*** : Natural disasters may affect more than one country and are more and more likely to lead to large scale displacement. For example, when successive cyclones hit south-eastern Africa in February 2001, rivers and dams overflowed throughout the region, resulting in widespread flooding in Mozambique, Swaziland, Botswana, Malawi, Zimbabwe and South Africa, which affected more than two million people. However, conflicts more frequently extend beyond the borders of one state, affecting large areas or regions and leading to the sustained displacement of thousands of people. One must look no further than the former Federal Republic of Yugoslavia, the Great Lakes region of Africa or the West African sub-region for examples of such spill-over effects. Responding to such crises requires a higher level of regional coordination and interaction with a greater multiplicity of actors.

Response Structures at International Level

Gentlemen, having seen the basic elements of response and their importance let us have an over view of organisations for international response.

United Nations

In the recent past as an immediate response to any disaster the local governments of various nations have increasingly called upon the international community to perform an ever-widening range of relief activities like provision of water, sanitation and food assistance. Due to the complexity of these crises, a myriad of actors with different areas of expertise are needed to address the full range of needs. These include the various UN agencies, elements of the Red Cross system, donor governments, non-governmental organizations (NGOs) and religious and civil groups. In complex emergencies, peacekeepers, other military forces or political authorities with varying degrees of understanding of international humanitarian law may also be involved. In natural disasters, highly specialized international search and rescue teams will work alongside civil authorities or everyday citizens mobilized to help in rescue efforts. The involvement of so many actors can lead to overlapping activities and a duplication of efforts in areas of common concern, while some critical needs go unmet. Unfortunately, competition among agencies for scarce aid, dollars and differences in opinion over the best way to help a country in crisis, may delay the response, at the expense of lives and a more timely return of peace and normalcy.

It was in this context that the international community began calling for better coordination of relief efforts and cooperation among the various aid actors. These calls led to the passage in December 1991 of General Assembly Resolution 46/182, which aimed to strengthen the UN's response to both complex emergencies and natural disasters and to improve the overall effectiveness of the UN's humanitarian operations in the field.

Soon after, the Secretary-General assigned the Emergency Response Coordinator (ERC) the status of Under-Secretary-General (USG) and established the Department of Humanitarian Affairs (DHA) to provide the USG/ERC with institutional support. As part of the Secretary-General's reform programme in 1998, DHA was renamed Office of the Coordination of Humanitarian Affairs (OCHA) and charged with three core functions:-

- Coordination of Humanitarian Response
- Policy Development
- Humanitarian Advocacy.

Today, these functions are supported by 137 staff in five branches at Headquarters in New York and Geneva and by 151 international and 366 national staff in the field.

Mission Statement

The aim of the United Nations Office for the

Coordination of Humanitarian Affairs (OCHA), a department of the UN Secretariat, is to mobilize and coordinate effective and principled humanitarian action in partnership with national and international actors in order to:

- Alleviate human suffering in natural disasters and emergencies.
- Promote preparedness and prevention efforts to reduce future vulnerability.
- Facilitate sustainable solutions by addressing root causes.
- Advocate for the rights of people in need.

Roles and Responsibilities

The basic roles and responsibilities assigned are :-

- Humanitarian Coordination, policy development, advocacy and information management.
- Service and added value.
- Field orientation, support and surge capacity.

UN's Guiding Principles for Humanitarian Aid (General Assembly Resolution 46/182)

- Humanitarian assistance is of cardinal importance for the victims of natural disasters and other emergencies.
- Humanitarian assistance must be provided in accordance with the principles of humanity, neutrality and impartiality.
- The sovereignty, territorial integrity and national unity of State must be fully respected in accordance with the Charter of the United Nations. In this context, humanitarian assistance should be provided with the consent of the affected country and in principle on the basis of an appeal by the affected country.
- Each State has the responsibility first and foremost to take care of the victims of natural disasters and other emergencies occurring on its territory. Hence, the affected State has the primary role in the initiation, organization, coordination, and implementation of humanitarian assistance within its territory.

- The magnitude and duration of many emergencies may be beyond the response capacity of many affected countries. International cooperation to address emergency situations and to strengthen the response capacity of affected countries is thus of great importance. Such cooperation should be provided in accordance with international law and nations laws. Intergovernmental and non-governmental organization working impartially and with strictly humanitarian motives should continue to make a significant contribution in supplementing national efforts.
- States whose populations are in need of humanitarian assistance are called upon to facilitate the work of these organisation in implementing humanitarian assistance, in particular the supply of food, medicines, shelter and health care, for which access to victims is essential.
- States in proximity to emergencies are urged to participate closely with the affected countries in international efforts, with a view of facilitating, to the extent possible, the transit of humanitarian assistance.
- Special attention should be given to disaster prevention and preparedness by the Government concerned, as well as by the international community.
- There is a clear relationship between emergency, rehabilitation and development. In order to ensure a smooth transition from relief to rehabilitation and development, emergency assistance should be provided in ways that will be supportive of recovery and long-term development.
- Economic growth and sustainable development are essential for prevention of and preparedness against natural disasters and other emergencies. Many emergencies reflect the underlying crisis in development facing developing countries. Humanitarian assistance should therefore be accompanied by a renewal of commitment to

economic growth and sustainable development of developing countries. In this context, adequate resources must be made available to address their development problems.

- Contributions for humanitarian assistance should be provided in a way which is not to the detriment of resources made available for international cooperation for development.

UN Agencies and Programmes

A variety of UN agencies and programmes will execute a UN relief effort including the UN Development Programme (UNDP), UN High Commissioner on Refugees (UNHCR), UN Children's Emergency Fund (UNICEF), World Food Programme (WFP), Food and Agricultural Organization (FAO), World Health Organization (WHO) and the UN High Commissioner on Human Rights (UNHCHR). Representatives from these agencies are often present in the country prior to the emergency.

Gentlemen, we shall now discuss the mandate and role of each of the UN agencies in emergency response.

United Nations Development Programme (UNDP)

UNDP plays an important role in humanitarian emergencies in the context of its broader goal of promoting sustainable social and economic development, by eradicating poverty and empowering the world's poor.

UNDP is present before, during and after the outbreak of crises and facilitates the transition from relief to development by emphasizing capacity building and long-term recovery. UNDP also manages the UN's Resident Coordinator (RC) system, which provides the overall framework for the coordination of operational activities in a given country. The merger of the Resident Coordinator (RC) and Humanitarian Coordinator positions ensures a more unified and integrated UN approach, and the early integration of a more long-term, development oriented perspective.

In particular, UNDP's Emergency Response Division (ERD) helps country offices support the transition between the relief and recovery phases in the areas of conflict, security, recovery and disaster reduction. Within ERD,

UNDP has also established a network of transitional recovery teams to help strengthen country office capacities, support strategy and operational coordination, enhance advocacy and public information programmes and establish and implement resource mobilization strategies.

UNDP is a pivotal partner for OCHA in the area of disaster response preparedness. Because preparedness falls under both mandates, UNDP and OCHA support each other's work in this area as a joint venture.

UN High Commissioner for Refugees (UNHCR)

UNHCR, the United Nations refugee organization, is mandated to lead and coordinate international action for the worldwide protection of refugees, or people who have fled their country due to a well founded fear of persecution. UNHCR is also authorized to become involved in the protection of other groups, such as people who are stateless and whose nationality is under dispute and, in certain circumstances, Internally Displaced Peoples.

The role of UNHCR in emergency operations is primarily to protect refugees. UNHCR assists and complements the work of the government by acting as a channel for assistance from the international community, and by coordinating the implementation of assistance. Whatever the organizational manner in which UNHCR provides emergency assistance, UNHCR is responsible for ensuring that the protection and immediate material needs of the refugees are met.

United Nations Children's Emergency Fund (UNICEF)

UNICEF is mandated to advocate and work for the protection of children's rights, to help the young meet their basic needs and to expand their opportunities to reach full potential.

UNICEF integrates approaches to emergency interventions and policies throughout all its divisions, but focuses on coordination within the Office of Emergency Programmes (EMOPs). EMOPs is the focal point for emergency assistance, humanitarian policies, staff security and support to UNICEF offices in the field, as well as strategic coordination with external humanitarian partners both within and outside the United Nations system, including OCHA.

In addition, UNICEF operates a New York based emergency operations centre that provides 24 hour emergency communications used by UN agencies.

World Food Programme (WFP)

WFP provides food to sustain victims of emergencies and disasters, to improve the nutrition of the most vulnerable people, and to promote the self-reliance of poor people and communities.

WFP's dual relief and development mandate allows it to play a key role in the continuum from emergency relief to rehabilitation and development, where priority is given to disaster prevention, preparedness and mitigation, as well as post conflict rehabilitation activities.

In humanitarian emergencies WFP plays an important role in the coordination of food aid and logistics, through the collection and dissemination of information on global food aid deliveries and requirements.

World Health Organization (WHO)

The WHO is responsible for health. In collaboration with and for the use by its partners at the global level, WHO develops, consolidates, publishes and disseminates best practices, strategies and guiding principles for emergency health management.

With offices in more than 200 countries, WHO is often in place before an emergency arises and will stay after the crisis phase. This long-term presence means WHO is well placed to respond to the health aspects of emergencies where it routinely works to improve country capacities for disaster mitigation, preparedness and response to limit the negative impact of disaster on health and health systems.

During emergencies, WHO will take the lead in rapid health assessments and surveillance, epidemic preparedness and control of tuberculosis and HIV, water sanitation, drug management and medical supplies, reproductive health and mental health.

Food and Agriculture Organization (FAO)

FAO is mandated to raise levels of nutrition and standards of living, to improve agricultural productivity, and to better the condition of rural populations. In addition to its development programmes, FAO also plays a major role in dealing with food and agricultural emergencies. In relief operations, it focuses on the provision of agricultural inputs such as seeds, farming tools, and emergency veterinary services. This involves working closely with relevant NGOs and in some countries with UNICEF. Furthermore, the organization operates an early warning system for taming that assesses shortfalls in food production. It also conducts joint assessments with WFP in countries of concern to assess food security and food assistance needs.

United Nations High Commissioner for Human Rights (UNHCHR)

The United Nations High Commissioner for Human Rights is mandated by the General Assembly to promote and protect the enjoyment of civil, cultural, economic, political and social rights, as well as to coordinate the human rights promotion and protection activities throughout the United Nations system. The HCHR operates with the support of the Office of the High Commissioner for Human Rights (OHCHR).

Promoting the goals of the Secretary General's reform programme, which identifies human rights as a cross cutting issue, OHCHR plays an important role in all activities of the UN system (peace and security, economic and social development, humanitarian affairs and international law). OHCHR engages in active collaboration, both at field and headquarters level, with governments, all UN agencies and programmes as well as with non-governmental organizations. OHCHR also supports the work of the UN's human rights treaty bodies, the Commission on Human Rights and its special mechanisms.

UN COORDINATION AT A FIELD LEVEL

Resident Coordinator and the UN Country Team

In the initial stages of a complex emergency or natural disaster, the UN resident coordinator (RC) plays a critical role in coordinating the policies, programmes and actions in all countries with a UN presence. The RC will also often represent OCHA in the early warning and initial response phase of an emergency. The RC is also typically the resident representative for UNDP and is usually in place and familiar with the nature of the crisis when an emergency erupts.

In his or her coordinating role, the RC convenes regular meetings of the UN country team (UNCT), which is composed of the resident representatives of the various operating UN agencies on the ground. In a crisis, the RC may also organize broader coordination forum comprised of NGOs, the Red Cross movement, donors and international organizations and include sub-committees, which help coordinate humanitarian relief in a particular sector or region.

Humanitarian Coordinator (HC)

When faced with the threat of a full-blown crisis, the Under Secretary General/Emergency Response Coordinator, may identify the need to designate a humanitarian coordinator (HC), who becomes the most senior UN humanitarian official on the ground and is accountable to the Under Secretary General/Emergency Response Coordinator to facilitate and ensure quick, effective and well-coordinated assistance. The appointment of a Humanitarian Coordinator signals both the need for a full-time coordinator of the humanitarian response during the crisis and the need for a long-term humanitarian presence in country.

Stages of Response

As a coordinating body, free from the day-to-day operations challenges, OCHA focuses on the full spectrum of issues associated with humanitarian assistance, anticipating changes in fluid operational environments and setting the agenda for common international humanitarian actions well in advance of events.

Its response has been divided and planned at various stages described as under: -

- ***Pre-Crisis Preparedness*** **:** Working closely with the RC and the UN country team, OCHA begins observing and evaluating countries at risk for war and vulnerable to natural disasters well before crises occur.
- ***Monitoring and Preparedness*** **:** Desk officers continuously monitor weather conditions,

earthquake bulletins and the news services in their assigned regions for potential natural disasters, environmental and technological emergencies and signs of social unrest. Though UNDP is mandated to carry out disaster preparedness, OCHA collaborates closely with them on activities such as improving links with national authorities, implementing lessons learnt or organising seminars to discuss coordination mechanisms.

- As soon as OCHA receives a warning of a foreseeable natural disaster – such as a cyclone or tropical storm warning – the USG/ERC may decide to dispatch individual delegates or interagency assessment missions to evaluate the local and international disaster response capability.
- ***Emergency Response*** : When a full-blown crisis erupts, the need for assistance frequently exceeds the ability of local governments to provide it. As the international community responds to the disaster, and more actors become involved, the need for coordination of the response becomes apparent.
- Governments affected by natural or environmental disasters may seek UN's help through its emergency hotline, through the RC or by contacting OCHA at headquarters. In complex emergencies, it is USG/ ERC, the RC and affected government, who assess the coordination needs and alert the international community.
- ***Determining a Response*** : In Geneva and New York, an on-call duty term provides emergency response coverage of new and ongoing emergencies 24 hours a day, seven days a week.
- ***On-Site Coordination*** : Once coordination structures are activated and in place, the R/HC, on behalf of OCHA, begins coordinating humanitarian response on the ground using a combination of rapid-response tools information services and consultative fora.
- In the immediate aftermath of a sudden-onset disaster, the USG/ERC, in consultation with the RC,

may field a rapid response team to support on-site coordination among donors. Known as United Nations Disaster and Coordination (UNDAC), these teams work under the R/HC's authority to reinforce the UNCT/DMT and, when requested by the affected government. UNDAC teams typically remain deployed for two to three weeks.

- ***Rapid-Response Tools*** **:** There are certain tools at OCHA's disposal for coordinating emergency response, primarily during natural disasters and environmental emergencies. These tools are managed by the Field Coordination Support Section (FCSS) in OCHA's Geneva-based Emergency Services Branch (ESB). These are :-
  - International Search and Rescue Advisory Group (INSARAG).
  - United Nations Coordination and Assistance (UNDAC).
  - Environmental Stand-by-Experts (ESBE).
  - UN Humanitarian Response Depot (UNHRD).

Gentlemen, in a nutshell, to conclude we can assume that UN system with large number of agencies working under it is an extremely complex and decentralized system. The web of mandates and capacities must be understood in order to be effective. Furthermore, it should never be forgotten that the United Nations is subordinate to the sovereign host and most relief efforts are local.

RESPONSE STRUCTURE AT NATIONAL LEVEL

> "Lives are lost, families ruined and property is destroyed. The only survivors are those who govern - politicians, bureaucrats and their retinue. They go about their business of harassing citizens and feathering their nests. Nothing happens to them...no one is ever brought to book. By implication, no one is held accountable for public safety. Thus, the very minimum requirement of governance is waived. Never mind disaster management, the government itself is the disaster."

The above comment from a journalist which is based on the government apathy seen during the destructive cyclone that hit the Gujarat Coast in 1998, is true for the system of disaster management prevalent in the country today because similar state of affairs was witnessed during the Super Cyclone in Orissa in 1999 and the Killer earthquake in Gujarat in 2001. On paper, India has a well defined disaster management policy under which the states have responsibility for managing all disasters. The Central Government only supplements the efforts of the state governments by providing financial and material assistance in the event of disasters that spread over several states and union territories or are otherwise of a grave nature. However, it does not generally translate to smooth action on ground during serious disasters due to a variety of reasons. We shall have a look at the existing system of disaster management in our country and would analyse the weaknesses and shortcomings in the system.

National Policy for Disaster Management

As per the existing national policy, the primary responsibility for providing relief and rescue effort in case of natural disasters is that of State Governments. The Centre's role has been restricted to one of providing resources to the States for this purpose acting in a supportive manner in relation to those economic activities and infrastructure mobilization, for which the constitutional responsibility rests with the Government of India.

Even though the State Government is primarily responsible for relief activities, the Central Government associates itself with measures aimed at alleviating the suffering of the people on account of these calamities. To this end, the Central Government provide its resources including the Armed Forces and financial support in case of major calamities depending upon their gravity, scale and the requirement of additional resources by the State Governments.

The four major components of Disaster Management planning at national level are :-

- Application of scientific inputs for forecasting and relief programmes,

- Timeliness and dynamism in management of relief operations.
- People's participation in relief delivery and monitoring.
- Contribution to resilience of societies and improvement in the quality of life.

National Approach to Disaster Management : At various levels, our approach to Disaster Management should be four dimensional as under :-

'All in One' : It is desirable to establish a single set of arrangements capable of encompassing all hazards.

Comprehensive : Four elements of emergency/disaster management, namely : prevention/mitigation, preparedness, response and recovery are crucial to success of the mission.

Integrated : Active participation amongst Central Government, State Government, local bodies, industries, voluntary organizations and communities will be required.

Prepared Community : Since disasters/emergencies usually affect communities, the vital links in dealing with such situations are the individuals, voluntary organizations and local bodies.

National Policy for External Assistance

The basic tenets of national policy for external assistance being followed at national level are :-

- No formal appeal for external assistance to be made for relief.
- External assistance, if offered as solidarity accepted with gratitude.
- Bi-lateral agreements suggested by some countries for emergency response may be considered.

Imperatives of a Dedicated Organization : In the absence of a dedicated organization, Disaster Management tends to be adhoc and leads to 'crisis management'. While the basic responsibility for undertaking Disaster Management rests with the State Government./UTs concerned, Central Government. has a supportive role, particularly in the pre-disaster stage and also in the post-disaster stage of a major disaster, which may be clearly beyond the means of the State/UT. In the post-disaster scenario, therefore, first priority is extending immediate rescue and relief aid to hapless victims, who need shelter, food, medical help and care. Only synergy of effort at all levels including non governmental agencies under a proper organisation and timely response can provide succor to victims. Hence the need to restructure/create a dedicated organisation at various levels. Second phase involves rehabilitation, relocation and redevelopment, which is best handlèd by the various State Government. Departments. with necessary support from the financial institutions, industry, NGOs and the Central Government.

The Response System at National Level

The National Disaster Management Division in the Ministry of Home Affairs of Government of India at New Delhi and the National Centre for Disaster Management in the Indian Institute of Public Administration at New Delhi are the nodal agencies for disaster management in India. The following ministries with the Government of India have been nominated as the nodal ministries for disaster management for various types of disasters :

Sl.	*Type of Disaster*	*Ministry*
1.	Natural Disasters	Home Affairs
2.	Air Accidents	Civil Aviation
3.	Civil Strife	Home Affairs
4.	Rail Accidents	Railways
5.	Chemical	Environment and Forests
6.	Biological	Health
7.	Nuclear Accidents	Dept. of Atomic Energy

The extent of national response depends on the gravity of disaster, the scale of relief operations required and the need of central assistance to augment the financial resources of the state. The policy response is provided by the Prime Minister, Cabinet Relief Commissioner in the DAC, functions as the nodal officer to coordinate all works in respect of disasters. He is supported by an Additional

Relief Commissioner and the Natural Disaster Management Division and by appropriate core staff for Disaster Management from concerned departments/ ministries in the cases of 'man-made' disasters. A control room functions under his charge to maintain the flow of information and coordinate with agencies and state governments during an emergency situation.

Organisation

In order to keep a disaster situation or an anticipated disaster situation under regular review, the Central Government has evolved a hierarchy of high-powered committees. Salient aspects of inter agency interaction have been explained as under :-

- ***Cabinet Committee (CC)*** : Usually chaired by the Prime Minister, this committee is activated during major disasters, whether they actually take place or are anticipated.
- ***National Crisis Management Committee (NCMC)***: Under the Chairmanship of the Cabinet Secretary, this committee has apex level representation of all concerned departments of Government of India. An empowered committee exercising all the powers of Government of India, it meets as frequently as required and at least once a day during the crisis period taking prompt decisions then and there for immediate action.
- ***Central Relief Commission (CRC)*** : The Central Relief Commissioner, who also chairs the Crisis Management Group, heads the commission. The task of the commission is to take account of the disaster situation during actual disaster or in anticipation of the same and to constantly review and coordinate all relief operations accordingly. A control room is established under his charge with appropriate staff to procure real time situation reports from the site of disaster. The Commissioner is assisted by an Additional Relief Commissioner and Natural Disaster Management Division along with the core staff for disaster management from concerned departments/ministries.

- ***Crisis Management Group (CMG)*** **:** Chaired by the Central Relief Commissioner, this group comprises senior operational officers of the concerned departments. During a disaster situation, this group meets daily and takes operational and coordinating decisions keeping in view the directions received from the NCMC. The CMG maintains close liaison with the concerned State Governments and obtain real time ground situation struck by the disaster. The Control Room acts as the information inflow/outflow hub for the CMG. The Group meets at regular intervals even during non-crisis periods to review the state of preparedness.

Organisation for Disaster Response at National Level

The Government of India's Contingency Action plan for natural calamities defines various organizational structures at national, state and local level which would handle disaster related matters in their respective jurisdictions, and lays down policy guidelines to be followed by them. The organization of the Scarcity Relief Division within the Central Relief Commissioner's (CRC) office is set up in the Department of Home Affairs. Salient aspects of this structural set up for administrative response are as under:-

- The CRC would receive information relating to warning of an impending disaster from the director, Indian Meteorological Department (IMD) or from the Central Water Commission (CWC). He would send the information up the chain of command to keep everyone informed viz, the Secretary, the Home Minister, the Cabinet Secretary, Secretary to the Prime Minister as well as to other government ministries and departments including the National Crisis Management Committee (NCMC). He would also disseminate the information to the affected State governments for appropriate action.
- The CRC also sets up an Emergency Operation Centre (Control Room) on receipt of first information about the impending occurrence of a calamity which is supposed to function round the clock for collecting and transmitting information, keeping in touch with

the state governments concerned and interacting with other central ministries and departments to coordinate the relief measures.

ORGANIZATION AND FUNCTIONING OF SCARCITY RELIEF DIVISION

Set Up at State Level

The State Governments are autonomous in organising relief operations in the event of a disaster as well as for undertaking long-term measures for preparedness and rehabilitation. The State Governments also have a similar hierarchical organization.

State Cabinet Committee : Chaired by the Chief Minister, this committee is activated when a major disaster in the State has actually occurred or is anticipated.

State Relief Commission : Every state has a Relief Commissioner who is the nodal officer to deal with disaster situations. The states which do not have a Relief Commissioner, the Chief Secretary or an officer assigned by him is given the overall charge of relief operations. The Relief Commissioner also chairs the State Crisis Management Group (SCMG). The task of the commission is to take account of the disaster situation during actual disaster or in anticipation of the same and accordingly constantly review and coordinate all relief operations. The Relief Commissioner is assisted by an appropriate staff as per disaster threats anticipated.

State Crisis Management Group (SCMG) : The SCMG is formed under the chairmanship of the State Relief Commissioner. The group has structured membership on 'as required' basis from Ministries of Commerce, Agriculture, Irrigation, Revenue, Home, Health, Finance, Transport, Industries, Public Works, Urban Development and Housing, Food and Civil Supplies, Water Supply, Forest, Labour and Publicity etc. depending on the nodal agencies involved. It also gets assistance from GOI, Defence Services, DOT/MTNL, Civil Aviation, Railways and Atomic Energy. Its task is to review and coordinate relief operations in the state, for disaster situations. While it meets at least once everyday during periods of crisis, it should meet on a regular basis even when there is no crisis, in order to update plans and review preparedness for disaster situations.

State Emergency Operations Centre or State Crisis Management Control Room **:** This is an operational centre/ control room established by the State Relief Commission, which receives real time information from all agencies related to management of disaster. It functions round the clock under the control of the Relief Commissioner. A close liaison is maintained by the SCMG, through its functionaries and the control room with the central government and divisional and district level. This hub centre also coordinates aid received by the state from Central Government, Defence Forces, friendly foreign countries, NGOs, *Sansthas,* community leaders or from other states. The aid received, or about to be received is taken stock of here, pre-directed to user destinations or collected and then distributed and directed to move to districts on 'as required' basis.

Set Up at District Level

General : At the district level, a 'Coordination and Review Committee' (CRC) is headed by the District Collector/ District Magistrate. This organization becomes the focal point for drawing up district action plans for management of any disaster situation. The State Government routes its instructions through the District Magistrate/Collector who in turn ensures that the total efforts of the district are geared in a coordinated manner to the provision of relief to the people. Sometimes, in emergency situations, 'the powers of the district magistrate are enhanced so as to ensure complete unison in the efforts of the concerned departments.' Each district is further divided into sub-divisions and tehsils. The Sub-Divisional Officer and the Tehsildar form part of the District Magistrate's team to provide succour in the event of a disaster.

Important measures undertaken at the district level for managing disasters are as under :-

- ***Contingency Plans*** **:** The District Magistrate is to develop a district level plan for the State Government's approval. The plan assigns measures to be undertaken by the different departments and their functionaries as well as the areas of coordination between departments and agencies.

- ***District Relief Committee*** **:** The relief measures are reviewed by the District Relief Committee which consists of official and non-official members including representatives of local bodies, people and the concerned members of legislative assembly and/or parliament.
- ***District Control Room*** **:** A district control room is set up in the District HQ as soon as a disaster occurs. It monitors the rescue and relief efforts on a continuing basis.
- ***Coordination*** **:** The District Magistrate also coordinates with the Central government authorities and the defence forces, if required and involved. He also synchronizes the voluntary efforts of NGOs with those of the district administration. Communication is maintained through police wireless network in the event of a break down of the normal means of communications such as the telecom and telegraph network.

Non-Governmental Organisations (NGOs)

A Non-Governmental Organisation (NGO) is an organisation that works in any capacity with relief assistance. The NGOs can be divided into two main categories, namely the international NGOs (working in the international field, even though they may not be an international organisation in the true sense of the name) and the local NGO (working within its own country).

NGOs are in principal autonomous and are independent of Government (hence the name) and are financed by private individuals or groups. Financing, however, has changed in recent years. The modern tendency for NGO funding goes towards receiving more and more funding from governments (usually their own governments) or inter government organizations (IGOs), e.g., the European Union. Whether or not this affects the authority, greatly depends on the individual NGO and the possible strings attached to the funding.

International NGOs are private, non-profit organizations

that operate in more than one country. Most are headquartered in western countries, although an increasing number are based in developing countries. Some NGOs only provide humanitarian relief (e.g., Medicines Sans Frontiers), while others manage development oriented programmes, but will become involved in humanitarian relief operations when a crisis occurs (e.g., Care International, Oxfam, Save the Children Fund). The humanitarian relief component of major international NGOs is in part funded by private sources, and donor governments may use them to channel large amounts of humanitarian assistance.

Some international NGOs also receive funding through UN agencies as implementing partners of the UN agency in question. NGOs' participation in the UN inter agency CAP is crucial because it allows collaborative programming within the broad humanitarian community.

Local NGOs operate only in their country of origin, and may have a wide range of programmes, often with a development perspective. These organizations may act as implementing partners with international NGOs, and may be funded and supported by them. OCHA often plays a key role in collaborating with non UN partners in an emergency by coaching and mentoring national NGOs.

NGOs work in all areas of the humanitarian field and provide the greatest international capacity to implement relief on the ground. Therefore, it is important to inter-relate with them as there is valuable information and help to be found. It is usually the case that one or more NGOs are actually physically in the area of an emergency before, during and after the impact, and will therefore have hands-on information and experience of the issues. NGO's also tend to specialize in one or two fields, or to direct their efforts towards one needy population group. They usually offer skilled staff, rapid deployment capacity (if they are not already in the area), operational flexibility, and resources that might not otherwise be available in the emergency. NGOs may organize themselves into NGO coordination bodies to streamline the activities. NGO umbrella organizations such as the International Council of Voluntary

Agencies (ICVA), an association of European NGOs, and Inter Action, a group of North American NGOs lead these efforts. OCHA integrates the activities of these coordinating bodies into its own coordination effort. The NGO community is becoming increasingly important in the humanitarian world. The period from around 1980 till the beginning of the 90s has rightly been called the decade of the NGOs. In the years after World War II, the number of international NGOs began to soar (from 832 in 1951 to 9398 in 1981). These NGOs include all aspects of relief work. In the 80s the number of international NGOs have nearly doubled to 16208 in 1990. Of these about 500 are involved directly with humanitarian work.

Inter Governmental Organizations (IOs)

Inter-governmental organizations exist outside the UN system and have executive boards composed of national governments. One such IO is the International Organization to Migration (IOM), which arranges resettlement and repatriation for refugees and assists with resettlement and repatriation of migrants.

Another humanitarian IO is the European Community Humanitarian Office (ECHO) that administers humanitarian aid victims of both man-made and natural emergencies on behalf of the European Union (the biggest donor of humanitarian aid in the world) to non- European Union countries. In carrying out this task, ECHO works in collaboration with more than 170 organizations worldwide including OCHA.

The Red Cross and Red Crescent Movements

The International Committee of the Red Cross (ICRC), based in Switzerland, is the founding institution of the International Red Cross and Red Crescent movements, which include the National Red Cross and Red Crescent Societies (National Societies), and the International Federation of Red Cross and Red Crescent Societies (IFRC). All three branches have distinct tasks.

International Committee for the Red Cross (ICRC)

Based in Geneva, ICRC's mandate is to operate in areas of armed conflict and internal disturbance. Focusing on protection work, ICRC also assists in complex emergencies, especially inside conflict zones and on both sides.

National Red Cross and Red Crescent Societies

The national societies of the Red Cross operate in more than 160 countries around the world (using the Red Crescent symbol in Islamic countries). Acting as auxiliaries to the public authorities in their own countries, they provide a range of services from disaster relief, health and social assistance to first aid courses. During wartime, national societies may support the army medical services.

International Federation of Red Cross and Red Crescent Societies (IFRC)

IFRC supports the actions of the various national societies. It assists with coordination of international assistance to victims of natural disasters, and to victims of man-made disasters outside of conflict areas.

Disaster Assistance Response Team (DART)

The US Agency for international Development's (USAID) Office of Foreign Disaster Assistance (OFDA) has developed a response capability called the Disaster Assistance Response Team (DART) as a method of providing rapid response assistance to international disasters, as mandated by the Foreign Assistance Act. A DART provides an operational presence on the ground capable of carrying out sustained response activities. A DART includes specialists trained in a variety of disaster relief skills who assist US Embassies and USAID Missions with the management of the United States Government (USG) response to disasters. The activities of a DART vary depending on the type, size, and complexity of disasters to which the DART is deployed.

Civil Society

During humanitarian emergencies, domestic civil society represents one of the most critical sources of humanitarian assistance and civil protection. In this context, civil society refers not only to local non governmental organizations and human rights groups, but also to religious congregations, charities, universities, trade unions, legal associations, independent activists and human rights defenders, families, clans and others.

In the initial stages of an emergency it is the local population and government that cope and provide the first wave of assistance. Only after they have exhausted their own resources, does substantial international response begin. An ongoing dialogue with the affected population is crucial for a number of reasons.

- To help with forward planning and early warning of major changes in future humanitarian needs, such as new flows of displaced persons. The affected population is usually the most well-informed and astute about the impact of military and political factors.
- To best plan and implement ongoing assistance. The affected population is well-placed to identify needs and effective mechanisms for distributing and utilizing the aid provided. Local emergency personnel who cope with crises in the early stages are often absorbed by the UN and NGOs as national staff.
- To ensure that the affected population maintains a sense of empowerment and control, and to avoid forcing them into a state of dependency. A process of information sharing from the grass roots level up is therefore important.

Donor Governments

In a natural disaster, donor response, whether financial or in-kind, is largely bilateral between the affected country and the donor government. Donor response in complex emergencies often involves a host of agencies.

Many donor governments to international relief efforts have embassy representation in-country. When they do not have an embassy, donors usually maintain a regional presence. Most of the larger donors have specialists within their embassies that focus on relief efforts.

In some emergencies, donors may form a coordination body on their own behalf. These bodies are usually created at the height of an emergency when donors they need to collaborate to get quick access to reliable information and may be sustained through the rehabilitation and reconstruction phase.

Shortcomings of the Existing System

- The existing system of managing disasters in India is just about functional but not in keeping with the global trends of using modern management techniques so as to optimize the efficiency of the machinery called upon to respond to disasters. The basic flaws in the present system are two outdated beliefs viz., people holding routine administrative posts can handle any emergency without sacrificing the basic functional requirements of their jobs and that generalists are as competent in command and control functions as specialists. According to an impartial analysis, 'the government of India has the requisite structure to cope with disasters....(but it) lacks the formal and official framework for strategic guidance and doctrinal development.' Thus, the country's disaster response strategy still appears to be reactive with emphasis on rescue and relief rather than on prevention and mitigation, the overall approach being tactical rather than strategic. Following specific shortcomings have been observed by the study conducted by the US Government on India's Disaster Response System:-
  - (i) Lackadaisical approach of authorities to tackling a disaster.
  - (ii) Delayed response by the government officers.
  - (iii) Absence of effective early warning systems.
  - (iv) Lack of adequate resources to undertake measures like mass evacuation.
  - (v) Inadequate coordination amongst various departments and agencies.
  - (vi) Non-existence of and non-familiarisation with Standard Operating Procedures for disaster relief procedures.
  - (vii) Failure to keep essential stores like boats, OBMs, *ballies* and sand bags, medicines in readily available stocks in the vicinity of disaster prone areas.
  - (v) Inadequate coordination by the civil authorities with the armed forces.
- In addition to the above shortcomings, following

weaknesses also need to be taken note of:-

- Absence of dedicated organization to handle disasters and affiliated issues.
- Undue and uncalled for reliance on the armed forces for coping with disasters. The armed forces have specific role and their over employment in disasters is likely to distract them from their primary task. Besides, it deprives other governmental agencies of a chance to develop efficient mechanisms for coping with the after math of disasters and learning from them. There is a need to create dedicated and specially trained manpower for coping with disasters.
- Lack of proper training for the people involved in managing disasters is another major weakness in the existing system of managing disasters in the country. *Time* magazine described relief work after the recent earthquake in Gujarat without meticulous planning, coordination and training as the 'second disaster'.
- Inadequate documentation of disasters so as to derive lessons for disaster responders in the future is yet another major shortcoming in the existing disaster management system in the country. There is no institutional framework to do this task in a methodical and objective manner.

(v) Absence of legal framework for dealing with disaster prevention and mitigation is another grey area which hampers efficient management of disasters.

Key Issues : The study also suggested that answers to key questions given in following paragraphs are yet to be found:-

- ***What has the strategic direction or doctrinal guidance provided disaster planners and managers?*** The country lacks a formal framework for strategic guidance and doctrinal development. Although, the confluence of efforts by the Indira Gandhi National Open University, the National Centre for Disaster Management and the Disaster Management Institute, Bhopal has developed a professional body of knowledge relevant to India's environment, more needs to be done at university, college and school levels to make an average citizen more aware of hazards and disasters and how to cope with them. The following doctrinal imperatives are a must for a more effective disaster management regime to come up in India:-

(i) A strong focus on disaster prevention and mitigation.

(ii) Long-term measures to fight earthquakes.

(iii) Control of economic development to reduce the impact on land and resulting changes to the flow of water run-off.

(iv) Set aside funding by states for disaster emergencies, augmented by central government grants.

(v) Need for networking amongst disaster management organizations, government agencies, NGOs and other voluntary organizations.

(vi) Emphasis on training and publication of literature.

(vii) Emphasis on human dimensions of disasters, particularly the social, medical and psychological aspects of long-term recovery.

- ***What is India's strategic plan and organization for disaster management?*** Except for an old regulation which dates back to colonial times, the Government of India does not have a national emergency plan for disaster management. The National Centre for Disaster Management is now working on a National Disaster Management Plan.
- ***Who is responsible for providing disaster assistance in India and who does the work?*** Under the constitution, responsibility for disaster management rests with the state governments but few state governments have up-to-date and efficacious disaster management plans that are backed up by in-place services and supplies. At the district and lower levels, the first responders are the staff of the District Magistrate, *Tehsildar* and

the superintendent of Police or the local police station who are neither trained nor equipped to handle various kinds of emergencies.

- ***What are the roles of NGOs in the national disaster response?*** Experience has shown that NGOs have been very effective in providing disaster assistance to the affected community as they have effective networks throughout the country. Other local volunteer organizations have the advantage of having intimate knowledge of the people, terrain and the situation so as to apply the required services efficiently where they are needed most. However, there is a lack of institutional framework for ensuring their integration and better coordination with the government agencies.
- ***How should international organizations and donor nations provide assistance?*** India prefers not to request disaster assistance from donor nations or international organizations due to its stated policy that the country will rely on its own resources to resolve disaster situations.
- ***Is there a common theme in India's disaster management planning and training?*** While professional disaster responders are emphasizing the need for an efficient mechanism for quick and effective rescue and relief operations, the academia is concentrating on prevention and mitigation measures which are generally theoretical in nature. Is there an agency which is to synergize these efforts towards a common goal and how?
- ***How is the country to leverage new conceptual and technological advancements in disaster management field?*** There is a need to encourage a free and active participation by the country's disaster management professionals including the members of the armed forces in international disaster management fora so as to derive maximum benefits from the ongoing conceptual, scientific and technological developments in the international community.

12

Relief Operations to Include Urban Search and Rescue

Introduction

Response to a disaster is the overall effect of planning and coordination at all levels within the nation. So far you have all seen the processes involved right upto the assessment of the disaster. You are also aware of the various organisations functional to mitigate the effects of any disaster. In the next 45 mins, I shall try and acquaint you with relief operations and urban search and rescue.

Speed of response to any disaster speaks of a highly oiled machinery at various levels. Speed of response is also directly proportional to awareness of the general public, effectiveness of the trigger mechanisms, a well-coordinated action plan at various levels and availability of resources. The local bodies are generally the first groups to react to any disaster, as they are present in the immediate vicinity. Immediate action can be helpful in saving a lot of lives. Having been personally associated with earthquake relief operations in Ahmedabad, I can vouch for the fact that 60–70 per cent of lives saved after the earthquake, was by the locals, within the first 10-12 hrs. I am sure others would have had similar experiences.

Relief operations are the mainstay of mitigating the effects of a disaster on the populace. Actions taken at various stages need to be coordinating between different groups to ensure a correct quantum of effort at the correct places.

Response Sequence

On a disaster striking, the response of the various agencies seen till now will be sequential at the site depending on the warning received, speed of moving of parties and distance of the teams. The agencies will buildup on each other and the sequence could be: -

- Local population present around the site or survivors who are not injured.
- Local/District administrative persons and local NGOs.
- State level response.
- National level agencies and NGOs. Their reaction would be governed mainly by their distance from the site.
- International response.

The army normally fits at the second stage of response to the disaster. The sequence given is not sacrosanct in any respect and there may be overlaps. Despite the coordination at the preparation stage, due to the number of different organisations taking part in relief operations, there is again a necessity to coordinate the efforts to ensure that there is no wastage of person and equipment.

PHASES OF DISASTER MANAGEMENT

For effective management of a disaster, there is a need to understand, prepare and phase the activities. The various phases into which these activities can be divided are as in subsequent paras.

Preparedness Phase

A response begins well before the mission, deployment with sound team organization ensures preparedness of personnel, equipment stock, and mobilization and operating procedures. Each state must have a single designated Focal Point, staffed 24 hours a day. This entity will be the official (and team) contact point for a state requesting team activation or to forward disaster related communications. All notifications, communications, or other interaction with teams must go through this focal point. The Focal Point is also responsible for any other administrative or reporting requirements.

Team management prior to any deployment must address a variety of administrative and personnel issues. Records of personnel data must be developed. The team should establish a programme to develop and conduct routine training and exercises to ensure the operational effectiveness of the team. Training should also be developed and conducted as needed to maintain team member qualifications, including :

- Basic knowledge of operations.
- Code of Ethics.
- Safety and security.
- Hazardous materials awareness.
- Cultural awareness.
- Extended incident stress management.
- Survival.
- Physical conditioning.
- Basic first aid.

Each team should have a written mobilization plan that addresses the necessary actions to activate and deploy the team. This plan should include team and country/ sponsoring agency notifications procedures; team member assembly point location and procedures; equipment packaging and loading plan; and a transportation plan to the POD or for ground travel directly to the Point of Arrival (POA) in the affected state. All aspects of team mob must be well documented in its plans and ex regularly to accomplish such a large undertaking. All personnel should have required personal items ready for deployment as well as essential equipment, tools, and supplies that support the team in the field. Load plans should be prepare well in advance for the moving of certain material on aircraft, with weights and cubic size already calculated. Additionally, load plans for ground transport should be in place that indicates similar placement of equipment on over-the-road trucks.

All agencies need to be well-coordinated to ensure results in the face of a disaster. All the bodies from the DC level upwards need to coordinate amongst themselves to ensure a smooth induct, requisite effort at the correct places and a clean pull out afterwards. These coordination meetings need to be held in the preparation phase, when all the agencies are free to discuss and there is time to plan and acquire resources. Certain essentials of good coordination to ensure an immediate response are enumerated in the succeeding paras.

Keep the Ball Rolling : Momentum in coordination is essential to maintain interest and commitment. One way to do this is to ensure rapid reporting of new and updated information. Decisions made in the coordination process must be documented in the form of minutes or aide memoirs and distributed. Even more important is to ensure follow-up and follow-through on decisions. Failure to implement conclusions will cause cynicism about the process to develop and ultimately destroy the Centre's credibility. Part of keeping momentum is keeping people in touch with one another and keeping channels of communication open. This may involve going out of your way to make the right connections.

Respect People's Time and Schedules : Don't let the coordination meetings get to be just another meeting. Ensure that the meetings need to occur and that there is vital and important work to be done. Don't be afraid to cancel a standing meeting if the agenda is not compelling enough. Publish an agenda for the meeting and stick to the schedule. Try to begin and end meetings on time. Practice good meeting facilitation skills, ensuring that everyone has a chance to say what's on their mind and that a small group or individual does not dominate the conversation.

Attack small Problems before they Grow : A small problem, be it a misunderstanding, a hurt feeling, or a perception of insensitivity can grow and fester resulting in a loss of faith and thus hamper the process of planning. This will have a bearing on the final outcome of the meeting and on the further operations being planned.

Clarify Co-ordination Parameters and Activities : Taking a little bit of the mystery out of coordination will go a long way in ensuring that it happens. Confusion would be present if organizations feel that it will be a waste of time in endless meetings or that the coordination effort will result in a veto of their plans and activities. The best way to clarify the coordination parameters is to have frank and open discussions on the goals expected to be reached through coordination efforts and the needs of the various organizations for coordination.

Secure Commitment of Staff and Other Resources for Co-ordination : Once the co-ordination parameters have been determined, a commitment of resources for coordination must be forthcoming. This may take the form of staff or equipment, but also publicly stated intentions to attend meetings and share information, and, if possible, a stated intention to adapt organizational activities to issues raised in the coordination process.

Write it Down : Some of the results of the coordination process, both from large groups and bilateral discussions, will be concrete enough to be developed into a formal document. Such items might include a preparedness plan or plan of operations. A signed document can serve as a point of reference for resolving or heading-off disputes as well as a useful mechanism for securing continuity when staff rotates over. Certainly all such agreements will require updating and, even in the best of cases, represent an intention to act or an agreement, in principle, subject to change as situations change.

Involve the Right People and Organizations in Appropriate Roles : All the members of the groups capable of a sizeable effort must be involved. Also major NGOs and NGOs with significant donor ties are important members. However, not everyone should be or needs to be involved in the coordination process. Smaller organizations with limited operations and resources may be left out as per the requirements of the groups assembling.

Train Others to Take Over Functions : It is an old cliché, but try to work yourself out of a job. If a Centre is going to need to function for a long time period, it will be best if as many functions as possible can be handled either by the other agencies or by local staff of the Centre. If someone else can and is willing to do your job, given them the chance. In almost every situation there is more to be done than can be done. Giving jobs to others can only help in freeing you up to take on another task.

Thank People and Acknowledge Their Contribution : Rewarding participation is an important technique in building commitment to the coordination process. When organizations have done good work; changed their programme or otherwise gone out of their way to put other's needs ahead of their own, they need to be thanked and acknowledged publicly. Few things will inspire more participation in coordination than the feeling of being a valued contributor.

Have a Party : It's a good idea to have a social gathering periodically. Non-work related gatherings sponsored by the Centre will promote the Centre as a place to "let down your hair". Much useful information will be shared at a social gathering and relationships will be made and strengthened. In general, it should be a common practice to celebrate successes and mourn failures.

Activation Phase

Requests for assistance go through several stages before reaching teams. When a disaster occurs, the first response will be from local officials and supporting services of the affected state. If additional assistance is required outside the local level, requests should be filled by the state government until the affected country's resources are exhausted or the requested level of assistance is not available. The affected country may then request international assistance.

For a developing country, like ours, it is but obvious that there is a need to collect resources, which are otherwise not kept collected due to an overall paucity. The groups have to be afforded a certain amount of time for collection of the resource. The need for a speedy dissemination of information assumes a greater importance in our context.

It is crucial that information pertinent to the disaster response is provided to the responding teams in the Advisory, Alert and Activation Notice. When a team is deployed to the affected area, often, limited information is known in the early phase of the mission. Team management must advise deploying personnel of weather and environmental condition so that appropriate clothing and equipment is packed. Equipment stock items may vary based on the type of disaster and the mission of the team. Team management will need to ensure that administrative requirements are identified. The security status of the effected state must be assessed and pertinent security issues that could affect a team's response are made in the action plan.

Team Deployment

- It is imperative that the determination of the team's assigned area be made as quickly as possible. These decisions will be made by the appropriate local authority.
- While it is most desirable to move the team directly to their assigned locality/work site, it may in some cases, be necessary to first route the teams through a Staging Area.
- ***Staging Areas***. A team may be required to move through a staging area enroute to its assigned area due to a change in the mode of transportation or for other logistical reasons.
- An advance or reconnaissance team may be sent ahead of the full team to liaison with the local auth. Upon arrival, they can ascertain the name and location of the contact person, possible sites, and current information on the situation. They should also identify resources needed at the assigned work site so the team can immediately integrate into the local rescue operation.

Operation Phase

Team management should attend initial briefing, provided by local authority, to discuss the current situation. Included in this briefing will be :-

- Existing chain of command.
- Formal lines of authority.
- Lines of communication.
- Strategic plans.

- Establish who the team's on-site contact is (local official in charge).
- Communications plan.
- Schedule of operational briefings.
- Local available support for the team.
- Available transportation.
- Safe shelter for the team.
- Interpreters (if necessary).
- Location and assignment of other teams.
- Food and water.
- Safety and security.
- Availability of cranes and other heavy equipment.

The specific team assignment should be discussed with representatives and include:

- Team assignment.
- Specific objectives of the assignment.
- General population demographics.
- Native language.
- Methods of communicating with the local population.
- Types of occupancies (schools, factories or residences).
- Anticipated number of victims.
- Maps of the area, site information, building plans, and utility information.
- Local medical policies and procedures, assessments, and patient hand-off information.

Coordination, at the site and at a central level when move than one sites are involved, is of immense importance to ensure that requisite effort is emp at the sites and duplication is avoided. For coordination, the local authority will setup a central control room, preferable at an easily accessible locality. 'Officials of the state/district/ municipality, controlling the overall efforts should staff the control room. Sub control rooms for areas also need to be establish. These control rooms at various levels should have the latest int reports of the disaster. Overall allotment of effort will be coordination by the central control room. The effort allotted to an area will be further control by the sub control rooms. Reports with specialised training will be detailed with each group/site so as to decide on method of functioning of the team. The report will provide feedback to the detailing control room at the various stages of operations.

There are two critical issues the team leader must address immediately upon arriving at the work site and commencing operations. The first is the operational work period scheduling and rotation of personnel. The initial deployment of personnel into rescue operation may have lasting effects on extended operations later in the mission. The Team leader must consider whether to commit all personnel to the rescue effort or hold some personnel in reserve for 24-hours operations or a combination of the two. The second issue is the site location and set-up of the team's control. An appropriate control site is essential to effective operations by the team. A safe and secure site must be obtained that considers environmental factors, team member stress reduction, and proximity to the work site. Any known specific support requirements for the team should be identified and resolved at this time. The locality should identify any political or sensitive considerations specific to the current situation. The Team Leaders should receivc clarification of authority specific to the locality or country.

As soon as possible, the Team must be integrated into the rescue operation. If the local rescue effort has not already identified potential victim locations, team operations may begin by sending out reconnaissance personnel into its assigned area. This size up may include identifying individual structures by address, physical location, or landmarks; performing a general triage of the area that includes identifying the structures that offer the highest potential for viable rescue opportunities; and a general hazard assessment and marking of the structural stability of the buildings the team may work in as well as the potential hazards that may be encounter during operations. One method of developing information for this assessment is to perform structural triage of the area. The triage process consists of a three-step process:

- Concise identification and location of buildings for reference.
- Rapid assessment of the affected area.
- The identification of locations that require a more detailed assessment.

After completion of the initial assessments and reconnaissance operations, the team should focus it priorities on searching and locating trapped, live victims; removal of trapped victims; and providing medical care to those rescued.

Search. Teams should have the capability to perform physical search, consisting of conducting interviews with survivors and a systematic movement across the site while listening for calls for help; canine search using specially trained dogs to locate living persons; and electronic search using sophisticated listening and seismic equipment. These three primary types of search will allow search personnel to focus on the most important potential rescue opportunities. Prior to initiating search operation, the team must determine the search strategy to be followed. This should be based on detecting and locating the greatest number of victims in the shortest amount of time. A plan should be developed which prioritizes the search opportunities based on a number of factors, including occupancy, time of day, and local information on missing persons. In most cases, if the local rescuers have not identified locations of trapped people, the team's search operations will begin with a rapid initial search of their assigned area followed by a more through main search.

Rescue. Rescue operations follow search operations and area focused on extricating the greatest number of victims in the shortest amount of time, prioritizing technical rescues that cannot be accomplished by local resources. Based on the search results, the team must prioritise the rescue sites and determine what resources to commit to a rescue site based on the potential success. Generally, rescue operations are prioritised based on rescues that are easily achievable and moving on to those that area more complex. A rescue plan will ensure that all efforts are brought to bear in a systematic and coordinated manner, using the most upto date intelligence about the victims and buildings.

Medical Care. Early in the incident, team medical personnel should meet with the local medical authority of the affected work area to determine the procedures to be followed. Team medical personnel should also develop a medical plan for the on-site operation that includes handoff procedures, re-supply needs, deceased victim management, indigenous health concerns, and evacuation procedures for injured team members or canine. The team medical personnel should work closely with the rescue lead to an untimely death form crush injury syndrome. Following the rescue of trapped victims, the team must provide an advanced level of medical care until such time as the personnel even prior to victim release to monitor and ensure proper care is provided to trapped victims. Medical actions may be necessary to prevent hypothermia and reduced oxygen consumption. Failure to provide necessary care to trapped victims can victim is handed off to the local medical system. Additionally, the medial team personnel must provide care to team member and canine from injury and illness while on-site and make recommendations to the Team Leader on the need for specialised care and/or evacuation to an appropriate medical care site. Medical operations will be covered in a subsequent part of the presentation.

Reassignment/Stand Down Phase

The state government will act as the central control point in demobilizing and/or reassigning teams.

Reassignment Considerations. The following factors, as a minimum, should be considered:

- Duration of operation already undertaken.
- Physical and mental condition of team personnel.
- Capability of the remaining equipment stock to support continued operation.
- Availability of other teams to handle the identified assignment.
- Availability of appropriate transportation.

Stand Down of Teams. Prior to issuing Standown Notices for either mission completion or inability to continue, state government officials and political leaders of the community should meet and bring to an end the team participation. If the mission is complete, all parties should review the objectives contained in the previously developed document of understanding. There should be complete agreement that all objectives have been completed before teams are returned home. The amicable agreement on the mission objectives completion will assist in the appreciation of the response by the affected country. Once the mission has been completed and no further activity or reassignment is warranted, the state government along with the local authority will begin to demobilize the teams. This information will be communicated to local officials through the state government.

The Team Leader should be considering standown issues several days before the assignment has been completed. The standown process needs to be discussed with the Planning Officer and Team Managers during action planning meetings and reviewed with the team members during briefing sessions. The Team Leader should ensure a standown plan is developed. This plan should cover all actions that must be completed before beginning the return home as well as the time schedule of events for leaving. Every effort should be made to comply with the time frames set in the plan, as they will be an integral part of the overall stand down plan.

URBAN SEARCH AND RESCUE

Responsibilities of Search and Rescue Operations.

Urban Search and Rescue (SAR) assistance is an extremely complex and fast moving form of assistance normally provided immediately on occurrence of an earthquake affecting an urban area. For it to be successful, each of the partners involved, i.e., the affected state and the assisting state/organisations must be aware of their responsibilities which are outlined below:

Affected State Responsibilities

- Affected state to provide in-state transport (personnel/equipment)
  - Will provide identified local transportation.
  - Fuels as required.
- Affected state needs to make available needed support facilities and a base of operations.
- Security for resources will be provided by the affected state for personnel, equipment and facilities.
- Affected state will issue proper waivers for:
  - Emergency medical practice, controlled drugs.

  - Canine/dog quarantine requirements, clearance/visa.
- Interpreters will be provided by the affected state.
- Ability to provide.
  - Compressed gases, fuels.
  - 24-hour point of contact.

Assisting State Responsibilities

- Assisting state to bear the cost of deployment.
- Getaway from time of activation.
  - Within 10 hours for air transport.
  - Within eight hours for ground transport.
- Self-sufficiency.
  - For 10 operational days.
  - Food, water, team medical support, shelter, etc.
  - Ability to self resupply.
  - Priority on taking care of your own.
- Incident Management Structure to include command and control.
- Responding resources place minimal burden on affected state exceptions are compressed gases, fuel, in-country transport.
- Internal/external communications.
- Perform search and rescue operations.
- Staff team with qualified personnel capable of performing multiple functions.
- Length of deployment of upto minimum of 14 days.
- Team members have appropriate training.
- Assisting state should have provisions to deal with:
  - Proper conduct of all team members.
  - Treatment of injury to team members.
  - Full responsibility for death(s) of a team member.
  - Damages brought by malicious, wanton and/or willful acts of its members.
  - 24-hour point of contact for deployment.

Basic Facts

A number of factors have a direct influence on the casualty rate in a disaster with many collapsed structures and on the survival chances of trapped victims.

Type of Construction and Collapse Profile : The material used for construction, the method and the type of structure hear a relationship to the type of collapse (collapse profile).

- Multi-storey structures of framed construction (reinforced concrete or rolled steel joints), with reinforced concrete floors and panelled walls of brick or building board. Upon collapse, this type of structure leaves cavities (lean-to or tent collapse) where casualties can be located with good prospects for survival.
- Medium-rise buildings of brick construction with poor bonding techniques. With this type of building, total collapse can be expected, the end result being a large pile of compacted rubble offering little chance for survival (compact collapse).
- Low-rise buildings constructed with local materials, such as single-storey dwellings of adobe construction with heavy roof structures. Upon collapse, the load-bearing members tend to disintegrate completely (pile of rubble), leaving little room for survivors.

Building Occupancy

- Some buildings (e.g., hospitals, old people's homes, boarding schools, mental institutions, etc.), have a permanent occupancy risk irrespective of the time of day. Others, (e.g., schools, offices, commercial centres) have a high-occupancy risk during working hours and low risk after this period.
- Residential property is at highest risk during the night, when occupants are in bed, causing the greatest number of casualties.

Hazards

- *Exposure hazard* : Climatic conditions and temperature are important factors. Although in some countries a comfortable temperature is enjoyed during the day, it can fall at night to below zero, creating a risk of hypothermia for exposed casualties.
- Trapped victims often suffocate due to a lack of oxygen or exposure to gas leaks or smoke.
- Water penetrating into cavities, particularly cellars and basements, may often lead to the drowning of

victims. The risk of electrocution may also be increased.

Time Factor

- Rescue efforts during the first 24 hours after an earthquake result in a very high percentage of victim survival. After that period, the survival rate dr operations dramatically.

Search and Rescue Phases After an Earthquake

- ***Phase 1*** : Informal, spontaneous search and rescue by families and neighbours. The emergence of on-the-spot citizen rescue groups. These informal groups perform the majority of rescues.
- ***Phase II : Light Search and Rescue*** : Coordinated localized searches by trained teams, often with dogs and other sensing resources, to rapidly search likely locations of survivors and rescue those not requiring major resources of equipment and manpower.
- ***Phase III : Intensive Search and Rescue*** : More-focused, intensive efforts through increased manpower and equipment, often involving tunnelling to search major buildings and gain access to buried spaces. All survivors who can be located without major cutting and lifting operations are extracted.
- ***Phase IV : Heavy Urban Rescue*** : Use of specialised equipment and manpower to disassemble and lift portions of collapsed structures to reach survivors and recover bodies not otherwise accessible.

Assessment and Response : The information collected by the local teams – particularly regarding the following subjects – should guide search and rescue teams already in the disaster area and those who plan deployment.

- ***Damage-related information*** : The type of construction and type of building have to be taken into consideration.
- ***Secondary threats*** : Such as the release of hazardous substances from chemical factories, pipelines and transport resources, storage facilities, power plants or nuclear facilities in the affected area.

- ***Teams already operational in the area (local, national, international)*** : The local SAR effort should be taken into account in deciding the need for outside assistance.
- ***Coordination Mechanisms at the site(s)*** : One should examine the organizational structure supporting SAR activities to see if it is a spontaneous effort by untrained locals. Uncoordinated, unstructured and with limited effect, or if it is an operation performed within the local Emergency Plan with identified tasks and priority setting.
- ***Specific equipment and expertise required*** : The local availability of specialist SAR equipment for both detection and rescue should be evaluated.
- ***Priority areas of intervention*** : The authorities with-expert advice should determine those areas where SAR operations can be most effective, taking into account resources already deployed. It should be borne in mind that SAR operations with scarce resources should be directed at those locations and buildings where the collapse profile and occupancy factor indicate that the largest numbers of live casualties are likely to be trapped. Coordination is extremely important for an efficient utilization of resources.

(SLIDE)

A guideline for necessary information to be provided to the various groups that are activated on the onset of a disaster are listed below:

Information Provided to Groups by Affected State Government

Disaster Advisory/ Alert Notice	*Disaster Activation Notice*	*Stand Down Notice*
• Type of event	• Type of event	• Reason for stand down
• Location	• Location	• Person
• Magnitude	• Magnitude	

Contd.

Disaster Advisory/ Alert Notice	*Disaster Activation Notice*	*Stand Down Notice*
• Weather condition • Current situation • Security Info	• Weather condition • Current situation • Damage assessment • Point-of-Arrival (POA) • Team radio frequencies • Reception Centre location • Other resources activated • Anticipated length of mission • Time of official activation • Person initiating activation • Identify and contact procedures • Security information	initiating stand down

13

Role of Armed Forces in Disaster Management

Introduction

A minister of home ministry receives a call on his mobile while he is busy arguing over some scam in the Parliament. The concern and confusion over the issue is clearly evident in the voice of the person on line. But the minister remains cool, as cool as cucumber. Unperturbed, he replies 'Summon Army'. This probably is the "Two Word" unwritten policy being followed in our country for Disaster Management. And the Armed Forces, true to its ethos and traditions as an organisation have always risen to the occasion and carried out commendable work in all the calamities, be it Bhuj earthquake or the Orissa cyclone.

Just to emphasize it further, it is only due to this selfless service done by our Armed Forces that 'India Today' chooses to put the Armed Forces on the topmost slot when selecting 55 things that India can be proud of. This in my view amply and concisely puts forth the roles of Armed Forces in disaster management.

Primary and Secondary Role

The primary role of the Armed Forces is to preserve national interests by safeguarding the territorial integrity of the nation against external threats, as well as the nation's strategic interests in the region. Their secondary role is to assist civil authorities in handling internal threats, maintenance of essential services, as also to assist the Central Government or States during natural and other calamities. In organisational and infrastructure terms, the Armed Forces provide speedy and efficient response in dealing with a disaster situation which is beyond the resources of the civil administration. They are also capable of providing emergency health operations and relief measures, particularly in search, rescue and evacuation; shelter for victims and damage assessment. Consequently, the Government often falls back on the Armed Forces during emergencies. As a result, efficient disaster management mechanisms incorporate the Armed Forces at each level when contingency plans are formulated, and specify the assistance likely to be required is disaster prone areas. This facilitates a more efficient response by the Armed Forces when called upon, and provides an interface mechanism in an emergency, thereby ensuring synergy and effective response. The Army's presence in underdeveloped areas along our borders help it contribute to the relief endeavours where the state governments relief mechanisms and resources are indifferent.

Types of Assistance

The Armed Forces may be called upon to provide the following types of assistance :

- Providing infrastructure of command and control organisation for providing relief is an important function. This would entail provision of communications and making available the technical and specialist manpower.
- Provision of medical care at the incident site and evacuation of casualties.
- Logistics support for transportation of relief material.
- Setting up and running of relief camps.
- Construction and repair of roads and bridges to enable relief teams/material to reach affected areas.
- Repair, maintenance and running of essential services especially in the initial stages of disaster relief.

- Assist in evacuation of people to safe places before and after the disaster.
- Coordinate provisioning of escorts for men, material and security of installations.
- Stage management and handling of international relief, if requested by the civil administration.
- Provision of communication infrastructure and equipment at the initial stages of disaster.

Principles of Employment of Armed Forces

The operations of the Armed Forces whenever called upon to assist the civil authorities in rendering relief are governed by certain guiding principles. These are enumerated below :-

- ***Judicious Use of Armed Forces*** **:** Assistance by Armed Forces should be requisitioned only when it becomes absolutely necessary, and when the situation cannot be handled by the civil administration from within its resources. However, this does not imply that the response must be graduated. If the scale of disaster so dictates, all available resources must be requisitioned simultaneously.
- ***Immediate Response*** **:** When natural and other calamities occur, the speed for rendering aid is of paramount importance. It is clear that, under such circumstances, prior sanction for assistance may not always be forthcoming. In such cases, when approached for assistance, the Army should provide the same without delay. No separate Government sanction for aid rendered in connection with assistance during natural disasters and other calamities is necessary. We must constantly improve our response times which are already the envy of several advanced countries.
- ***Command of Troops*** **:** Army units while operating under these circumstances, continue to be under command of their own commanders, and assistance rendered is based on task basis.
- ***No Menial Tasks*** **:** While assigning tasks to troops, it must be remembered that they are not employed

for menial tasks, e.g., troops must not be utilised for disposal of dead bodies.

- ***Requisition of Aid on Task Basis*** : While requisitioning the Army, the assistance should not be tasked for in terms of number of columns, engineer and medical teams. Instead, the civil administration should spell out tasks, and leave it to Army authorities to decide on the force level, equipment and methodologies to tackle the situation.
- ***Regular Liaison and Co-ordination*** : In order to ensure that optimum benefit is derived out of armed forces employment, regular liaison and co-ordination needs to be done at all levels and contingency plans made and disseminated to the lowest level of civil administration and the Army.
- ***Advance Planning and Training*** : Army formations located in areas prone to disaster must have detailed plans worked out to cater for all possible contingencies. Troops should be well briefed and kept ready to meet any contingency.Use of the Vulnerability Atlas where available must be made.
- ***Integration of all Available Resources*** : All available resources, equipment, accommodation and medical resources with civil administration, civil firms and NGOs needs to be taken into account while evolving disaster relief plans. All the resources should be integrated to achieve optimum results. Assistance from outside agencies can be superimposed on the available resources.

Procedure for Provision of Aid

General : Assistance during a disaster situation is to be provided by the Defence Services with the approval and on orders of the Central Government. In case the request for aid is of an emergent nature, where government sanction for assistance is not practicable, local military authorities, when approached for assistance should provide the same. This will be reported immediately to respective Services Headquarters (Operations Directorate) and normal channels taken recourse to, as early as possible.

Requisition Procedure : Any state unable to cope with a major disaster situation on its own and having deployed all its resources will request Government of India for additional assistance. Ministry of Defence will direct respective Service Headquarters to take executive action on approved requests. The Chief Secretary of Sate may initiate a direct request for emergency assistance for example, helicopter for aerial reconnaissance, to a corresponding officer of local formation headquarters (Command/Area Headquarters) or naval base or Air Force Station.

Coordination : The responsibility for coordination of disaster relief operations at various levels is as follows:

- ***Inter-Service Coordination at Central Level* :** Cabinet Secretariat (Military Wing). A case for co-opting a Tri Service RRF to cater for emergency situations within India and in the region is under consideration and directing all rescue/relief operations to ensure synergy of effort of all three services in management of disasters.
- ***Service Headquarters* :**
  - Military Operations Directorate (MO-6) at Army Headquarters.
  - Director of Naval Operations at Naval Headquarters.
  - Directorate of Operations (Transport and Maritime) at Air Headquarters.
- ***Command and Lower Formation Headquarters*:** Senior General Staff Officer (Operations).
- ***State level* :** Service liaison officer deputed to form part of Joint Control Centres.
- ***Local level* :** Nominated commander of troops and senior civil administration in charge of relief.

In the present system planning, provisioning and coordination of disaster relief operations is primarily the responsibility of operational branch down the chain of command which is already overburdened with other important tasks. Therefore, there is a need of creating a dedicated entity in the form of Disaster Management cell at all headquarters down the chain of command which will responsible for dealing with the disaster management in its entire spectrum.

Stages of Disaster Relief

Disaster Management could be broken up into the following four sequential, though not necessarily exclusion stages:

- ***Preparatory Stage*** : This corresponds to the pre-disaster period and includes disaster prediction, warning and alert systems, preventive measures and issues of contingency plans and check lists for potential disasters. During this stage appropriate organisation-infrastructure formulated, equipment and communication provisions and rehearsals conducted.
- ***The Emergency Stage*** : This stage commences from the warning of disaster to the period immediately after the disaster strikes and aims at providing immediate succor to the affected people and bringing a semblance of order in the disaster affected area.
- ***Rehabilitation Stage*** : This period covers short time measures to restore essential services, communications and normal community life.
- ***Reconstruction Stage*** : This is a long term measure aimed at providing adequate relief to the affected people.

Organisation in the Army for Disaster Relief

All formation and units located in various places in the country have instructions to be ready to move in case required for aid to civil authorities. All formation headquarters prepare detailed contingency plans to meet any eventuality, which may arise due to any natural or other disaster situation. All units located in the areas which are prone to recurring natural disasters like floods etc have detailed plans worked out which are frequently rehearsed. The task of co-coordinating aid to civil authority is generally given to static headquarters like Area and Sub Area Headquarters who report to the theatre commands. Additional units may be placed under the static headquarters on an as required basis.

- ***National level*** **:** At the national level a tri-services integrated organisation has been formed and is already functional. HQ IDS monitors, assesses and provides immediate and coordinated response of the three services at the national level. It also carries out coordination at national level with the national government, ministries of home and other ministries responsible for various disasters. Close liaison with various humanitarian organisations like UN and various NGOs both international and national is maintained. Timely mobilisation of resources of the three services becomes much easier and coordinated. To cite a more recent example of the floods in the state of Bihar, HQ IDS responded in a very effective manner by providing immediate relief in terms of mobilisation of engr boats from nearest location at Roorkee and helicopter sorties from the nearest Air Force station. This greatly reduces the minor hiccups in coordination among three services as a well structured organisation already exists with prior plans and procedures. Furthermore, in Armed Forces various organisations are more comfortable executing instructions and orders of their higher formations than evolving a coordinated policy at every level, which may not be feasible due to a large number of players involved.
- ***State level*** **:** At the state level, the Area and Sub Area headquarters of the Army interact with the state administration for coordinating various aspects of military assistance to civil administration. Important issues are also discussed during the annual Civil Military Liaison Conferences held in each State Capital in which the Chief Minister and the commander-in-chief of the Army's Regional Command also participate. At the Army's initiative and as the result of decisions taken during the recent civil military liaison conferences, many states have prepared State Disaster Response Plans in consultation with the Army and are in the process of finalizing District level plans.

Emergency Response

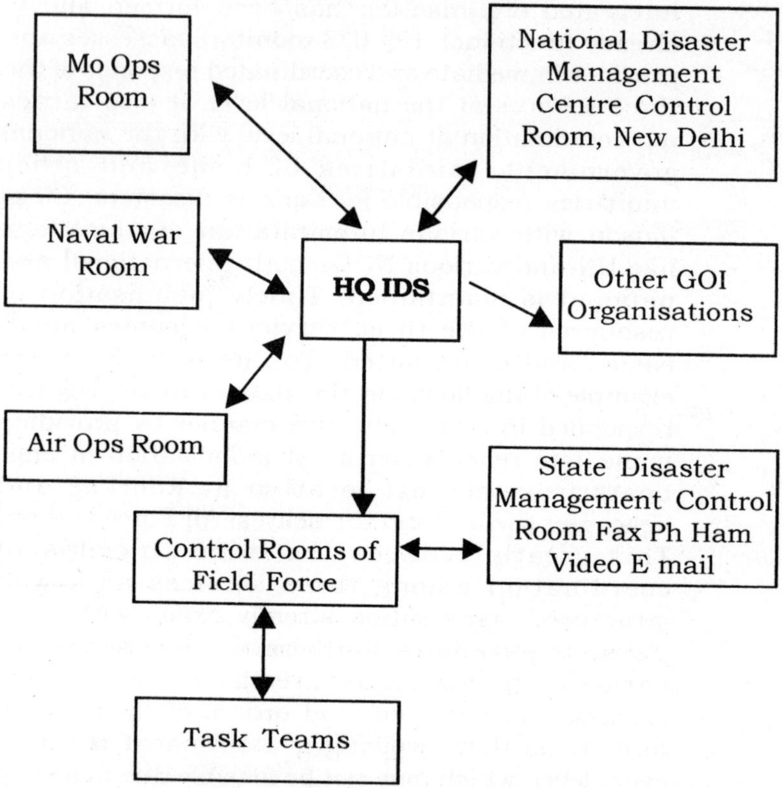

- ***District level*** **:** At the district level it is the station HQ or the commander of the unit stationed in the district or earmarked by the army for aid to civil authority who interacts and carries out close liaison for possible aid. The Army has system of Internal Security (IS) and Flood Relief schemes in respect of each command, area and sub area which earmark units and formations for each district in the country. The officers of the unit earmarked for internal security as well as for flood relief for the district carry out annual liaison with the district authorities including area familiarization for disaster relief operations. In case of any disaster situation in the district, an IS or a Flood Relief column is dispatched

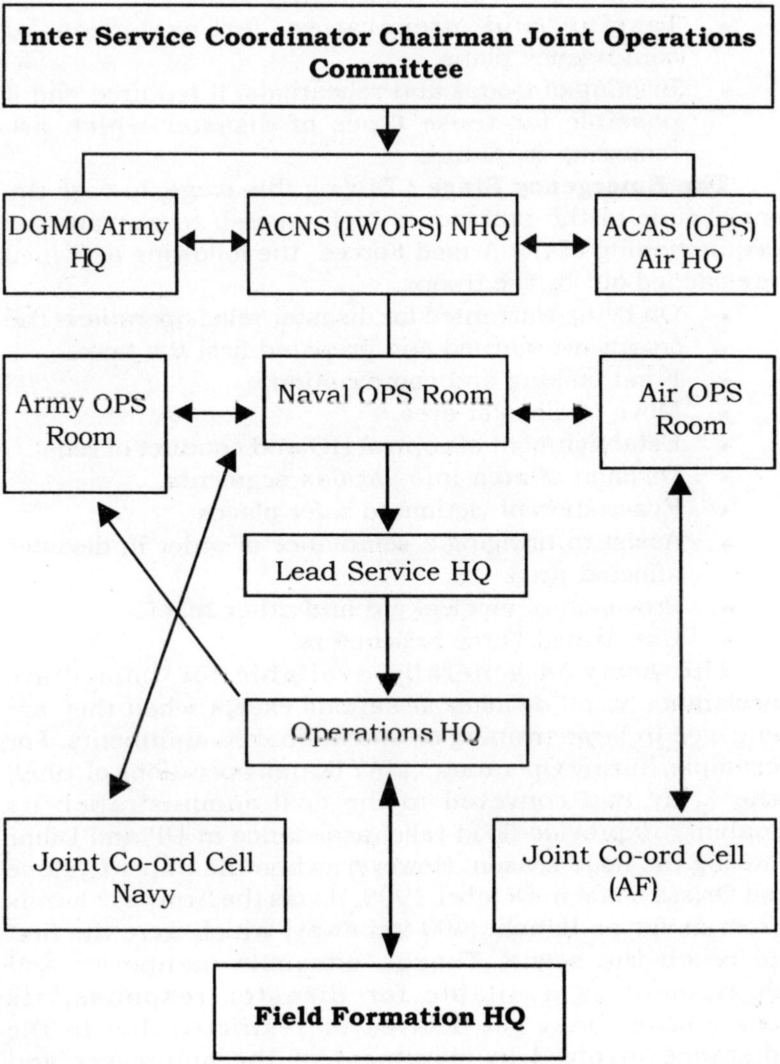
Inter Service Coordinator Chairman Joint Operations Committee
DGMO Army HQ
ACNS (IWOPS) NHQ
ACAS (OPS) Air HQ
Army OPS Room
Naval OPS Room
Air OPS Room
Lead Service HQ
Operations HQ
Joint Co-ord Cell Navy
Joint Co-ord Cell (AF)
Field Formation HQ

- Establishment of Liaison with State and Local Level Authorities.
- Identification of possible areas of employment.
- Understanding the overall disaster relief plan and formulation of own contingency plan.
- Tasking and preparation for execution of contingency plans.
- Briefing of troops and rehearsals. If required and if possible for those types of disaster which are recurring in nature.

The Emergency Stage : During this stage, in case the magnitude of the problem is high enough to warrant the requisitioning of the Armed Forces, the following activities are carried out by the troops.

- On being warranted for disaster relief operations the troops are warned and prepared first the task.
- Final tasking and coordination.
- Move of disaster area.
- Establishment of control HQ and conduct of relief.
- Division of area into various segments.
- Evacuation of victims to safer places.
- Assist in bringing a semblance of order in disaster affected area.
- Provision of medical aid and other relief.
- Use Armed Force helicopters.

The Army is generally available for immediate assistance in all disaster situations except when they are engaged in large training or operational commitments. For example, during Operation VIJAY (Kargil operations of 1999) the Army had conveyed to the civil administration its inability to provide flood relief assistance in UP and Bihar during the flood season. However, when the Super Cyclone hit Orissa coast in October 1999, it was the Army's columns from as far as Ranchi (400 km away) which were the first to reach the scene. Though adequate manpower and equipment is available for disaster response, its employment may get delayed or restricted due to the distance involved in movement of the manpower and personnel and the need to conserve operationally critical equipment. For example, no troops are stationed in the states of Bihar and Orissa and have to be moved from locations as far as 400-600 km. away in Jharkhand, UP or MP which requires time.

In order to emphasize this fact further, I would like to elaborate the role played by the armed forces in Bhuj earthquake. Aid was requisitioned by the state Government of Gujarat from GOC, 11 Infantry Division at 1115 hrs. on 26 January 2001.

- ***0945HR, 26 Jan. 01*** **:** WO received by rear party of the unit.
- ***1030HR, 26 Jan. 01*** **:** Rescue column of two JCOs and 22 OR moved out.
- ***1530HR, 26 Jan. 01*** **:** WO received by CO at Operation Area.
- ***1645HR, 26 Jan. 01*** **:** CO alongwith his recce party move to Ahmedabad by road.
- ***NI 26/27 Jan. 01*** **:** Recce of affected areas by the CO.
- ***2200HR, 26 Jan. 01*** **:** Loading of vehicals commenced at OP Area.
- ***0700HR, 27 Jan. 01*** **:** Move of convoy from operation area to Ahmedabad.
- ***NI 27/28 Jan. 01*** **:** Recce by Company Commander.
- ***0830HR, 28 Jan. 01*** **:** Relief and rescue work commenced at three sites (Akshar, Vishad and Giriraj apartments
- ***1800HR, 01 Feb. 01*** **:** Rescue work completed. Relief work continues.
- ***1800HR, 06 Feb. 01*** **:** Relief work completed. Dem of dangerous buildings commenced.
- ***1800HR, 14 Feb 01*** **:** Dem of dangerous buildings completed and colns derequisitioned.

Rehabilitation Stage **:** During this stage the Armed Forces may be utilised to assist the civil administration to restore essential services, communications etc. The Armed Forces need to be derequisition the moment semblance of normalcy is restored.

Reconstruction Stage **:** The Armed Forces have limited role to play during this stage.

Conclusion

The armed forces of the country have played a vital role in times of disaster, providing prompt relief to the affected people even in the most inaccessible and the remotest areas of the country. The 'organisational strength of the armed forces, their high sense of discipline, the enormous manpower at their disposal and their excellent human resource management makes them an extremely useful tool in providing disaster relief'. In fact, it is only the armed forces which are increasingly seen as the only agency to provide quick relief and rescue operations – both during natural as well as man-made disasters in the country. Consider the following comment in the editorial of a leading national daily during the communal violence in Gujrat during March 2002. 'The army's performance thus stands in stark contrast to that of the police and the state administration....Such is the Army's reputation for restoring normalcy that in any situation of emergency, the public invariably demands its early deployment.'

14

Health Aspects of Disasters

Disaster are a major cause of premature death, impaired health status and diminished quality of life. The direct effects of disasters on human, on the environment or on physical structures important to humans, usually defines whether a phenomenon will be viewed as a disaster. To therefore recall the PAHO definition of disaster which is aptly described as "an overwhelming ecological disruption occurring on a scale sufficient to require outside assistance"

Since there is no evidence to suggest that frequency of natural disaster will alter significantly in near future, appropriate plans leading to a well-coordinated public policy is required for disaster prevention, preparedness, emergency response and reconstruction. One of the critical elements in these disaster management procedures, is 'health care'.

Disasters are frequently classified as Natural and man-made disasters, while some authors subdivide man-made disasters into sudden disasters, slow or insidious onset disasters and war and armed conflicts.

Health management in disasters should be a continuous process covering the pre-disaster, disaster emergency and post-disaster phases. Disaster plans and preparedness to deal with disaster situation are necessary for every community and particularly for the health care system with its critical component, the hospitals, which are to be prepared consistently to mobilise all their facilities for maximum use.

Effects on Natural Disasters on Health

	Earth-quakes	*High Winds*	*Tidal Waves*	*Floods*
Deaths	Many	Few	Many	Few
Severe Injuries Requiring Medical care	Overwhelming	Moderate	Few	Few
Risk of Infectious Diseases	Problems in all major disasters			
Food Scarcity	Rare	Rare	Common	Common
Major population movements	Rare	Rare	Common	Common

Disaster management in India : While Central and State Government share the responsibility for disaster management, the primary responsibility for disaster planning, preparedness, rescue and relief is of the state Government. Health being a state subject, health care in disaster comes under its purview.

Similarly, Indian Armed Forces are the key resource and response organisation for relief and rescue, of whom Armed Forces Medical Service is a critical element in emergency response.

Health problems related to a disaster : Though all disasters are unique in that they affect areas with different social, medical and economic backgrounds there are still similarities between disasters, which if recognized can optimize the management of health relief and use of resources. The points to be noted are :-

- Relationship between type of disaster and health (Earth-quake and Floods).
- Some disasters effects have potential rather than inevitable threat. For example population movement causing rise in disease transmission.

- Actual and potential health risks after disaster do not all occur at the same time. Instead, they arise at different times with different degrees of importance, e.g., casualties rise with decreased sanitation and over-crowding.
- People generally recover quickly from their immediate shock and spontaneously engage in search and rescue, transportation of injured and other relief activities. Disaster created needs for food, shelter and primary health care are usually not total. Even displaced persons often salvage some of the basic necessities of life.

Effective health relief management hence depends on anticipating, and as they arise identifying problems, and delivering specific materials at precise times and at points where they are needed. What is less essential is to transport maximum supplies and personnel to a disaster area.

Health Problems Common to All Disasters

- **Social Reactions**
  - ***Spontaneous Reactions***: - Highly organised individual action occurs. Victims recover rapidly from shock and begin search and rescue activities immediately after an impact and within hours have organised themselves in groups to transport the injured to health posts. Only rarely there is generalised panic or stunned waiting.
  - **Rumours about epidemics**: As a result of rumours, considerable pressure is put on authorities to undertake mass vaccination against diseases like Typhoid and Cholera, for which there is no sound technical reason.
  - **Conflicting Roles**: Key individuals involved in disaster management being health officials and also being family heads, have in some instances not reported for duty on time, until their relations and property are safe. An otherwise rational spontaneous reaction of such nature may also be detrimental to higher interests of community.
  - **Antisocial behaviour.** Such as widespread looting occurs only in exceptional circumstances.

These behaviour patterns have two major implications :

* Demands for relief can be limited and modified by keeping the population informed about disaster impact and relief measures and by also obtaining necessary information before embarking on extended relief programmes.
* Victim population will itself provide most rescue and first aid, take the injured to hospitals if they are accessible, build temporary shelters and carry out other essential tasks. Additional resources should therefore be directed towards meeting the needs that survivors themselves cannot meet.

• **Communicable diseases :**

Disasters do not usually result in the outbreak of infectious diseases although in certain circumstances it does increase the potential for disease transmission. This transmission may be influenced by following factors:

– **Pre-existing disease in the population**: A disease, which already exists in low levels, may show signs of an outbreak. For example, Diarrhoea, Dysentery, Cholera, Plague and Malaria. It is rarely seen that an exotic disease, non-existing in a population earlier, is introduced in post-disaster scenario.

– **Ecological changes**: Following disasters, altered ecological conditions result in rise in transmission of diseases by mosquitoes and other vectors or water-related diseases. A case to point is the plague outbreak in Beed in Maharashtra following earthquake.

– **Damage to Public utilities**: This results in water-borne and excremental diseases due to mixing of sewage disposal with water supplies.

– **Interruption of Public Health Services**: Disruption of vector control programme, maternal and child health efforts and the ongoing vaccination programmes result in rise in communicable diseases. Increased mosquito breeding sites and washing away of residual insecticides from buildings caused 75000 cases of malaria in Haiti in 5 months following a hurricane in 1963.

- **Population displacements :** This occurs due to large and spontaneous or organised population movements to urban areas but where the public services cannot cope with the exodus, due to increased load on water, food and raised risk of food contamination, as in refugee camps. An example is the 6000 excess deaths in Bangladesh which took place after floods in 1974.
- **Climatic exposure**: The need to provide emergency shelter varies greatly with local conditions. As long as the population is dry and reasonably well-clothed or able to find windbreaks, the death from exposure does not appear to be a major risk.
- **Food and Nutrition**: Generalised food shortages, severe enough to cause nutritional problems, do not occur after earthquakes. Flooding and sea surges damage household stocks, crops and its distribution and cause local shortages. These are the only two probable causes of food shortages viz food stock disaster or disruption of distribution system.
- **Psychological Reactions to Disaster**

  Common age-wise reactions include

  Pre-school (1 – 5 years)

  Fearfulness, Night terrors, clinging to parents.

  Early childhood (5 – 11)

  Night terrors, nightmares, fear of darkness, aggresive behaviour in home/school, stomachaches and headaches, clinging or whining, poor concentration in school.

  Pre-adolescence (11 – 14)

  Rebellious, refusal to do chores, stomach-aches, headaches, loss of interest in friends, school problems, attention seeking behaviour.

  Adolescence (14 – 18)

Loss of interest in dating, irresponsible or delinquent behaviour, poor concentration, hypochondria.

Adulthood

Distressing and intrusive memories of disasters, flashbacks of upsetting feelings, intense distress at reminders, irritability, being easily started, blunting of feelings, lack of interest in pleasures, estrangement from people, troubling dreams, insomnia, poor concentration.

Health problems related to a type of disaster

- **Earthquakes** : Depending on dwellings may cause deaths in more than 10 per cent population and injure large number of people. This depends on : -
  - **Housing Type** : Poor concrete constructions as seen in Gujarat earthquake of 2001, results in damage and destruction to life. Stone construction even if one storeyed, is more susceptible than wooden-framed house of higher construction.
  - **Time of the day** : Whether more people are outdoors/indoors as in Gujarat earthquake.
  - **Population density** : Ratio of death to injured due to primary shock has been around 1:3 and decreases as the distance from epicentre increases. Iran earthquake in Sept. 1978 at Tabas-e-Goldan killed 11000.of its 13000 residents at its epicentre.
  - **Age groups** : Fit adults survive better than extremes of age.
  - **Secondary disasters** : Are usually caused by fires though less now. The majority of injured present with minor cuts and bruises, smaller group suffers from simple fractures and another group with serious multiple fractures or internal injuries requires surgery. Most demands for health services occur within first 24 hours. Injured appear in medical facilities during first 3 – 5 days after which sickness falls into normal presentation pattern.

- **Destructive winds** :

Cause relatively few deaths and injuries unless complicated by secondary disasters such as in floods or sea surges. The 1974 cyclone in Darwin, Australia with 45000 people, destroyed major part of city, but caused only 51 deaths and total 145 admissions. Effective warning before such windstorms limit morbidity and mortality.

- **Flash Floods and sea Surges**

  Cause much deaths but few injuries. Deaths commonly occur from drowning amongst weakest. 1977 cyclone complicated by sea surge in Andhra Pradesh affected 700,000 people leaving 10,000 dead and only 177 orthopedic cases.

- **Floods**

  Slow flooding causes limited morbidity and mortality. There are rare reports of slight increase in snakebites unsubstantiated and trauma causing limited health care needs.

Health Aspects of Disaster Management

A well coordinated public policy for disaster prevention, mitigation, preparedness, emergency response and reconstruction is essential for disaster management.

- ***Disaster prevention*** : Natural disasters are more or less unpredictable and cannot be prevented. Man-made disasters like industrials accidents, oil spills into sea, fires, train accidents and those with wars or conflicts are preventable and require control procedures, surveillances systems and early warning elements in place. All research and experience goes to show that efforts taken against disasters may not prevent them in most cases, however can definitely reduce their impact on life and property. Most of the opportunities for primary prevention of sudden disasters/insidious slow occurring disasters lie in the political realm. These include tighter regulation of chemical plants, policy on management of nuclear wastes, implementation of already existing national and state environmental standards and regulations, insistence on the construction of hazardous industries away from communities, personnel testing in companies transporting chemicals, oils and nuclear wastes.

- ***Disaster Mitigation (Secondary Prevention)*** : The consequence of disaster can be reduced in some of the following ways :
  - **Implementing land use and building codes** : Lack of exercising the stringent building codes and land use management problems lead to increased mortality and morbidity after earthquake, hurricanes and fires where people remain at high risk. The converse is true in the developed world.
  - **Public Education** : This should also be an ongoing process, more so before the event and as it is happening such as how to prepare for disaster (storing food reserves, obtain an emergency radio) or more specific to situation (standing in doorway when earthquake occurs). Evacuation alternatives for hurricanes and tornados should be discussed in the media well before the event. April 10, 1975 Texas tornado left 44 dead, 1871 injured, 6000 families homeless. 25 deaths associated with passenger vehicles included 16 who got into cars to avoid the tornado and 11 of homes of these persons escaped major damage.
  - **Preparation of Relief plan** : Relief plan might include some or all of the following activities :-
    - Rescue of victims
    - Provision of emergency medical care
    - Elimination of physical dangers (Fires, gas leaks)
    - Evacuation of population
    - Provision of preventive and routine medical care
    - Provision of water, food, clothing, shelter
    - Disposal of human waste or solid waste
    - Control of vector borne diseases
    - Disposal of human bodies
    - Support activities:-
      - Coordinate volunteer assistance
      - Management of facilities
      - Storage and distribution of materials
      - Management of communication facilities
      - Management of transport
      - Management of public information and rumour control services

- Management of registration and inquiry services
- Traffic and crowd control.

– **Early warning**: Weather warning, public address systems, satellites, radars and aircrafts predicting tornadoes and hurricanes.

– **Civil Defence** : Especially in wars and armed conflicts.

- ***Disaster Preparedness***

This is the next crucial stage where following aspects used to be addressed:

– Development of realistic and adaptable disaster plans
– Development of resource plans for health care
– Assign roles and responsibilities of resource organisation
– Plan for logistics, equipment and supplies required
– Communication, transport and evacuation
– Coordination and control
– Disaster drills

Coordination of National Relief Activities

Chairman of Nation: nergency Committee

↓

Disaster Re Coordinator

↓

Health Rel :oordinator

↓

Health Re Committee

↓

← →

Medical Attention	Supplies
Environmental Health	Transport
Epidemiological Surveillance	Coordination of volunteers
Nutrition	Requests and donations
Temporary settlements/Camps	Public information

Most important issues in the disaster preparedness are:-

– **Arrangements for on-site medical support**
  - Altering and dispatching mobile teams
  - Staff, equipment, transport and communication
  - Arrangements for on-site coordination for rescue and relief
  - Triage, First Aid and evacuation team.

– **Hospital Disaster Plans:**
  - Alert, recall and deployment system
  - Triage, First Aid and Emergency care arrangements
  - Critical area response like OT, ICU, etc
  - Support services like Blood Bank, Radio diagnosis, Pharmacy
  - Expansion and creation of facilities for disaster victims
  - Sustaining the plan and matching resource allocation.
  - Drill

– **Training:**
  - Creating awareness of the risk, vulnerability and hazards among health care workers
  - Dissemination of disaster management plans
  - Awareness of role and responsibility of various functionaries
  - Arrangements for mobilisation and its practice
  - Training of hospital staff in operationalising the hospital disaster plans.

- ***Disaster response*** **:**

The rapid disaster response is heavily dependent on appropriate disaster plan and preparedness. The initial response is hinged on rescue and relief. Rescue in specific disasters requires trained personnel and special equipment like rescue in case of earthquakes to find survivors in debris/collapsed buildings. Important features of disaster response are :

– **Rapid survey and assessment**: Needed for immediate and medium-term requirements for rescue and relief. Surveys must be organised in three stages:-

  - **Initial rapid survey** : Is an aerial survey which delineates area, assess physical condition of health care, transport and communication facilities and status of relief activities.This is generally the responsibility of Armed Forces and serves as a basis for mobilising specific relief. These personnel should be prohibited, whenever possible, from giving medical care and backup medical assistance should be provided.

- **Detailed multi-disciplinary survey**: Includes all affected areas. Information is collected on: -
  - Total casualties and dead
  - Number requiring evacuation and their major diagnostic categories
  - Number requiring local treatment
  - Availability of essential health supplies and personnel
  - Facilities for continued after care for those needing emergency treatment
  - Need to supply or reconstruct medical facilities
  - Impact on water quality and availability
  - Need for food, shelter and protective clothing
- **Surveys of specific problems**:
  Surveys to assess damage to health facilities and utilities by engineers and competent technicians for reconstruction cost estimates and to channelise international relief funds.

– **Management of mass casualties**: Most injuries are sustained in the initial impact and thus the greatest need for emergency care occurs in the first two days. Little effective help from International agencies is likely during the period of greater need because of response time required.

- **Search, Extrication or Rescue and First Aid** : After a major disaster the need for this is so great that organised relief service will be unable to meet more than a small fraction of the demand. Most individual help comes from injured survivors and they provide whatever First Aid they can.
- **Transport to health facilities and treatment**: Injured should be treated near own homes whenever

possible. Most would converge into nearest health facility but some may avoid or be unable to seek medical care hence active case finding is important in casualty relief. For this mobile health care team along with fixed first-aid stations are important.

Bed capacity and surgical services should be expanded. Responsibilities to staff delegated fully such as non-physicians to assist physicians. Arrangements made for round the clock manned centre for dissemination of information to relatives and friends.

Triage: Principle of first come first treated, applied in routine medical care, is inadequate in mass emergencies. Triage consists of "rapidly classifying the injured on the basis of benefit they can expect from medical care and not according to severity of injuries". For example moribund patients who require much attention for questionable benefit should be given the lowest priority.

Three categories in general use are: –

P I Seriously injured to be attended first

P II Seriously injured to be attended first

P III Ambulatory whose injuries are less severe

P IV Cannot benefit from treatment available under emergency conditions.

Triage should be carried out in two stages :-

- At disaster site to decide on transport priority.
- On admission to *hosp* or treatment centre in order to reassess the patient's needs and priority for medical attention.

Triage, should ideally be performed by field health workers or First Aid personnel at disaster site and an experienced clinician in a hospital. First Aid at the site by trained persons and evacuation to nearest hospital facility is essential without causing secondary accident to patient.

Tagging : Patients should be tagged with plated stating name, age, sex, place of origin, triage category, diagnosis and initial treatment given. Standardised tags should be chosen in advance.

- **Redistribution of patients between hospitals when necessary :** Due to damaged health care facilities in a disaster area and under pressure of mass casualties, the patients could be distributed to hospitals outside disaster area. Unplanned and possibly unnecessary evacuation can cause more problems than it can solve, and therefore should be restricted to a limited number of patients.

  If the country's total health care capacity is insufficient to meet disaster related needs then the best alternative is rapid expansion of country's own permanent facilities and staff for fulfilling immediate needs and permanent long time benefits.

– **Communicable Disease Control** : Prevention and control measures of communicable diseases rest on following broad principles :-

- Public Health and Administration measures to reduce risk disease transmission.
- Investigate unconfirmed reports of disease outbreaks promptly for avoiding unnecessary dispersion of scarce resources and disruption of normal programmes.
- Organise a more reliable disease reporting system, initiate control measures and evaluate ongoing sanitary or public health programmes.

Steps :

- **Setting up a surveillance system** : The information collection system could be from existing standard surveillance system, unofficial community sources and relief workers reports. It is established to collect, collate and interpret the data and will need the services of an epidemiologist/ public health specialist, paramedical and health professionals and clerical staff.
- **Disease surveillance** : To identify disease outbreaks, investigate them and instigate control measures. The diseases considered are those known to be endemic to the area. Where

this is not possible, a symptom based surveillance system should be instituted like searching for cases of fever, fever and diarrhea, fever and cough, trauma, burns etc.

- **Lab Services** : Basic blood and stool examination should be established by field reporting units. Bacteriological and viral tests must be performed by laboratories.
- **Vaccination and vaccination programmes** : Mass vaccination programmes against typhoid, cholera and tetanus, though instituted at times, prove to be of little use. These are prompted by exaggerated reports of risks of outbreaks which should be thoroughly investigated. Even at best of times, mass immunization against typhoid and cholera is avoidable.

– **Environmental Management** : Natural disasters expose people to danger by disrupting or threatening to disrupt their immediate environment. Effective management of environmental health, after a natural disaster, is of primary importance. The measures will entail action in following areas :

- **Water Supply** : Survey of all water points should be made with priority to drinking water distribution system to determine any sewage/chemical contamination with water supply which should be disinfected if found contaminated. Chlorine levels should be checked in distribution system before supply. All repaired pipelines, tanks and reservoirs should be properly cleaned and disinfected. Individual level or centralised disinfection may be resorted to.
- **Basic Sanitation :** To be ensured to protect environment from human wastage normally responsible for contamination of food and water. These include:-
  - Establishment of a sanitary solid waste disposal system (Emergency latrines).
  - Camps and relief worker settlements should have trench disposal facilities.
  - Education programme for demonstrating proper

usage of these facilities to upkeep sanitation in camps.

– Repair of public sewage systems.

- **Shelter** : Organised to accommodate displaced persons. In some cases public shelter could be provided temporarily like schools, meeting halls or hotels. Important to underscore that once individuals have been located and established at a site it is difficult to ask them to move again. Individuals encouraged to stay with family/friends and as soon as possible encouraged to return to their homes.
- **Food Sanitation**: Locally available food products become degraded or contaminated in natural disasters, by polluted waters, disease vectors and unsanitary handling in mass feeding facilities. All food needs to be inspected especially that which is locally made or available. The activities of mass feeding should be supervised by a specialist.
- **Vector Control** :
  - – Elimination of breeding places by water management and not by draining, filling of stagnant pools and over-turning receptacles.
  - – Enforcing personal protective measures.
  - – Indoors and outdoor spraying with insecticides against mosquitoes.
  - – Control of houseflies.
  - – Control of rodents - Improve environmental sanitation, store foods in closed areas, hygienic disposal of solid wastes and use of rodenticides.
- **Personal Hygiene** : Usually falls off in disasters in densely populated areas. Diseases such as scabies, meningitis are usual dreads during such times and can be avoided by:-
  - – Provision of washing, cleaning and bathing facilities.
  - – Avoidance of overcrowding in sleeping quarters.
  - – Information and encouragement about habits of pers hygiene.
- **Burial/Disposal of Dead**: Unlikely to cause out-

breaks of disease but presents a delicate social problem. Local methods of burial or cremation to be used but bodies should be identified before cremation and identities recorded.

- **Food and Nutrition** : Food requirements should take into account probable effects of disaster on food availability, approximate size of population affected, normal food supply and variations within the area and impact of seasonal factors.

Food supplied should be simple, acceptable and palatable. It is better to give cooked food when fuel shortages are likely. No detailed calculation of calorie required. A cereal, concentrated source of fat and a protein such as *khichdi* with vegetables and butter/ghee mixed in it will meet most Indian requirements.

It is also essential to monitor the long-term food supply and nutrition problems in the community.

– **Management of health relief supplies**: During first week supplies consist of drugs and medical equipment and later sanitary engineering equipment, vehicles, food articles, construction materials etc. Individual needs should be met primarily by the affected country, its closest neighbours and well equipped Armed Forces. Usually the aspects to be covered are :-

- Use of locally available stocks wherever available.
- Preparing national list of essential drugs on lines of UNICEF, Red Cross societies and WHO.
- Requests for International assistance.
- Labelling and marking consignments.
- Colour coding – Red for food stuffs, Blue for clothing and household equipment, green for medical supplies and equipments.
- Inventory and distribution of incoming supplies : Critical supplies sent at request of the affected country compete for storage space and transport with the bulk (up to 90 per cent) of unsolicited supplies. Such unsolicited supplies should be expected and procedures devised to handle them.
- Expired drugs, perishable products: Some drugs close to or past their stated expiration dates are often

donated or offered. Some of these can be suitably used after storage.

- Medical need for blood donated from abroad is generally limited.

– **Management of refugee camps** : Through health authorities are not directly involved in setting up and managing camps and temporary settlements, many aspects of camp management affect health of its occupants and health relief coordinators should therefore be involved in its decision making earliest. Camp services include : -

- Water supply: Camp should be close to a public water supply. Tube and Dug wells may also be used. Temporary storage facilities such as collapsible tanks or household containers should be used. Water chlorination and bacteriological monitoring is essential.
- Excreta disposal: one latrine for 20 people.
- Health services.

• ***Post Disaster Reconstruction/Re-establishing normal programmes*** : The first few weeks after disaster, pattern of health needs will change rapidly from casualty treatment towards normal primary health care. Priorities will shift from secondary health care towards environmental health measures and construction of temporary shelters.

The health relief coordinator faces decision making in three main areas:-

– **Long-term problems caused by disaster including**:

- ***Extended need for medical care***: 1 per cent casualties will require long-term nursing at home, institutions or specialized rehabilitation for months or years, like paraplegics, patients with severe brain damage, amputees and patients with chronic infections. Wherever long-term care and rehabilitation is limited, this will put a strain on health services. International resources are reluctant to take on such expenditures.
- ***Surveillance of communicable diseases***: As weeks pass after disaster, public is less likely to become concerned about risk of epidemic

diseases though outbreaks can still occur. Disease surveillance remains important and should be continued till normal disease reporting systems are restored.

- ***Care of orphans***: Institutionalised care should be the last resort since it presents administrative difficulties and social harm. Due to extended family networks in most developing countries, surviving relations undertake a child's care. Red Cross can also be asked for assistance.
- ***Psychological support and care***: Provided by psychologists to victims of disasters. People should be educated in recognising the signs of psychological trauma particularly in young children.

– **Re-establish normal health services**: This is a critical area since the affected country's resources are exhausted for disaster relief and massive voluntary or foreign government aid may temporarily exceed what country can afford to repay.

This period provides an opportunity for making major changes in health care methods since people are receptive to new ideas.

– **Reconstruction of damaged facilities and public utilities in buildings**: This should keep in view the water supply and sewage systems, hospitals and other health facilities (including stores and administrative buildings) which have been damaged.

15

Post Disaster Damage Assessment Need Analysis and Actions

Introduction

If officials responsible for organising post-disaster relief operations are to make effective decisions about deployment of sources it is essential that the model agencies are informed properly and in time. They must have timely and appropriate informations about what has happened, what needs to be done and what resources are available.

The correct decisions can save lives, minimise injury, damage and loss, prevent escalation, secondary hazards and inform people who need to know. Well-organised response in certain situations will also help build confidence and enhance credibility.

Relief operations are, in essence, management of informations and resources, based on assessment and reports. Information is needed at all levels of administration but the nature of information will vary from one level to another. Good assessments and reporting require forethought and vision.

Damage Assessment

Damage assessment is the process of determining the impact of a disaster on a specific society. Damage assessments include the preparation of specific qualified estimates of physical damage resulting from a disaster. It may include recommendations concerning the repair/ reconstruction of structures, replacement of equipment and restoration of economic activities.

Damage assessment is a prerequisite for all disaster management practices. Assessing level of damage is required at two basic levels of intervention. Firstly, for emergency relief measures, for which purpose, a quick assessment of damage would become the basis for the amount of medical relief and food stocks to reach the disaster affected area. At the second level would be a detailed technical analysis of damage for long-term restoration and rehabilitation works. From a long-term perspective, realistic damage assessment provides the mechanisms of failure that took place during the disaster.

Objectives of Damage Assessment : The basic objectives of damage assessment are :-

- To make rapid assessment of areas affected and the extent of impact, for the purpose of immediate rescue and relief operations.
- To prepare estimates for amount of relief to be provided and mode of relief, in terms of food, clothing, medicines, shelter and other essential items.
- To make detailed assessment for long-term relief and rehabilitation planning.
- To identify areas for purpose of retrofitting actions in similar situation.

In short, damage assessment is an important tool to assimilate the extent of disaster management actions.

Assessment must be carefully planned and managed. The assessment process includes :-

- Identification of information needs and sources of reliable data.
- Collection of data.
- Analysis and interpretation of data.
- Report writing. This aspect would be discussed in greater details a little later.

- Drawing conclusions and forecasting.
- Prepare databank for planners and decision makers.

The official agency for reporting estimates of disaster damages is the revenue department of the state governments as they are also the authority for distribution of the relief to the affected persons. As usual there is a hierarchy of officials who report from the lowest levels of villages / panchayats through blocks/ talukas, subdivisions and finally to the districts.

What Can be Damaged

Damage to Buildings : The damage caused to buildings by various disasters may be categorised to as losses under following heads :-

- Loss to main building.
- Losses due to failure of other components whose damage is attributed to the main building damage.
- Area covered by the collapsed structure.
- Death or injury to life due to building collapse.
- Loss incurred in terms of debris removal and restoration.
- Loss of revenue during the idle period.

Building damages on the wider scales usually are most relevant in terms of damage to the houses, than other types of buildings. Damage to house property is estimated in terms of number of households, percentage reporting damage and repair cost per household. This estimation is required to be carried out for all houses but presented under categories *pucca, kutcha* and semi *pucca* houses. This is required in order to carry out a value based assessment.

Besides the house structure damage itself, there is also an aspect of household asset damage which has to be taken into account. Damage to house structure can cause resultant damage to household goods, artisan assets and other productive assets stored in the house. These need to be accounted for in terms of average value of damages per household in rupees.

Damage to Land : Damage to land due to disaster could be short-term damage, as the land is rendered useless due to coverage by debris of sand and loss of standing crops or else it could be long-term damage as in lava or ash deposit or loss of productivity of land. The most important in the immediate post-disaster scenario is the aspect of agricultural loss through land destabilisation.

Crop damage is assessed in terms of percentage of households reporting damage under following heads :-

- Area damaged per household.
- Production loss per household.
- Value of production loss per hectare in rupees.
- Value of production loss per household.

Besides the damage to direct land attributes such as crops, there is also a long-term impact on the productivity of the land itself, which is felt even after the disaster, mainly in case of floods, has receded. The long-term impact on crop production could either be favourable or unfavourable. The favourable effect could be in the form of deposit of fertilising silt on the land resulting in rise in soil fertility which would manifest in crop yields or a better crop after the monsoon season due to water availability. The unfavourable effects would be in the form of sand castings rendering the land unfit for cultivation. This generally affects the production of Rabi crops after the floods. This damage can be assessed in terms of variation in production of crop after floods :-

- Yield per hectare (Quintals).
- Normal yield per hectare (Quintals).
- Percentage variation.

Damage to Human Lives : The most disastrous and immediate impact on human lives is in terms of loss of lives by deaths that may occur due to direct impact of the disaster or through indirect impact as in case of building collapses, fires etc. Injuries are the second level of impact of disaster on human lives, and result from the same sources as deaths. The impact on lives in terms of deaths and injuries due to death or injury, as also the loss of productivity of the persons affected.

In longer perspective, impact of disaster is also manifested in morbidity. Usually after a gestation period, which may be about two weeks after disaster, diseases start to set in due to the unhygienic living conditions and contamination of drinking water and food. The affected persons who may be housed in make shift relief camps, have no access to proper civil services and as a result of vector borne diseases affecting them, it may even take the form of an epidemic if unchecked. Once again impact of sickness due to disaster is felt in terms of expenditure on treatment and loss of employment during the sickness period. This may be assessed under following heads :-

- Total number of sample households.
- Percentage of households reporting sickness.
- Average number of persons reporting sick per household.
- Average duration of sickness (days).
- Average expenditure on treatment per household (Rs).
- Average employment lost per household (days).
- Average loss of income per household (Rs).

Beside the physical impact of death, injury and morbidity and then resultant financial implication, there is also a purely economic impact on human lives which is in terms of loss of employment due to dislocation and disruption of routine activities due to the disaster. For assessment of this impact, it is necessary to first collect information on the average number of wage earners per household in the affected areas.

Damage to livestock : The damage to livestock, namely cattle, other animals and poultry, which are very important assets in rural household, is generally assessed in terms of the number of households reporting loss and the per household value of livestock lost. It is generally observed that loss of livestock takes place because they are not moved out at the time of disaster threat or because people flee the area leaving livestock behind.

Damage Reports

The basic items usually covered in damage assessment report are :

- ***Rapid Assessment Report***
  - Name of sub division.
  - Area in square km.
  - Area affected in square km.

- Total number of villages.
- Population/Percentage affected.
- In case of floods, area still under water.

• ***Detailed Damage Assessment*** **:** The detailed damage assessment goes further than the rapid assessment and includes the following aspects :

- Verified number of lives lost.
- Cattle lost.
- Details of damage to crops and estimated cost of produce.
- Loss to public works and utilities including local bodies properly.
- Rough estimates.

Some of the data required is already available in the form of baseline data, i.e., maps, population statistics etc which must however be accessible but this baseline data must be supplemented by real time information which is mostly in the form of incoming reports from various sources after the disaster.

There is a clearly defined sequence of the process of managing information converting raw data into useful information. This is done in the following sequence: -

- Information in.
- Sorting (grading, collating, discarding what is unreliable).
- Evaluation.
- Decision Making.
- Action.

"Passing of information is every bit as important as receiving it".

Types of Assessment

There are two types of assessment :-

- ***Situation (Damage) Assessment*** **:** A description of what has happened.
- ***Needs Assessment*** **:** A statement of what needs to be done.

Reports

Flash Report : This report is sometimes called a SOS report and is submitted very quickly. Its purpose is simply to confirm that the disaster has actually occurred, that the steps are being taken to cope with it, to give a first indication of the sort of external relief that might be required and to inform the recipients that further reports will follow shortly. Flash report contains four parts. Each part contains the following information: -

- ***Part I*** **:** Situation :-
  - Type of Disaster.
  - Affected Area.
  - Date and Time.
  - Possibility of after effects.
- ***Part II*** **:** Initial estimate of effects:-
  - Dead.
  - Injured.
  - Missing.
  - In need for shelter and / or clothing.
  - In need of food.
  - In need of water.
  - In need of sanitation.
  - Damage to lifeline system.
  - All information required in approximate number.
- ***Part III*** **:** Possible need for external assistance for :
  - Search and Rescue.
  - Evacuation.
  - Protection.
  - Medical and Health.
  - Shelter and clothing.
  - Food.
  - Water.
  - Sanitation.
  - Repair of lifeline system.
  - All answers are required in terms of Yes/No.
- ***Part IV*** **:** The next report with more details will be sent at ______ (Date & Time).

Initial Report **:** This report should follow the flash report as soon as possible. The purpose is to inform the recipients of the severity of the disaster and more importantly by relating the severity of the disaster to coping capacities, providing the information needed to start mobilising resources from outside the affected area to help. This report should briefly summarise: -

- The severity of the disaster (without necessarily providing precise figures).
- Actions being taken locally.
- Local coping capacities (including locally available resources).
- The immediate priorities for external relief, where it is required and approximately what quantities.
- Alternative means of logistics.
- Forecast of possible future developments including new risks.

The situation, needs and priorities will change over a period of time. As assessment only describes the state of affairs at the time that the assessment is made. An initial assessment should therefore also establish the system for subsequent reports.

Interim Report : This report should build on the earlier reports providing additional and more precise information. To begin with, interim reports should be submitted every 24 hours at the same time everyday. The time is determined by the recipient according to his needs. The frequency thereafter is again decided by the recipient. As the operations progress, the emphasis of interim reports will shift from the needs of relief to needs of rehabilitation and reconstruction. It is not necessary to repeat what has already been said in earlier reports unless the earlier details require updating. Interim reports should provide forecasts which should include inputs from specialists and people who have experience of previous disasters and highlight information which may otherwise be obvious to the recipients for example, the potential problems, changes, patterns, trends and indicators and particular of especially vulnerable groups and any other special concerns.

Specialist or Technical Report : This provides the supplementary technical details for specialists, e.g., engineers and officials responsible for emergency health case.

Final Report : This will be summary of: -

- What happened.

- How the response was managed.
- Lessons learnt.

Salient Aspects for Preparation of Reports : The originator of report should put himself in the position of the people to whom he is reporting and ask himself "what do they need to know in order to meet their responsibilities and make the right decisions.[9] A report should not be packed with unnecessary data nor should it be delayed because of insufficient information. It is better to say "We do not have as much information as we would like but on the basis of what we do know and our experience, in broad terms the situation is as follows and we estimate the needs to be in the following range, we shall provide more details as soon as we can".

The details provided in the reports should be consistent. Conflicting report from different sources can cause confusion. Desirably, report from one level of administration to another should be consolidated.

Format of Reports

As envisaged the reports will be received from many sources, it is essential that the format should standardised so as to facilitate the process of analysis and collation. There should be common understanding of the terminology used. All reports should have a format where it can be transmitted electronically. Format should be as simple as possible and should include checklists, guide the reporter through sequence of: -

Stating the problem

Identifying current status

Identifying unmet needs

Decision-making

Suggested parts might include: -

- Search and Rescue.
- Evacuation.
- Protection.
- Medical and Health.
- Shelter and Clothing.
- Food.

- Water.
- Sanitation.
- Lifeline systems.

The person responsible for each part should be clearly designated. Each part should indicate the need for relief workers, supplies and relevant logistical requirements. Unless and otherwise stated, the provider should assume that the relief he supplies must be self-sufficient. It is often helpful to indicate what is not needed.

Identifying Needs

At some stage it will be necessary to quantify needs. Do not assume that everybody is a helpless victim requiring every sort of assistance. Initial assessment should concentrate on the effects of the disaster and not attempt to rectify the chronic. In quantifying needs it is sometimes appropriate to use internationally accepted standards and planning factors.

- X Search and Rescue teams per Y missing people.
- X items per family.
- Shelter of X per cent of homeless people.
- X grams of staple food per person for Y days.
- X grams per child per day for Y days.
- X litres per person for Y days.
- X tons/litres to create reserves.

Victims should always be described in terms of needs rather than give total population as effected. Damage can best be described in terms of casualty, for example.

%	*Damage Meaning*
• 100	Structure is unusable. Cannot be repaired.
• >75	Major structural damage. Unsafe for use. Repairable within one month
• >50	Significant structural damage. Unsafe for use. Repairs will take more than one week.
• <25	Minor structural damage. Usable.

(All above figures are based on WHO damage assessment form)

Priorities

There is a consistency of priorities for relief items after certain types of natural disasters. They can be understood by following table :-

Needs	*Typhoons*	*Floods*	*Earthquakes*
• Search & hence	Marine SAR	Rescue Boats	Usually No extremes SAR teams
• Medical	Supplies	Bandages, Spints not Medicines	Surgical sets, Bandages sutures
• Water supply	Treatment supplies	Treatment supplies	Treatment supplies
• Shelter	Tents Blankets Mosquito nets	Tents Blankets Mosquito nets	Tents Blankets
(e) Expertise	-	-	Structural engineers.

POST DISASTER ACTIONS

Earthquakes

- Detailed survey of building for assessment of damage and decision regarding repair, reconstruction and strengthening or demolition.
- Repair, reconstruction and seismic strengthening or demolition.
- Selection of sites for new settlements, if required.
- Execution of the reconstruction programme.
- Review of the existing seismic zoning and risk maps.
- Review of seismic codes and norms of construction.
- Training of personnel, engineers, architects, builders and masons.
- Statistical studies regarding the earthquake.

Floods

Post-disaster management could inter-alia include the following essential requirements:

- Speedy restoration of roads, rail routes and the postal services.
- Normal water supply in the affected areas either by arranging tankers or fire tenders.
- Repair of the power, telephone and sewerage lines on priority basis so that normalcy is restored.
- Proper arrangements for the supply of food, shelter and clothing to the marooned people.
- Ensuring adequate supply of POL and kerosene oil and keeping the supply line moving.
- Constitution of a survey team to assess the loss and compensation to be given to the affected population.
- Assistance for repair/rebuilding of private properties.
- Desilting and dewatering of the inundated areas.
- Taking up appropriate measures according to Contingency Plan for the agriculture sector.

Floods are not an unmixed evil as they bring beneficial silt and help in procuring a better Rabi harvest. While an attempt can be made to minimise damages on account of a flood of 25 Years return, it is by no means easy to do so against a 50-year or a 100-year flood return. This is exactly what happened in Haryana in 1995. There against an average annual rainfall of 600-700 mm in the state, the average daily rainfall from 26.8.95 to 30.8.95 and again from 2.9.95 to 4.9.95 was 200-300 mm which engulfed a population of over 2.5 million involving a colossal loss placed at Rs. 1800 Crores. The damage caused by floods can at best be minimised and not altogether eliminated and the old-age philosophy of living with the floods has to be adapted to the emerging situation with all the concomitant pressures of population and developmental activities.

Cyclones

The initial response by local authorities could include:-

- Evacuation.
- Emergency shelter.
- Search and rescue.
- Medical assistance.
- Provision of short-term food and water.

- Water purification.
- Epidemiological surveillance.
- Provision of temporary lodging.
- Reopening of roads.
- Reestablishment of communication networks and contact with remote areas.
- Debris clearance.
- Disaster assessment.
- Provision of seeds for replanting.

Cyclone Shelters : One of the most successful means of reducing loss of human lives during cyclones is the provision of shelters. In densely populated coastal areas, where large scale evacuations are not always feasible, community buildings and buildings used for gathering of large number of persons, like school, *dharamshalas*, hospitals, prayer halls, etc, can be used as cyclone shelters. These buildings can be so designed, so as to provide a blank façade, with a minimum of apertures in the direction of the prevailing winds. The shorter side of the building should face the storm. Alternately these buildings can be designed on a circular/ellipsoidal plan, so as to impart least wind resistance. Earth beams and green belts can be used in front of these buildings to reduce the impact of the storm. These shelters should be located in relatively elevated areas with provision for community kitchen, water supply and sanitation. Another alternative, though expensive is to have individual cyclone shelters attached to dwelling units. The shelter is fabricated in concrete and steel and designed for installation on that ground adjacent to the house. The shelter is installed 4 feet in the ground, the dirt from the excavation is placed around the shelter to help increase the shelter's effectiveness in protecting its occupants.

Drought

- Close monitoring of the emerging drought scenario so as to develop an advance warning system.
- Relief measures required for providing immediate succour to the affected population and the cattle wealth, and if possible to integrate it with long-term objective and

- Hammering out an alternative crop strategy for maximum possible retrieval of the Kharif crop and a better ensuring Rabi crop.

Landslides

In general the chief mitigatory measures to be adopted for such areas are

- Drainage correction,
- Proper use of land,
- Reforestation of the areas occupied by degraded vegetation, and
- Creation of awareness among local population.

Importance of Information Technology in Disaster Management

The major areas for computerisation in disaster management are:-

- **Pre-disaster System**
  - Risk Analysis System.
  - Contingent Plan System.
  - Forecasting/Simulation and Warning Dissemination.
- **During Disaster System**
  - Rescue and Relief System.
  - Damage Assessment and Full Allocation System.
- **Post-disaster System**
  - Restoration and Rehabilitation.
  - Damage Analysis.

Conclusion

Timely and correct passage of information is the most essential aspect of any post-disaster management actions. This facilitates minimising the effect of the disaster by timely relief thus reducing casualties. Each person responsible in the chain of reporting and distribution of relief plays an equally important role. The correct and uniform format ensures that minimum information required by all is always available to orchestrate own resources for maximum gains.

Bibliography

Books and Articles

1. Abelson, P.H. (1971) *Changing Attitude towards Environmental Problems.*
2. Adams, L., J.A Finn and R.E Wetmore. (1971) *Stress and Behavior as Components of a Population Control Mechanism.* Bull. Ecol. Soc. Amer.
3. Agarwal, Anil; "*Human – Nature Interactions in a Third World Country*" *In Ethical Perspectives on Environmental Issues in India.*
4. Akula, Vikram K; (1995) *Grassroots Environmental Resistance in India In Ecological of Radical and Popular Environmentalism,* Albany – State University of New York, *Press.*
5. Alaspe RE, ed. (1995) *Reducing Traffic Injuries from Inappropriate Speed.* Brussels, European Transport Safety council.
6. Alaspe RE, ed. (1999) *Safety of Pedestrians and Cyclists in Urban Areas.* Brussels, European Transport Safety council.
7. Alley, Kelly D; (1994) "*Ganga and Gandagi; Interpretations of Population and Waste in Banaras*" *Ethology 33.*
8. Alm H, Nilsson L (1975) *The effort of a mobile telephone task on driver behaviour in a car following situation. Accident Analysis and Prevention.*
9. Altshuller, A.P.; *(1966) Air Pollution: Photochemical Aspects.*

10. Amory, Cleveland; (1974) *Man Kind.* Harper and Row; New York.
11. Anderson, P.K, Omega: (1971) *Murder of the Ecosystem and Suicide of Man.* Dubuque: Wm. C. Born,
12. Anderson G, Nilsson G. (1997) *Speed Management in Sweden Linkoping,* Swedish National Road and Transport Research Institute.
13. Anjou, G. (1963) *The Formation of the Bible.* St. Louis and London: Herder.
14. Arnold, David, and Ramachandra Guha, eds; (1985). *Nature, Culture, Imperialism: Essays on the Environmental History of South Asia;* Oxford University Press, Delhi.
15. Ashton S J, Mockay GM (1983) *Benefits from Changes in Vehicle Exterior Design.* In: proceedings of the Society of Automotive Engineers. Detroit MI, Society of Automotive Engineers.
16. Atwal, D.S (1971) *Semi-dwarf Rice and Wheat in Global Needs. Quart. Rev of Biology.*
17. Banuri, Tariq and Frederique Apffel- Maarglin, eds; (1993) *Who will save the forest ? Knowledge, Power and Environmental Destruction:* Zedf Books, London.
18. Barron's (January 22, 1990). "*Land That Time Forgot*".
19. Barron's (February1, 1988), *Fresh Disaster at Bhopal Indian Politics Threaten To Compou. Volume 68, Issue 5.*
20. Barrons, (Feb 20, 1989) *"Second Thoughts on Bhopal".* Volume 69. Issue 8.
21. Battan, L.J.; (1966) *The Unclean Sky: A Meteorologist Looks at Air Pollution.* Doubleday, Garden City, N.Y.
22. Bates, M. The Forest and the Sea. (1960) *A Look of the Economy of Nature and the Ecology of Man.* New York: Menton Books.
23. Battan, L.J. The Unclean Sky: (1966) *A Meteorologist looks at Air Pollution.* Garden City,, N.Y: Doubleday.
24. Bharara, L.P.; (1982) *"Notes on Experience of Drought: Perception, Recollection, and Predication." In Desertification and Development: Dry Land Ecology in Social Perspective,* London and New York: *Academic Press.*
25. *Bhopal: Absolutely Liable* (*July 23, 1988*) Economist, Volume 308 Issue 560.

26. Bookchin, Murray; (1996) *The Philosophy of Social Ecology* Rawat Publications, Jaipur.
27. Bookland John, Hora Cheryl and Carter Nick: (1985) *Injury, Damage to Health and Quel Treatment of Live,* Fauna EIA, London.
28. Bridger, C.A & Helpand (1968) *L.A. Mortality from Heat during July 1966 in Illinosis International Journal of Biometeorology.*
29. British Disaster Management Pamphlet. *Disaster Management- A Business Systems Approach.*
30. Brown I D Tickner AH, Simonds DCV. (1969) *Interference between Concurrent Tasks of Driving and Telephoning. Journal of Applied Psychology.*
31. Brown, H. (1954) *The Challenge of Man's Future. New York: Viking Press.*
32. Boulding, K.E. War as a Public Health Problem (1965). *Conflict Management as a Key to Survival. In Behavioral Science and Human Survival,* Palo Alto, California.
33. Bouma, M.J & Dye.C. (1997) *Cycles at the Malaria Associated with EL Nino in Venezuela.* Journal of the American medical association.
34. Bryerton, G. (1970) *Nuclear Dilemma.* New York: Ballantine Books.
35. Cassels, Jamine (1993) *The Uncertain Promise of Low: Lessons from Bhopal.* University of Toronto Press Incorporated.
36. Cerrelli E. (1998) *Crash Data and Rates for Age. Sex Groups of Drivers; 1996* Washington: DC, National Centre for Statistics and Analysis.
37. Chakraverty, Chiranjit; (1996) *Environment for Everyone, Augustan Publishers and Distributors, Delhi.*
38. *Changnon, S.A et al. (2000) Human factors explain the increased losses from weather and climate extremes.* Bulletin of the American Metrological Society 81 (3).
39. Chakrovarty, Surata N. (December 10, 1990) *'The Ghost Returns' Forbes, Volume 146, Issue 13.*
40. Checkly.W. et. al. (2000) *Effects of EL Nino and Ambient Temperature on Hospital Admissions for Diarrhoeal Diseases in Peruvian Children.*Lancet 355.
41. Champion H.G. (1936) *A Preliminary Survey of the Forest*

Types of India and Burma. Indiàn Forest Record (Silvi Culture Series) Vol.1, No.1.

42. Chiu Wetal. (2000) *The Effect of the Taiwan Motorcycle Helmet Use Law on Head Injuries.* American Journal of Public Health.
43. Dasmann, R. *(1968) Environmental Conservation.* New York: Wiley.
44. Davidson, Basil (1959) *The Host Cities of Africa. Boston: Little, Brown.*
45. Dematte, J.E. et al (1998) *Near: Fatal Heat Stroke during the 1995 Heat-wave in Chicago. Annals of Internal Medicine.*
46. Diaz, H.F. et al. (2000) *Climate and Human Health Linkage on Multiple Timescales. Climate and climatic impacts through the last 1000 years.* Jones.P.D. et. al. *Cambridge, UK Cambridge University Press.*
47. Donaldson, G.C et al. (2001) *Outdoor Clothing and it Relationship to Geography, Climate, Behaviour and Cold related Mortality.* International Journal of Biometeorology
48. Dunn, F.L. *Health and Disease in Hunter Gatherers. Chap. 23 In the Man the Hunter, Lee and Devore (eds), Chicago*: Aldine (1968) Neel, J.V. *Lessons from a "Primitive" people.*
49. Editorial: Toxic Futures (January 26, 1990) *New Statesman and Society. Volume 3, Issue 85.*
50. Ehrlich, P.R.;(1970) *"Famine, 1975: Fact or Fallacy". In the Environmental Crisis.* New Heaven, Yale University Press.
51. Elton (1933) *C.S. The Ecology of Animals.* London: Methuen.
52. Eluik R, Mysen AB, Vaa T.. (1997) *Trafikksikkerhetshandbok, tredje utgave,* Olso, Institute of Transport Economics.
53. Engelthaler, D.M. et al. (1999) *Climate and Environmental Patterns Associated with Hantavirus Pulmonary Syndrome,* Four Corners region, United States. *Emerging Inflections. Disease.*
54. Epstein, S., Brown, L., and Pope C; (1982). *Hazardous Waste in America, Sierra Club, San Francisco.*

55. European Road Safety Action Programme. *Halving the number of Road Accident Victims in European Union by 1010: A Shared Responsibility*. Brussels, Commission of European Communities 2003.

56. Finch D Jetal. (1994) *Speed, Speed Limits and Accidents*. Crowthorne, Transport Research laboratory.

57. *Freaks of Nature: Errors of Man. (January 1991) World Health.*

58. Friends of Vrindavan; (1993) *"Protecting Sacred Forest: Linking Leicester's Community with the Sacred Forests of India"*

59. Gagnon, A.S et al (2001) *Dengue Epidemics and the EL Nino Southern Oscillation. Climate Research.*

60. Ghash, Arun; (1993) *"Ecology and Environment". In Nature, Man, and the Indian Economy*. Oxford University Press, Delhi and New York.

61. Giddens, Anthony; (1990). *The Consequences of Modernity*. Stanford, Calif Stanford University Press.

62. Githeko, A.K S Ndegwa(2001), W *Predicting Malaria Epidemics in the Kenyan Highlands Using Climate Data, a Tool for Decision on Makers*. Global Change and Human Health.

63. Glantz, MS Jamison, D.T. *Societal Response to Hurricane Mitch and Intra versus Inter generational Equity Issues. Whose norms should apply? Risk Analysis 20(6).*

64. Goldsmith, E.; (1985) *The World Bank : Global Financing of Impoverishment and Famine. The Ecologist, Vol. 15, No-1/2.*

65. Guha-Sapir, D Rapid (1991) *Assessment of Health Needs in Mass Emergencies: Review of Current Concepts and Methods*. World Health Statistics Quarterly.

66. Gupta,A.: (1986) *"Drought and Deprivation: Socio-Ecology of Stress, Survival and Surrender." Paper Presented at the Seminar on Control of Drought, Desertification and Famine. Delhi.*

67. *Guthrie, D.A. (1971). Primitive Man's Relationship to Nature.*

68. Hobbes CA, Mills PJ. (1984) *Injury Probability for Car Occupants in Frontal and SideImpacts*, Crown Thome, Transport Research Laboratory.

69. Harold Issacs (October 1979) *Power and Identity: "Tribalism in World Politics."* Headline series of the Foreign policy Association, No 246.

70. Harris, Robert and Paxman, Jeremy; (1982) *A higher Form of Killing: Secret Story of Gas and Germ Warfare. Chatto & Windus, London.*

71. Hortley LR, Arnold PK. (1996) *Recommendations from the second international conference on fatigue in transportation, Fremantle, Western Australia, 11-16 February 1996.* Fremantle Institute for Safety and Transport Murdoch University, Western Australia.

72. Haworth NL. (2000) *Alcohol in Motorcycle Crashed. In; Laurell H, Schlyter F, eds. Proceedings of the 15 th International Conference on Alcohol, Drugs and Traffic Safety, Stockholm, 22-26 May 2000.* Stockholm, Swedish National Road Administration.

73. Helfrich, H.W., Jr (ed);. (1970) *Agenda for Survival. The Environmental Crisis-II,* New Haven: Yale Univ. Press.

74. Hizat M, Trastle J, Bronfman M. (2003) *Pedestrian Injuries in Mexico: a Multi Method Approach Social Science and Medicine.*

75. Horsfall, J.G. (1970) *The Green Revolution :Agriculture in the Face of the Population Explosion. In the Environmental Crisis.* H.W Helfrich, Jr, New Haven, Yale University Press.

76. *India's Environmental Policies. Programmes and Stewardship (1997).* London: Macmillan, New York; St. Martin's Press

77. Institute of Environmental Epidemiology (IEE). *Health Guidelines for Vegetation Fire Events. Schwela, D.H et al.eds. Singapore.* Singapore: Institute of Environmental Epidemiology 1999.

78. Jodha N.S: (1986) *Market Forces and Erosion of Common Property Resources, ICRISAT, Hyderabad.*

79. Jasanoff Shcila. (1994). *Learning From Disaster: Risk Management After Bhopal.* University of Pennsylvania Press, Philadelphia.

80. Keall MD, Frith WJ, Petterson TL (2004). *The influence of Alcohol, Age and Number of Passengers on the Night-time Risk of Driver Fatal Injury in New Zeland.* Accident Analysis and Prevention.

81. Khayesi M. (2003). *Liveable Sstress for Pedestrians in Nairobi: the Challenge of Road Traffic Accidents In: Whitelegg J. Hag G,eds. The Earthscan Reader on World Transport policy and Practice.* London Earthscan Publication.
82. Khera, S.S (1963). *The Establishment of The Heavy Electrical Plant at Bhopal. Committee of Case Studies.* The Indian Institute of Public Administration, New Delhi.
83. Kopits E, Cropper M (2003). *Traffic Fatalities and Economic Growth.* Washington, DC, the World Bank.
84. Koornstra MK, ed. (2003). *Transport Safety Performance in the EU. Brussels.* European Transport Safety Council. Transport Accident Statistic Working Party.
85. Kumar, Sanjay (May 8, 1993). *"India: The Second Bhopal Tragedy"* Lancet, Volume 341, Issue 854.
86. Kushwaha, Col M.K. *Inter-Agency and Inter-institutional Coordination during Disaster Response Operations.*
87. Kurzman Dan (1987). *A Killing Wind. Inside Union Carbide and the Bhopal Catastrophe.* Mc Graw Hill Book Company.
88. Lam Lt etal (2003). *Passenger Carriage and Car Crash Injury: a Comparison between Younger and Older Drivers.* Accident Analysis and Prevention.
89. Lappen, Alyssa A. (December 10, 1990). *"Breaking Up is Hard to Do"* Forbes, Volume 146, Issue 13.
90. Lee, R.B and I.De Vore (ed). (1968). *Man the Hunter.* Chicago: Aldine.
91. Leighly, J (ed) (1967). *Land Life. A selections from the Writings of Carl Ortwin Saure. Berkeley.* University of California Press.
92. Leopold, A (1949). *The Land Ethic. An Essay in a Sand Country Almanac.* New York, Oxford University Press.
93. Lewis F Richardson, *(1960) Statistics of Deadly Quarrels.*
94. Litman T.(2003). *If Health Matters, Integrating Public Health Objectives in Transportation Planning.* Victoria BC, Victoria Transport Policy Institute.
95. Mackay GM. *Some Features of Road Trauma in Developing Countries. In ; proceedings of the International Association for Accident and Traffic Medicine Conference,*

Mexico, DF September 1983. Stockholm, International Association for Accident and Traffic Medicine 1983.

96. Mackey M, Hassan AM (2000). *Age and gender effects on injury outcome for restrained occupants in frontal crashes.* In: Proceedings of the Association for the Advancement of Automotive Medicine conference. Chicago IL, Association for the Advancement of Automotive Medicine.
97. Mackey GM, Wodzin E (2002). *Global Priorities for Vehicles Safety. In : International Conference on Vehicles Safety 2002.* I Mech E conference Transactions London, Institution of Mechanical Engineers.
98. Marsh, G.P. *Man and Nature.* D.Lowenthal (ed), Cambridge: (1864) Harvard University Press 2nd Printing, 1967.
99. Martin, P.S and H.E Wright (1967). *Pleistocene Extinctions. Proc. 7th Cong. Int. Assoc for Quaternary Res,* Vol.6. New Haven. Yale University Press.
100. Mc Cromick, J. Forest Ecology (1959). *New York: Harper & Bros.*
101. Mclean J, Kloeden C. (2002). *Alcohol, Travelling Speed and the Risk of Crash Involvement In: Mayhew DR, Dussoult C, eds. Proceedings of the 16th International Conference on Alcohol,* Drugs and Traffic Safety, Montreall, 4-9 August 2002. Society de I' assurance automobile du Quebec, 2002.
102. Mclean AJ et al (1990). *Regional Comparative Study of Motorcycle Accidents with Special Reference to Licensing Requirements. Adelaide,* National Health and Medical Research Council Road Accident Research Unit. University of Adelaide.
103. Miller Tetal (1999). *Is it Safe to Travel by Bicycle, Car or Big Truck?.* Journal Crash Prevention and Injury Control.
104. Mishra BK, Banerji AK, Mohan D (1984). *Two Wheeler Injuries in Delhi, India: A Study of Crash Victims Hospitalized in Neurosurgery Ward. Accident Analysis and Prevention.*
105. Mitchell, R Short Days – *Shorter Lives. Studying Winter Mortality to get Solutions.* International Journal of Epidemiology (2001).

106. Mock C, Amegashi J, Dartch K (1999). *Role of Commercial Drivers in Motor Vehicle Related Injuries in Ghana. Injury Prevention.*

107. Mohan D, Tiwari G (1998). *Road Safety in low income countries: Issue and concerns regarding technology transfer from high income countries. In: Reflections on the transfer of traffic safety knowledge to motorizing nations.* Melbourne, Global Traffic Safety Trust.

108. Morehouse, Ward and Subramarian M.Arun (1986). *The Bhopal Tragedy: What Really Happened and what it Means for American Workers and Communities at Risk.* Council on International and Public Affairs.

109. Muden JM (1967). *The Relation between a Driver's Speed and his Accident Rate.* Crowthorne, Road Research Laboratory.

110. Munich Re Group Topics: (Pan American Health Organization (PAHO) (1999) Natural Catastrophes 2000-2001. *Disasters and Health in 1998. A Report of the Pan American Health Organization Emergency Preparedness and Disaster Relief Coordination Program.*

111. Nafukho FM, Khayesi M (2002). *Livelihood Conditions of Work, Regulation and Safety in the Small Scale Sector Public Transport Sector: A Case of the Matatu mode of Transport in Kenya. In:GodardX, Fantonzoun I, eds. Urban Mobility for all.* Proceedings of the Tenth International CODATU Conference Lome. Togo, 12- 15 November 2002. Lisse, AA Balkema Publishers.

112. Nantula VM, Muli-Musiime F (2001). *Uncovering the Social Determinants of Road Traffic Accidents in Kenya, In : Evans T et al; eds Challenging Inequities, from Ethics to Action. Oxford.* Oxford University Press.

113. National Centre for Disaster Management (2001). *Report of High Powered Committee to the Government of India,* Delhi.

114. National Oceanic and Atmospheric Administration (NOAA). *An Experiment in the Application of Climate Forecasts: NOAA-OGP activities related to 1997-98 EL Nino event.* Boulder, US office of Global Programs, US Dept of Commerce.

115. Nico Nellissen, Straaten and Klinkers; (2001) *Classics*

in Environmental Studies', Kusum Publishing, New Delhi.

116. Nilsson G. *The Effects of Speed Limits on Traffic Accident in Sweden.* Sartrych, Swedish National Road and Transport Research Institute (1982).
117. Noji, E.N (1997). *The Public Health Consequences of Disasters.* New York, US Oxford University Press.
118. Omvedt, G; *Anti-Drought Movement.* Economic and Political Weekly Vol XXI, No 18, 3 May 1986.
119. Olsen, K.W; *Manmade Drought in Rayalseema.* Economic and Political Weekly. Vol XXII, No 11, 14 March.
120. Osborn, F (1948) *Our Plundered.* Baston Little Brown.
121. Pasonen E (1991). *Ajonopeudt ja JalankulkijanTturvalisus. Espoo, Teknillinen Korkeakoulu, Liikennetekniikka.*
122. Perkins D. Jr Fauna of Cattle Huyuk (1969). *Evidence for Early Cattle Domestication in Anatolia.*
123. Red Cross*(2002). Death Toll Rise in Central Europe's Epic Floods.*
124. Rienow, R. and L.T. Rienow. *Moment in the Sun (1967).* New York: Ballantine Books.
125. Rodriguez DY, Ferrandez FJ Velasquez HA (2003). *Road Traffic Injuries in Colombia.* Injury Control and Safety Promotion (2003).
126. Ross-(1976). Macdonald, Malcolm *Life in the Future,* Interiberica S.A; Madrid Spain.
127. R.P. Richardson (1970). *An Analysis of Recent Conflicts.*
128. Saggs, H.W.F. (1962). *The Greatness that was Babylone.* New York: Hawthorn Books.
129. Salifu M. (1996). *Urban Pedestrian Accidents in Ghana. Research Journal of the International Association of Traffic and Safety Sciences.*
130. Sartor, F.et al. (1995) *Temperature, Ambient Ozone Levels and Mortality during Summer 1994 Heat-wave in Belgium. Environmental Research 70 (2).*
131. Sauer C.O. (1938) *Theme of Plant and Animal Destruction in Economic History.* Jour of Farm Econom.
132. Sauer, C.O Land and Life (1967). *A Selection from the Writings of Carl Ortwin Saur. John Leighly(ed).* Berkeley : University of California Press.

133. Sears, P.B.- Norman (1935). University of Oklahoma Press.

134. Simpson, D (1968). *The Dimensions of World Poverty. Scientific American.*

135. Singh, Mendal and Graham (2000). *Disaster Response in India.*

136. Singer, S.F (ed); (1970). *Global Effects of Environmental Pollution. AAAS Sympasium.* New York: Springer – Verlag.

137. Sinha, Anil; (2001). *Disaster Management ; Lessons Drawn and Strategies for the Future; In Training Document on Disaster Management.* II PA- UP Regional Branch.

138. Sinha, PC; (1998). *Encyclopedia of Disaster Management.* Vol-1, New Delhi.

139. Smeed R.(1949). *Some Statistical Aspects of Road Safety Research.* Journal of the Royal Statistical Society.

140. Sweedler BM (1995). *The Worldwide Decline in Drinking Water and Driving, In: Kloeden CN, Mclean AJ, eds. Proceedings of the 13th International Conference on Alcohol, Drugs and Traffic Safety. Adelaide, 13-18 August 1995.* Adelaide Road Accident Research Unit.

141. Taylor MC, Lynam DA, Baruya A. (2000). *The Effects of Divers Speed on the Frequency of Road Accidents. Crow Thorne.* Transport Research laboratory.

142. Taylor MC, Baruya A, Kennedy JV.(2002). *The Relationship between Speed and Accidents on Rural Single Carriageway Roads.* Crownthrone, Transport Research Laboratory.

143. Thomas, W.L.(ed) (1955-1956). *Man's Role in Changing the Face of the Earth.* Chicago: University of Chicago Press.

144. Tingvall C. The Zero Vision. In (1995). Van Holst H, Nigren A, Thord R, eds *Transportation, Traffic Safety and Health: the New Mobility. Proceedings of the 1st international conference Guthenburg, Sweden, 1995.* Berlin Springer – Verlag.

145. Toffler, Alvin; (1946). *A Study of History.* Dell Publishing Co..Inc, 750, Third Avenue, New York (USA).

146. Toffler, Alvin; (1991) *Power Shift, Bantam Paper Books Edition, Bauxam.* Double day Publishing Group, INC, New York, (USA).

147. Toffler, Alvin and Heidi : (1993). *War and Anti-War.* Little Brown and Company, Canada (USA).
148. Toynbee, Arnold; (1946), *A Study of History.* Dell Publishing Co. Inc, 750. Third Avenue, NewYork (USA).
149. Turner: (1976) *The Role of Flexibility and Improvisation in Emergency Response; In* British Pamphlet on Disaster Management, op.cit.
150. Varghese M (1990). *Analysis of 198 Medical-legal Records of Road Traffic Accident Victims Treated in a Delhi Hospital.* Journal of Traffic Medicine.
151. Gogt, W.(1948). *Road to Survival.* New York, William Sloane Associates.
152. Wall Bank, W.T (1958). *A Short History of India and Pakistan.* New York: Scott Foresman.
153. Weir, David (1987). *The Bhopal Syndrome: Pesticides,* Environment, and Health. Sierra Club Books, San Francisco.
154. Weir; David: (1987). *The Bhopal Syndrome Earthscan,* London.
155. White, L (1967). *The Historical Roots of Our Ecologic Crisis.*
156. Williams AF (2003). *Teenage Drivers: Patterns of Risk.* Journal of Safety Research.
157. Woodhouse P.R. et al. (1993). *Seasonal Variation of blood Pressure and its Relationship to Ambient Temperature in our Early Population.* Journal of Hypertension.
158. Woodhouse P.R. et al. (1994). *Seasonal Variation of Plasma Fibrinogen and Factor VII Activity in the Elderly: Winter Infectious and Death from Cardiovascular Disease.*
159. Zodor PL, Krawckuk SA, Voas RB (2000). *Relative Risk of Fatal Crash Involvement by BAC, Age and Gender. Washington, DC.* National Highway Traffic Safety Administration.

Reports, Organisations, Newspapers and Documents

160. *"After Bhopal"* (1988). July 16 *Lancet, Issue 603.*
161. Aroon Purie in *India Today,* (07 Sep. 78).
162. *Booklet on Post- Disaster Damage Assessment and Need Analysis* by ADPC Bangkok, Thailand.
163. *Booklet on Trigger Mechanism* by Department of Agriculture and Cooperation, Min of Agriculture,

Government of India.

164. *Book on International Travel and Health* by WHO, Geneva.

165. *Book on Staying Alive* by International Committee of the Red Cross.

166. *Coping with Disaster (August 1988) Technology Review*, Volume 91, Issue 6.

167. *Centre of Excellence for Disaster Management and Humanitarian Assistance; Disaster Response;* Hawaii. USA.

168. Darwin, C.G. (1953) *The Next Million Years*. New York: Doubleday.

169. Downing A. (1991) *Pedestrian Safety in Developing Countries. In proceedings of the Vulnerable Road User.* International Conference on Traffic Safety. New Delhi, 27-30 January 1991. New Delhi, Macmillan India. 1991.

170. Ehrlich, P.R. and A.H. Ehrlich. (1970) *Population, Resources, Environment: Issues in Human Ecology.* San Francisco: W.H. Freeman & Co.

171. *Hearing before the Subcommittee in Asian and Pacific Affairs of the Committee on Foreign Affairs House of Representatives. (December 12, 1984). Ninety Eight Congress, Second Session.*

172. *India Disasters Report (2000).*

173. *Manual on Natural Disaster Management in India by NDM,* Government of India.

174. NDM; *Manual on Natural Disaster Management in India.* Government of India.

175. Pan American Health Organization (PAHO) (1999a) *The Devastating Path of Hurricane Mitchin Central America. Disasters: Preparedness and Mitigation in the Americas.*

176. "*Poison Gas, Up Two Bucks*" (March 6, 1989) Nation, Volume 248 Issue 9.

177. *Police Enforcement Strategies to Reduce Traffic Casualties in Europe.* Brussels, European Transport Safety Council 1989.

178. *Promotion of Mobility and Safety of Vulnerable Road Users PROMISING. Leidschendom, Institution for Road Safety Research, (2001).*

179. *Report of the HPC on Disaster Management.*

180. *Report of the HPC on Disaster Management. (2000) (Grouping of Disaster is at Annexure A).*
181. *Report of the HPC on Disaster Management. (2001).*
182. *"Round the World: India – Long Term Effects of MIC" (April 29, 1989).* Lancet, Issue 644.
183. "*Spectrum: Update –Reforestation, Chernobyl, Bhopal*" (June 1988). Environment, Volume 30, Issue 5.
184. "Surviving Bhopal" (November 16, 1990). *New Statesman And Society Volume 3 Issue 127.*
185. The Concise Oxford Dictionary (1989); Bombay. Oxford University Press.
186. "*The Ghosts of Bhopal*" (Feb 18, 1989) Economist, Volume 310. Issue 580.
187. *The Risk of Using a Mobile Phone while Driving.* Birmingham, Royal Society for the prevention of accidents. 2002.
188. "Toxin Town" (December 2, 1994). *New Statesman and Society* Volume 7, Issue 331.
189. *UN Document of Disaster and Humanitarian Assistance: Geneva, (1991).*
190. *UN Report on Natural Disaster (1997).*
191. *WHO Reports on Climate Change 2003,* WHO Geneva.
192. World Toxic Trash Bin; (13 July 1995). *"India Accepting Toxic Products from Industrialized Nations"*. India Current Magazine.

Index

P

R